THE BEST OF DQR

NEW SERIES VOLUME 43

COSTERUS

Rodopi

Amsterdam 1984

THE BEST OF *DQR*

Edited by

F.G.A.M. Aarts / J. Bakker / C.C. Barfoot /
G. Janssens / M. Buning / W.J. Meys

ISBN: 90-6203-626-0
Printed in the Netherlands

A.G.H. BACHRACH, Emeritus Professor of English Literature, University of Leiden, is author of *Sir Constantine Huygens and Britain,* 1596-1687 (1962) and editor and translator (with R.G. Collmer) of *The English Journal 1651-1652 of Lodewijk Huygens* (1982). Founder and former director of the Sir Thomas Browne Institute for the Study of Anglo-Dutch Cultural Relations (now re-established as the "Werkgroep Engels-Nederlandse Betrekkingen/ Sir Thomas Browne-Institute"), he has been responsible for exhibitions in the Netherlands and in London and has written several articles in Dutch and English journals on the work of J.M.W. Turner.

J. BAKKER teaches American Literature at the University of Groningen. His books include *Ernest Hemingway: The Artist as Man of Action* (1972) and *Fiction as Survival Strategy: A Comparative Study of the Major Works of Ernest Hemingway and Saul Bellow* (1983); with J.C. Riewald he is the co-author of *The Critical Reception of American Literature in the Netherlands 1824-1900* (1982). He is one of the co-founders and editors of *DQR.*

C.C. BARFOOT teaches English Literature at the University of Leiden. Since 1970 he has contributed an annual survey of current criticism of nineteenth- and twentieth-century literature to *English Studies* and has published articles on Goldsmith, Wordsworth, Keats, Dickens and Hardy. In 1982 he published *The Thread of Connection: Aspects of Fate in the Novels of Jane Austen and Others.* He is a co-founder and editor of *DQR*.

SARAH BETSKY-ZWEIG is Professor of American Literature at the University of Leiden. Her professional interests are nineteenth-twentieth-century American and British literature on which she has published several articles. The third edition of *Onions, Cucumbers and Plumbs* translations of 46 Yiddish poems) appeared in 1982.

T.A. BIRRELL is Professor of English and American Literature at the University of Nijmegen. His professional interests include literary criticism and the history of English libraries in the seventeenth century. He recently published: *The Library of John Morris* (1976), *Engelse Letterkunde* (4th edn, 1978) and *Amerikaanse Letterkunde* (1982).

W.J.M. BRONZWAER, a co-founder and now advisory editor of *DQR,* has been Professor of Comparative and General Literature at the University of Nijmegen since 1974. He is a co-editor of *Textboek Algemene Literatuurwetenschap* (1977) and has published *Rilkes Elegieën van Duino* (1978) and *Keuze uit de Gedichten van T.S. Eliot met inleiding en commentaren* (1982).

PAUL P.J. VAN CASPEL holds Degrees in Dutch (Amsterdam) and Sanskrit (Groningen) and has published a study of Dutch post-war poetry, *Experimenten op Experimentelen* (1955) and articles on Joyce in *Neophilologus, English Studies,* and *DQR.* Doctoral thesis: *Bloomers of the Liffey: Eisegetical Readings of James Joyce's "Ulysses" Part II* (Groningen, 1980). He is a regular contributor to the *James Joyce Broadsheet.*

J. VAN DORSTEN is Professor of English Renaissance Literature in a European Context at the University of Leiden, and author of *Poets, Patrons, and Professors* (1962), *The Radical Arts* (1970) and *Op het kritieke moment: Zes essays over Nederlandse poëzie van de 17de eeuw* (1981). In 1974 he edited *Ten Studies in Anglo-Dutch Relations* and regularly contributes a critical bibliography of sixteenth- and seventeenth-century literature to *DQR.*

ROBERT DRUCE teaches language acquisition and English Literature at the University of Leiden. In 1972 he published a novel, *Firefang* and in 1974, *In Focus*, an anthology of poetry and prose. Articles on *Jane Eyre* and on "Pulitzer Prize Novels", Best-sellers and *Jaws* have appeared in *DQR.*

ROGER FOWLER is Professor of English and Linguistics at the University of East Anglia, Norwich, England. Since his contribution to DQR he has continued to publish extensively on linguistic-criticism and radical sociolinguistics. His more recent works include *Linguistics and the Novel* (1977), *Literature as Social Discourse* (1981) and, with R. Hodge, G.R. Kress and A. Trew, *Language and Control* (1979).

RICHARD GRAY is a Reader in the Department of Literature at the University of Essex. He is the author of *The Literature of Memory: Modern Writers of the American South* and has edited a collection of essays on Robert Penn Warren. At present he is editing a collection of original essays on American fiction.

L.C. KNIGHTS, King Edward VII Professor Emeritus of English Literature, the University of Cambridge, and author of *Drama and Society in the Age of Jonson* (1937) and *Some Shakespearean Themes* (1960). Selections from other books have recently appeared as *"Hamlet and Other Shakespearean Essays* (1979) and *Selected Essays in Criticism* (1981). He was a member of the editorial board of *Scrutiny.*

GEOFFREY N. LEECH is Professor of Linguistics and Modern English Language at the University of Lancaster since 1969. His recent books include *Explorations in Semantics and Pragmatics* (1980) and (with Michael H. Short) *Style in Fiction: A Linguistic Introduction to English Fictional Prose* (1981).

WILLEM MEYS studied English and Linguistics at the Vrije Universiteit, Amsterdam and Southampton University. Published a dissertation on word-formation, *Compound Adjectives in English* in 1975, and articles on morphology, grammar and applied linguistics. An editor of *DQR* since 1977. Now teaches English Linguistics at the University of Amsterdam.

DEREK PEARSALL is Co-Director of the Centre for Medieval Studies at the University of York. His recent publications include *Old English and Middle English Poetry* (1977) and an edition of the C-text of *Piers Plowman* (1978).

SIR ANGUS WILSON, knighted in 1980, is one of the most distinguished post-war English novelists. His most recent novels have been *As If By Magic* (1973) and *Setting the World on Fire* (1980). He has written critical works on Zola, Dickens and Kipling and has been Professor of English Literature (now Emeritus) at the University of East Anglia since 1966.

DAVID WYKES is a specialist in Restoration and eighteenth-century literature, with excursions into the moderns, notably Evelyn Waugh and George Orwell. He published *A Preface to Dryden* in 1977. He is Associate Professor of English at Dartmouth College, New Hampshire, USA.

CONTENTS

The Best of DQR: Introduction

The appearance of an anthology of articles from the first ten years of *DQR* is not the occasion solemnly to consider the part played by academic journals. But since the existence of *DQR* itself arose out of a dispute over the role of a familiar Dutch journal concerned at one time with the study of modern languages in the old-fashioned broad philological sense and increasingly appealing to pedagogic interests, a few reflections on the matter are not out of place.

To many teachers of foreign languages and literature in the Netherlands at the end of the sixties it seemed that the journal of the Dutch Modern Language Association, *Levende Talen*, was beginning to devote too much space to classroom techniques, to the extent that it was almost possible to envisage a generation of superbly equipped teachers in full control of their pupils but increasingly ignorant of the subject they were supposed to be teaching; and as has become even more evident in recent years, the means and the theory of communication were beginning to outstrip the matter and the ends. Of course, sensible people realized that most teachers were not devoted entirely to the practical skills of their profession and some of the more sceptical might still be inclined to believe that an imaginative and continually extending grasp of their subject might make them more inspiring and more effective encouragers of the young than a bandwagon of theory. Still, regrettable though the split may be, it was felt by some of us in 1970 that its pedogogical dissussions were going to squeeze literature out of *Levende Talen* (and the powers-that-be, or would-be, seemed to be in favour of such a change in emphasis), to the extent that the imaginative and creative uses of language seemed to be but a peripheral concern to the latest students of "living languages". It was then thought better to take some of the material left in the files of the older journal to use as a basis for the foundation of a new publication. This would cater for the traditional readership of schoolteachers who actively maintained and tried to sustain their interests in literature and of university teachers who not only regretted the division between pedagogy and literature but also feared that the increasingly specialized approach of current academic journals tended to ignore the intelligent and educated general reader.

Indeed it might be claimed that from the beginning *DQR* has hoped to successfully fill a space between competing specializations: on the one hand pedagogical journals and on the other bi-monthlies and quarterlies that printed articles intended to appeal to a handful of colleagues with comparable expertise in increasingly narrow fields of research. As our editorials in the first issues of 1971 and 1972 make clear, we felt that *DQR* was required to occupy a position between the practical concerns of the classroom and the somewhat aloof heights or remote depths of the university seminar. At the same time we wanted to be more balanced in our presentation of the whole range of literature in English from the Middle Ages to the present day and less concerned with instant journalistic appeal and coterie advancement than many of the more popularly based or glossy literary magazines. We wished *DQR* to be confined neither to the shelves of the university library nor to the coffee-table in the sittingroom: both places are worthy enough, but we hoped that our journal would also be read, enjoyed and filed in the private study.

However, visible tokens of reader participation have been few. It would be ludicrous to use this occasion as a platform for self-centred lamentation, but at the beginning we set out to found a journal that would serve language and literature in and out of the classroom, that would be responsive to the requirements of the teacher and the general reader, that would provide information and commentary in reviews and articles as well as critical surveys and we had expected, as those early editorials reveal, rather more signs of reaction from our readers.

As editors we are bound to wonder about our readership, which has never expanded much beyond the seven or eight hundred that we established in the first couple of years, when we were published by the Assen firm of Van Gorcum. It is hardly likely that it has been the same seven or eight hundred throughout the last ten years: subscriptions have been lost, others gained; with occasional moments of crisis when it appeared that more were being lost than won. In the first three or four years of *DQR*'s existence we were supported either by direct subsidy or by paid subscriptions by the English section of *Levende Talen*, and by the United States Information Service and the British Council, to whom we remain grateful for helping us to get off the ground. But in 1976 this help ceased, since it was felt by that time that if there was any real call for the journal it should be able to make its own way. However other kinds of assistance, particularly in respect to the access to visiting guests for interviews and the publication of appropriate sponsored lectures have come from the two latter cultural offices, in more recent years from the British Council especially.

The first editorial meeting was in February 1971 and the first issue of *DQR* appeared four months later. Looking back it is clear that despite the need to squeeze numbers 3 and 4 together that first year, the material was somewhat thin: too many old reviews, and too many pieces written by the editors themselves – always a bad sign. We have never thought that the editors themselves should be banned from writing for *DQR* – it seemed right and proper to contribute the occasional article and keep the critical surveys going – yet clearly one of the problems for any new publishing venture of this kind is not only to appeal to subscribers but also to attract a wide variety of contributors. It has always been a deliberate policy of the editors to use as much local skill and talent as possible, to encourage young Dutch scholars and critics as well as calling on the abilities and experience of the older generations of academic colleagues. It has not always worked. We are pleased to remember, and occasionally to remind ourselves of, the many contributors, both Dutch and non-Dutch, and not all of them university teachers or students, whose articles have maintained a consistent level of interest in the pages of *DQR* in the first decade. As we have become better known, and the title of the journal began to appear in various international bibliographies (including the Academy of Science in Moscow, from where, however, we have never received either a subscription or a contribution!), so articles have been increasingly forthcoming from Britain and the United States, as one would expect, frequently from Germany, only occasionally from elsewhere. As far as we can remember we have heard from Norway, but not from Denmark or Sweden, from Belgium but neither from France nor from Italy.

The bias of *DQR* has been literary, mainly because linguistic articles have become increasingly technical and many linguists have felt that they prefer to publish where they can speak to their fellow technocrats. However, we have always tried to find or to commission the right kind of linguistic article for our purposes, apart from the reviews and surveys, that could be read with interest and pleasure by the unprofessional student of linguistics and anyone generally interested in language. This anthology reprints two or three such articles. It is a regrettable aspect of developments in language studies in the last ten years or so that despite the philosophical claims that have been made by linguists for their discipline, their work has become less accessible to the interested general reader.

The editors of *DQR* have always tried to keep the essential figure of the common reader, who is yet not so common, in mind. Not every good article submitted for publication to us has been found suitable for such an ideal figure, and on occasions we have suggested re-writing for the less specialized reader. It is clear that we have never met the typical *DQR* reader, but we have always pretended that he or she exists: "would it do for a *DQR* reader?" is a question the editors have regularly asked themselves and each other at the quarterly meetings at which the issues are put together. And this touches upon another important *DQR* principle and custom which has been maintained from the beginning: that all the editors read all the material submitted and whatever our individual specialities may be we are equally responsible for the selection and arrangement of copy. In recent years we have decreased the number of separate reviews of new books, since our coverage was bound to be somewhat random; but we are continually trying to find ways to increase the range and scope of our valuble survey articles. Since 1976 we have had a number of important interviews with Angus Wilson, William Gass, Seamus Heaney, Tom Stoppard and Malcolm Bradbury; and we have published certain special issues devoted to a single topic: "Women and Fiction" in 1976, "Modern American Fiction" in 1977. In 1980 we published a choice issue of commissioned articles as a retirement present for A.G.H. Bachrach, an article from whom we had published earlier and which is to be found again in this book alongside two contributions by colleagues to that mini-Festschrift; and in our eleventh year we were responsible for the appearance of an Early- and Middle-English number which is also available in book form. During the last four or five years we have enjoyed lightening the letterpress with the imaginative and sometimes exuberant illustrations of Hendrik van Leeuwen.

Although not all the authors in this anthology are Dutch or even based in the Netherlands, we have attempted to give something of a Dutch flavour to the collection. One or two articles are on Dutch themes, or are Dutch variations on a theme; other items are from distinguished visitors who were passing through and who thought they would like to commemorate their brief stay with a contribution to *DQR*, which in such cases has served as a more than usually interesting guest book.

The present day publishers of *DQR* and of this anthology are Rodopi, who took us up (mainly through the rare enthusiasm of the late Piet Schippers) when Van Gorcum were themselves taken over by a widely based and far flung publishing empire which was very little concerned with local ventures. Rodopi as a small local Amsterdam firm with the right kind of casually directed energy for the publication of unprofitable journals has been a good friend to *DQR*: we have not always managed to come out on time (sometimes their fault, sometimes ours), but we have continued to come out.

We hope that this anthology will convince new readers and remind old ones that possibly *DQR* has been worth while. In order to give a full account of ourselves, at least in outline, for the last ten years, we also provide with this anthology a cumulative index, which will show newconmers what they have missed and help old friends and subscribers to find favourite articles. And browsing through an index is the quickest and most appetizing manner of discovering things you never knew were there (in those old unopened copies, perhaps?). The index indicates that the most discussed authors (for some reason) in *DQR* over the first ten years were Shakespeare (no surprise), Joyce, Chaucer, Dickens, D.H. Laurence, Conrad, Hemingway, Charlotte Brontë and Coleridge. No particular significance, we hope; probably pure accident. But perhaps we ought to encourage subscribers and contributors to place bets now on a list to be compiled recording the coverage of the next ten years: after Shakespeare, who then? Stay with us and we will all see. This is part of the excitement of editing any journal: you never know what may turn up in the next post, and we firmly believe that there always will be a post for magazines like *DQR*.

The Editors

TURNER'S HOLLAND

A.G.H. Bachrach

In the international world of art the bi-centenary of Turner's birth resulted in making 1975 a Turner Year on an hitherto unprecedented scale. Two major events stand out. Both at Turner's own Royal Academy and in the British Museum commemorative exhibitions were organised which showed numerically not only a unique richness of items which had not been brought together since they left the painter's studio, but also an almost unbelievable variety. Where the Royal Academy exhibition concentrated on oils, the British Museum presented watercolours. Each added, besides, a judicious sprinkling of sketchbooks which as footnotes were hardly less fascinating than the main text. Together the two exhibitions enabled the public at long last to "read" Turner.

It would, of course, have been impossible to relay all his various messages. Hence the present essay which is part of the opening chapters of Turner's Holland, *a forthcoming study of the special role of the Low Countries in Turner's evolution.*

The beginnings of the undertaking go back to 1970 when I was privileged to be given the chance to turn a dream into reality. This was the exhibition organised to illustrate the special relationship between Dutch seventeenth-century landscape and marine painting with British Romantic art. Somewhat brazenly entitled "Shock of Recognition", the exhibition was shown first at the Mauritshuis in The Hague and in 1971 at the Tate Gallery in London. On each occasion Turner's "The Dort Packet-boat from Rotterdam becalmed" was a pièce de résistance. *And in both exhibitions it was clear to the visitor that there could well be more in the background of the Dordrecht waterfront than met the eye – a feeling strengthened by the impression made on the history-conscious spectator by the same artist's "Van Tromp going about to please his Masters". Indeed Turner's interest in Dutch life and times had already emerged from a necessarily summary consultation of the sketchbooks for the catalogue.*

The search pursued ever since, together with Mrs Harriet Jillings as a truly invaluable collaborator, resulted in 1974 in Turner and Rotterdam, *a slender volume privately printed for Mr. W. H. Fockema Andreae, the out-going President of the Rotterdam Chamber of Commerce.*

With its 130 reproductions of unpublished sketches it was a Rotterdam-centered fragment of the overall picture which in Turner's Holland *will be made generally available. It is to the preface of the latter book that I would like to refer in acknowledging the great help and many courtesies received throughout. Even at this stage, however, I would like to make an exception for Mr. Andrew Wilton of the Department of Prints and Drawings in the British Museum, Mr. Martin Butlin of the Tate Gallery, and Mr. Evelyn Joll of Messrs. Agnew's, to all of whom I owe a great debt of gratitude.*

I

The following pages constitute an attempt to explore, within a frame of reference not usually touched upon, the relationship between Turner's sources and his finished works. Its aim will not be to prove that Turner was a Dutchman in disguise. What will be endeavoured is only to redress the balance between a conventional over-emphasis of his link with Claude, and an equally conventional underestimate of his Dutch allegiances. Both by Turner's own testimony and in contemporary reviews the Dutch connection was seen from the start. How it fared at his hands, however, when its batteries were recharged, and what its effect was on the development of his art has not really been pursued since.[1] Yet the artist's first biographer, Walter Thornbury, put this on record:

> Mr. Trimmer and Turner were one day looking over some prints. "Ah! that", said Turner with emotion, taking up a particular one, "made me a painter". It was a green mezzotinto, a VanderVelde – an upright; a single large vessel running before the wind and bearing up bravely against the waves.[2]

1. Cf. Luke Herrmann, *Turner. Paintings, Watercolours, Prints & Drawings*, 1975, p. 237.

2. W. Thornbury, *The Life and Correspondence of J. M. W. Turner*, 1862, I, p. 18.

1. "Ships in a Gale", mezzotint by E. Kirkall after a painting from the school of Van de Velde. The original is now lost; a similar composition is in the Rijksmuseum, Amsterdam, where sales of modern reproductions show how popular it still is.

Although the passage has been dismissed as probably apocryphal, the book contains another such reference. When drawn into a discussion of Turner's basic unpretentiousness, the same informant is quoted as having told the author:

> We were one day looking at a VanderVelde, and on someone observing "I think you could go beyond that", he shook his head and said "I can't paint like him".[3]

That Thornbury's biography, published eleven years after Turner's death, was a shallow and often slipshod piece of journalistic hackwriting need not invalidate the information thus preserved. Thornbury had after all been able to approach many who had known the painter personally; one of these was the Rev. H. S.

3. Thornbury, pp. 125-26.

2. "Fishermen at Sea", 1796 (Tate Gallery): Turner's first oil-painting (the Cholmeley Sea-piece). It represents what was to be an ever-recurring theme in his work: simple people plying their trade in a danger-fraught marine context. The rendering of various types of illumination and their successive reflections both behind the Needles and around the vessels and fishing-net floats is very effective; the lantern was obligatory.

Trimmer who had been a friend of Turner's father.

The first time that Turner wrote the word "Dutch" in an artistic context was on the right-hand edge of an ink, wash and white chalk drawing, where his neatly penned "Last Study to the Dutch Boats D of B" indicated, perhaps with some relief, that he was by then able to begin work on his first commission for an oil painting. This was to be the "Dutch Boats in a Gale" for the Duke of Bridgewater, intended to hang as a companion to a picture of the same size in his collection – the "Fresh Breeze with Men-of-War in the Distance" by Willem van de Velde the Younger[4] – and exhibited at the Royal Academy in 1801.

Neither the green mezzotint after Van de Velde, nor the Duke of Bridgewater's oil by this prodigious Dutch master, need actually have been the origin of "that made me a painter" or of "I can't paint like him". But Van de Velde did more than net the twenty-six year old Turner £250 for "a sea-piece five feet high and seven

4. Also entitled "A Rising Gale".

feet wide". As the usually appreciative art critic of the *Sun* admitted somewhat patronisingly after the rumour had reached him:

> Far from presuming to hint that this is too high a price, we hope the report is well-founded and we are disposed to honour His Grace for such a liberal patronage of rising abilities.[5]

This passage – possibly inspired by private knowledge of Turner's unsuccessful attempt at obtaining another £ 20 for the frame[6] – does not seem to have voiced the general feeling among the establishment. A week later William Cobbett, as the ever socially critical Porcupine, printed the entire review verbatim in the *Political Register* – the one paper at the time with a nation-wide significance – but left out this particular sentence.[7] It is interesting to note that whereas in his article Turner's picture was called "one of the greatest ornaments of the present exhibition" and proof that "nothing little appears from his hand", exception was taken to his "free touch" and the resulting "carelessness", "obscurity" and absence of a "firm, determined outline". The *Star* described it as "executed in the best manner of the Dutch marine painters", yet also complained of its "liberal style" which left "the supply of many of the minutiae" to the beholder.[8] The *St. James's Chronicle* applauded "the skill with which the boats are grouped" and "the motion of the water", but said of the general effect that it seemed "to unite the merits of Vandervelt (*sic*) and Rembrandt".[9] Had this critic heard the President of the Royal Academy refer to it as "what Rembrandt thought of but could not do", or the Academy's Professor of Painting describe it as "the best picture there, quite Rembrandtish"? [10] For the *Monthly*

5. The *Sun*, 1 May 1801.
6. Farington, *The Diary*, ed. J. Greig, 1922-28.
7. *Weekly Political Register*, 7 May 1801.
8. The *Star*, 4 May 1801.
9. *St. James's Chronicle*, 9 May 1801.
10. Farington, MS-Diary, 25 April 1801 (British Museum, Dept. of P. & D); A. J. Finberg, *The Life of J. M. W. Turner, R. A.*, ed. 1961, p. 71. The comments of West and Fuseli may just possibly have referred to Rembrandt's "Christ in the Storm on the Lake of Gallilee" which in the late eighteenth century entered the Hope collection at Dorking (cf. Evelyn Joll and Martin Butlin in *A Catalogue Raisonné of Turner's Works*, forthcoming). But

Mirror, at any rate, the picture had "with the justest claims" become "a peculiar favourite of the spectator", although the writer could not refrain from adding "the artist's good sense will teach him, to be on his guard against the effects of public favour".[11]

"Dutch Boats in a Gale; fishermen endeavouring to put their fish on board", as the full title reads, almost overnight acquired the status of Picture of the Year. Turner had successfully combined the prestige of a great tradition with a dash, flair and directness that were personal and new. To him could well be applied the first public pronouncement that Coleridge had made in an *Epistle,* (curiously enough) *written . . . near Bridgewater,* on the unknown Wordsworth:

> a Poet, whose versification is occasionally harsh and his diction too frequently obscure; but whom I deem unrivalled amongst the writers of the present day in manly sentiment, novel imagery, and vivid colouring.[12]

This many felt about Turner as well. There was, moreover, no danger of an unflattering comparison with its model in his patron's collection. The Van de Velde was in the Duke's drawing-room at Old Hall, Worsley, and another thirty-six years were to pass before both pictures were publicly exhibited together.[13] But, above all, the composition – arrived at after a whole series of pen-and-wash studies and offered at a time when "poetic", that is "historical", painting was considered to rank highest in the artistic hierarchy –

Turner would hardly have had to fall back on Rembrandt for a dangerous positioning of boats in heavy seas. His sketchbooks contain many instances of realistically drawn rowing-boats and fishing-dinghies in similar near-perpendicular situations. West and Fuseli could not have known this, nor, in fact, were they likely to have had any first-hand knowledge of such scenes.

11. *Monthly Mirror,* June 1801.

12. In *Poems on Various Subjects,* April 1796.

13. In 1837 Lord Egremont lent both his Van de Velde and the Turner, commissioned as its pendant, to the British Institution's Exhibition of Old Masters – with interesting critical results.

3. Willem van de Velde II, "A Rising Gale" (Sutherland Collection): the seascape for which Turner was commissioned to paint a pendant. The vessel in the right foreground, with its heavy rubbing strakes, is a *beurtschip* or packet-boat. The men-of-war in the left background are bearing up for anchorage.

would surely have been recognized as more than merely another sea-piece. What would have been registered by the contemporaries of Wordsworth, Coleridge, Crabbe, and Cowper, was the socio-political message at the core – even if this was never formulated in so many words. For like the meteorologically much calmer "Fishermen at Sea" of 1796, "Dutch Boats in a Gale" represented not only the elements of air and water in threatening conflict but also the everyday business of simple men in their relation to these elements. Besides, it was a picture of one of their occupations in a marginal situation, that is: a situation potentially as full of triumph as of defeat, since in the pursuit of their livelihood, they had constantly to contend with both the most brutal forces of nature and the most debilitating weaknesses of man.

When Turner painted the Bridgewater sea-piece his knowledge of seamanship would still have been in its infancy. But he did

4. Turner, "Dutch Boats in a Gale. Fishermen endeavouring to put their Fish on Board", 1801 (Sutherland Collection). Both in conception and execution this picture (the Bridgewater Sea-piece) is at once consistently reminiscent of, and boldly different from, the Van de Velde by the side of which until recently it still hung – the picture has just been sold for £ 374,000, a record for an English painting.

know that a flat-bottomed fishing-vessel, broad-reaching on the starboard tack in increasingly bad weather, would have her port leeboard up, particularly if and when another vessel could be expected to close with her. In general, people in those days were more familiar with the sea than they are now.[14] Coastal transport – say, from London to Margate, a route that Turner would have taken many a time when visiting relations – was much preferred to road transport. For a contemporary peruser of the painting it would certainly not have been necessary to be himself a sailor in order to see that the smaller vessel in the foreground (which was "endeavouring to put her fish on board"), stood in danger of

14. Cf. D. Cordingly, *Marine Painting in England 1700-1900*, 1974, p. 96.

5. "Dutch Boats in a Gale": detail showing the perilous situation in which the small *pink* in the foreground will be if her skipper fails to back his jib before the large smacks under full canvas are upon him, blanketing his sail. The port leeboard of the nearest smack can be seen to be raised in order to protect it in view of the threatening collision and at the same time have the vessel drift to leeward while the net is still down. The jib-sheet in the nearest smack has already been fastened to the cringle at the end of the reefing line to enable the crew to shorten sail.

collision if her helmsman failed to bear away in time before the two large fishing-smacks under full canvas were upon him and blanketed his backed jib. This applies even if the smacks were about to round up into the wind in order to shorten sail and lie hove-to while the squall passed.

As to the other, even smaller, boat that can be observed behind the first group, this had presumably already taken over part of the catch and was heading for the shore; every detail in the picture suggests that in a rising gale it would not have an easy passage either.

In the background, finally, there are three men-of-war riding at anchor in a narrow band of light. Naturally facing into the weather

6. "Dutch Boats in a Gale": detail showing three men-of-war "peacefully" at anchor in the right background, the horizon lit up and indicating better weather.

– two of them darkly silhouetted and one brilliantly lit up – their stationary position presents a marked contrast to the main theme. Indeed these anchored ships may even be seen as symbolizing what could be called "distant peace in present turbulence". The composition, in that case, is doubly striking when we consider that they are doing so as warships, precisely. Following a seventeenth-century Dutch marine painters' device, long practised for its psychologically harmonising effect – like that of the light sails against a dark sky and the dark shadow-outline of a vessel against a strip of sunlight on the horizon, which had its parallel in landscape painting – these men-of-war would thus constitute another element in the Bridgewater sea-piece to heighten the impact of the drama. It was a very different drama from that depicted in the Van de Velde. In fact a closer analysis of Turner's model reveals that Van de Velde's figures, though in a way protagonists too, were not fishermen whose living depended on God, their skill, and their daring; they were *beurt-schippers*, that is to say packet-boat skippers who operated what even then practically amounted to a regular, time-tabled service.

So far we have been mainly concerned with reading the story in the scene depicted. But there is also the general psychological climate of England in which this story was told. It can hardly be considered negligible, for instance, that for the five years before the picture was commissioned Britain had been at war. The aftermath of the French Revolution and the reaction produced by the Reign of Terror had caused one Kingdom after another to take up arms against the tidal wave of "liberation" that threatened to engulf Europe. The papers had been full of it, and for Britain as an island, ships – and the mental and physical qualities needed to sail and fight in them against any odds – had acquired a new and special glamour.

A side-effect of this had been that although the enemy was France and the British Navy the only bulwark between comparative freedom and total subjugation, Dutch boats had become of considerable topical interest. The situation was not unlike that of May 1940. As in so many European wars, the Low Countries, and especially their ports, waterways and shipping, were felt "geographically calculated to be vitally fatal to England".[15] This feeling, however, was not only printed as such in *The Times* but shared by the enemy.

In Holland the Republican faction had at first won the day. By 1794, with the United Provinces surrendering piecemeal to the French Republican armies in their winter-favoured advance across the frozen river-lines and inundations, there appeared to be little alternative. The result was that the "Hereditary Stadtholder" Prince William V of Orange and his entourage had been compelled to flee to England (with "specie, family plate, jewels, and principal archives").[16] In their wake had come hundreds of refugees – then called "fugitives" – in Dutch vessels that had dotted with their white sails the entire passage between Scheveningen and the East Coast. The sight would have been picturesque enough. As to

15. *The Times*, 22 January 1795.
16. The *Oracle*, 21 January 1795.

the significance of this Netherlandish influx, the refugees were families which could neither be described as destitute nor as physically persecuted; they were mostly affluent and traditionally Loyalist.[17]

Three years later at the battle of Camperduin – the last naval engagement between the British and the Dutch – the Dutch Republican fleet had been largely destroyed. In April 1798, however, Coleridge had written "Fears in Solitude" and the addition to this title of "During the Alarm of an Invasion" indicates how widespread the apprehension still was. Then in 1799, after weathering severe gales, a British Expeditionary Force, strengthened by Russian troops of the Czar, had landed under the command of the Duke of York and conquered the best part of North Holland. This had been possible because the new fleet of the Batavian Republic had surrendered without a shot, the crews having refused to fight ships flying the Orange colours. The Allied leaders had not hesitated to press their advantage. As soon as the Prince of Orange had set foot again on Dutch soil at Den Helder, he had succeeded in attracting thousands of Dutch deserters from the French command, while many Dutch men-of-war elsewhere had chosen to repair to British harbours or had been impounded following a British embargo on all Dutch shipping. Dutch boats had been used for the transport of stores or had stationed themselves as "living" buoys to mark passages and channels for the big ships of the line. But in the autumn before Turner began to paint his picture the tide had turned once more; the Expedition had proved abortive and its evacuation was completed by December – again with the help of fishing-boats and other vessels, many of which were owned or manned by Orangists.

It is in this wider perspective, then, that the extraordinary success of "Dutch Boats in a Gale" becomes understandable: to the British public its narrative and symbolic content must have been close to their heart, their experience and their interest, while in its representation of near-catastrophe it was not only topical but almost aggressively Romantic.

With an articulate minority Turner's first commission for an

17. *St. James's Chronicle,* 29-30 August 1799.

oil-painting was not universally applauded. In fact what it had elicited was critical comment that was double-edged, occasionally malicious, and even when full of praise not without a grudging undertone. In a professional context the situation was not exactly flattering either: after those numerous topographical drawings and watercolour-copies of places and pictures by which he had first made his name, this commission was not for an original Turner but merely for a Van de Velde by Turner's brush. However, the Duke of Bridgewater's realistically specified order was more than a *nouveau riche*'s passion to indulge in some form of art speculation. It forced Turner to regard Willem van de Velde the Younger as a personal challenge. The nine extant pen-and-wash studies in his large *Calais Pier Sketchbook* are revealing. Ranging from flimsy memoranda of the foreground boats in the Duke's Van de Velde (in reverse), and the outlines of two background vessels of his own invention against a mere chalk line as horizon, to detailed drawings which in their ingeniously balanced variations could each be considered fully-fledged water-colours – this whole set testifies to the seriousness with which he had undertaken his task.[18]

The prelude to the genesis of the Bridgewater sea-piece is not without irony. The considerable fortune of Sir Francis Egerton, the third and last Duke, had been founded largely on his Lancashire coalmines and transport canals. As "props" of the Industrial Revolution both of these were in themselves to prove extremely significant for the Romantics' perception of the Picturesque in nature. For the general public at the time the mines fired the imagination by the novelty of their specific mystery, and the canals first gave rise to a new form of tourist-travel. For us, to-day, the point of interest is that the Bridgewater millions had been turned to good use in the purchase of pictures from the collection of the Duc d'Orléans. After the guillotining of their *ci-devant* owner these pictures had been put up for sale in London by his grandson in 1798, in the very middle of the war that was to lend such special interest to Turner's "Dutch Boats in a Gale". Upon the formation of a syndicate with two other Peers, the Duke's operation had been successfully accomplished. In a way, therefore, it demon-

18. Cf. Finberg, *Life*, p. 70 and *Turner's Sketches and Drawings,* 1910, repr. 1968, pp. 33-6.

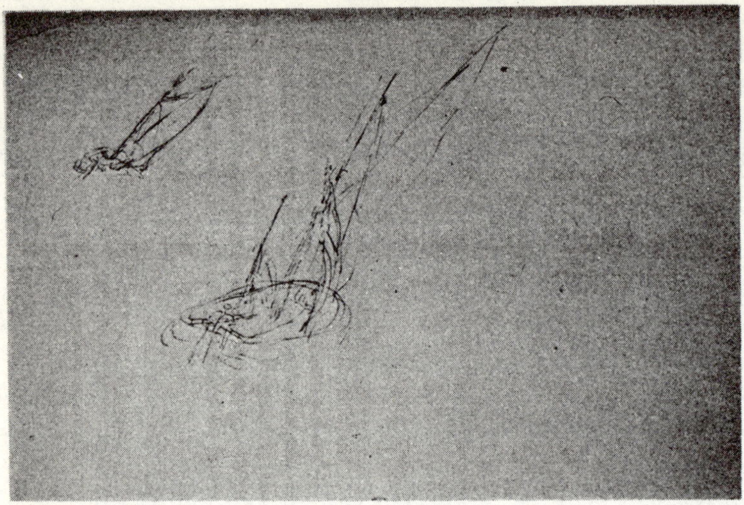

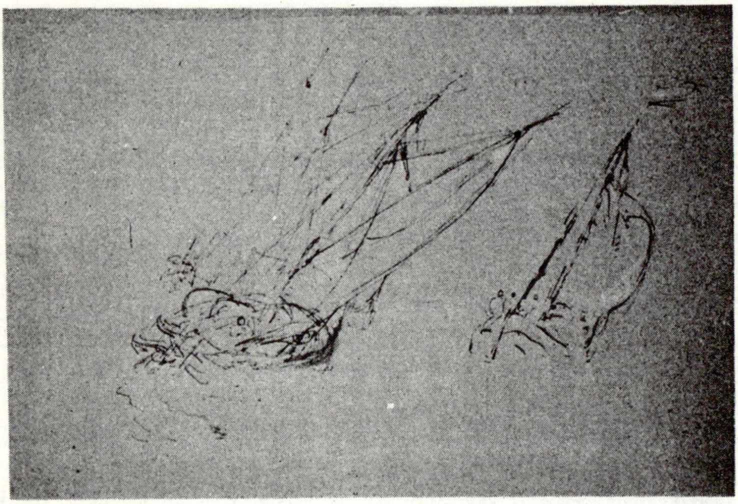

7. Early studies for "Dutch Boats in a Gale" (*Calais Pier Sketchbook,* LXXXI, 146 & 148). When compared to Van de Velde's "Rising Gale" it would seem that Turner first merely wanted to have the spritsail rigged vessels in his own composition on the port tack so as to obtain a mirror effect. The gaff-rigged fishing-boat on the right, in the lower study, was used in his "Calais Pier" of 1803; this is characteristic of what may be termed Turner's documentary economy.

8. Study for "Dutch Boats in a Gale" (*Calais Pier Sketchbook*, LXXXI, 118/119); artist's note: *Duke's Picture*. The background of the picture was clearly to be centred on a man-of-war at anchor. In this study the composition, as in the Van de Velde, includes another warship, sailing towards the spectator. In the version finally painted this was eliminated.

strates to perfection the cultural repercussions of this link, nowadays only too easily overlooked, between some aspects of the Industrial Revolution in Britain and of the political revolution in France. In a way, again, perhaps nothing could be more "romantic".

II

At this historical juncture almost any work by a landscape or marine painter of the Dutch School had become a safe bet for collectors, especially the new collectors who like Turner's first patron could be indicated as a by-product of the Industrial Revolution. Towards the end of the eighteenth century there had been a major exodus of highly prized works of art from the Continent across the Channel. The trend continued with even more vigour during the Napoleonic era, not only in spite of but precisely

9. Study for "Dutch Boats in a Gale" (*Calais Pier Sketchbook*, LXXXI, 122/123). In this study there is only one large fishing-smack with a smaller vessel still at some distance from her in the left foreground. In the background the man-of-war at anchor is identical with the previous study, while the one under sail has been shifted to the extreme right, thus mirroring the design of Van de Velde. Proportions and distances, however, do not match: the foreshortened frigate on the left being too high on the horizon in comparison to the other in profile.

10. Studies for "Dutch Boats in a Gale" (*Calais Pier Sketchbook*, LXXXI, 126/127); artist's note: *Study to the Duke of Bridgewater's Picture.* The foreground vessel shows great activity of the sailors, with the helmsman starting the manoeuvre to wear her round and one crew member coiling up the halyard of the downed mainsail. On the right a sketch of the second small boat in the painting's middle distance, the crew again very active.

11. Study for "Dutch Boats in a Gale" (*Calais Pier Sketchbook*, LXXXI, 108/109); artits's note: *Duke's*. Van de Velde's packet-boats have become fishing-smacks; these are in the same position as in the painting but the small vessel in the foreground is a rowing-boat under their lee. The figures in the second rowing-boat, half-hidden behind the smacks, are just visible, whereas the figure in the third boat, evidently meant to link pictorially the smacks and the anchored vessel, is disproportionately large. The contrast is only between movement and rest. A fishing-hooker has replaced, as a try-out, the men-of-war on the horizon. The practice of taking an early catch ashore in small boats was widely spread, these boats being called *ventjagers* and operating in the Thames estuary as well as in Dutch home-waters. Turner must often have seen the fishing fleet from Middelharnis at work in this fashions.

12. Study for "Dutch Boats in a Gale" (*Calais Pier Sketchbook*, LXXXI,106/107); artist's note: *Last Study to the Dutch Boats D. of B.* The foreground shows another variation, the small pink and the rowing-boat have successfully cleared the fishing-smacks. The background is busier than in the painting with one ship-of-the-line riding at anchor in front of a whole squadron, one man-of-war approaching downwind, and others under sail or at anchor, partly in the lighted area, partly in the shadow of an undefined squall.

because of the continued warfare and political upheavals. These again and again dislodged countless items that had been regarded as permanent fixtures. The nineteenth-century continental connoisseur who visited England found that although museums had barely begun to be established, the country seemed to house more Old Masters – pictures as well as sculptures and other antiquities – than almost any other country in Europe. But then in eighteenth-century Britain the special circumstances touched upon above had produced a special situation. As a result, private collectors laid out vast sums to enable the new "gardenists" to create on their estates the kind of landscaped environment that did credit to the Man of Taste, and spent fortunes at the great London auctions in order to live surrounded by the paintings, tapestries and *objets d'art* which had formed, and confirmed, their scale of values.[19]

In every one of the stately homes that Turner had visited on his practically annual sketching-tours of the kingdom since 1792, Dutch art would be in ample evidence – whether the owner was a recently created coal-baron, such as Bridgewater, a cultured eccentric, like Beckford, or a nobleman of ancient lineage, such as Leicester. The pedigree collections took precedence, of course, but at the other extreme were the salerooms, educative for the collector and informative for the artist, as a guide to fashions and prices. And in between came the annual exhibitions of the Royal Academy and British Institution, as well as the private shows of dealers and artists, which together had changed quite radically the pattern of patronage from agreed commission to selective purchase. Thus was constituted what could be termed a Stock Exchange of polite commodities. Indeed, writing of an exhibition at the British Institution in 1818, the *British Press* said in so many words: "Its influence on public taste, the mart it furnishes for the sale of pictures, the fame and reward which it has been the means of distributing among young Artists of merit, present a combination of superior advantages."[20]

For the curious and the less affluent there was the trade in prints, which in those pre-camera days provided an index of taste for those who were currently referred to as the "thinking middling

19. See F. Herrmann, *The English as Collectors*, 1972.
20. The *Examiner*, 9 February 1818.

classes". This trade was also an accessible source of lasting documentation for amateurs and professionals alike, and tended to increase demand. As early as 1736 James Thomson, himself a collector and in so many other respects the poetic spokesman of what moved his contemporaries in the field of nature perception, had apostrophised "engraving" as:

. . .the kind of art that, of unvalued price,
The famed and only picture easy gives,
Refine(s) her touch, and, through the shadowed piece,
All the live spirit of the painter pour(s).[21]

Involved as its syntax is, this expression of the feeling that through engravings a unique work of art can reach the many could hardly have occurred in a more suitable poetic effusion than that of his famed *Liberty.* Now three quarters of a century later but in hardly less lofty a strain, the *Examiner* declared: "Our native Artists create and satisfy the cravings of the connoisseur. They not only gratify us with . . . the general design of the painted originals, but the heart, the soul, and the strength; not only an intelligent but a luminous translation".[22] And in 1834 the point was taken up again when the well-known engraver John Pye, in a statement before the Select Committee on Arts and Manufactures, declared that the international success of English engravings was due to their being "free translations from pictures instead of being cold, rigid copies".

In his formative years Turner's visual memory was filled, as any English artist's memory naturally would be, with works of the great French and Italian masters. But it was also crammed with Dutch pictures, both from the collections or exhibitions that he had visited or the sales he had attended and from the prints he had bought or "looked over". His early training had been varied and

21. Thomson, *Liberty,* 1736. The passage, characteristically, begins:

Let Gallic bards record . . .
From Rome, awhile, how painting counted long;
With Poussin came – ancient design, that lifts
A fairer front and looks another soul . . .

22. The *Examiner,* 5 April 1818.

intense. First he had copied engravings. Thereafter he had begun to wash in the backgrounds of architectural drawings. Next, about 1788, had come his somewhat haphazard apprenticeship with Thomas Malton, the architectural draughtsman who must have taught him a good deal about the drawing of buildings and structural perspective. Between 1794 and 1796 there had been his years of salaried copying at the house of Dr. Thomas Monro – the curious climate of which years can only be guessed at when one considers that this uncommon physician was not only a collector and an amateur-painter but also a self-appointed art-teacher, besides being the alienist of Turner's schizophrenic mother and the director of the Bedlam Hospital where she died insane.

In Monro's service Turner had met Girtin and other young painters and – outwardly – soon developed into an extremely competent topographer in the style then current. His formal tuition, begun at the Royal Academy to which his father had generously sent him in 1789, had tended in the same direction. After all, in those days this tuition had to be based on a strict adherence to tradition and a faithful imitation of the Old Masters. Sir Joshua Reynolds, first President of a Royal Academy that had been established explicitly "to revive the dignity of a dying art", had a typically British predilection for the Italian style, conditioned by the deeply ingrained convention of the Grand Tour. It coloured every opinion expressed in the context of an institution where Turner had been admitted a student at fourteen, was to exhibit at fifteen, to be elected to full membership at twenty-seven and at thirty-two be made a Professor of Perspective – perhaps the most challenging assignment the Academy had to offer at a time, when psychologically, every single perspective in the life of European man either had been or was being re-adjusted. Yet in his description of "A Journey through Flanders and Holland in the year 1781", Reynolds had written:

> Painters should go to the Dutch School to learn the Art of Painting, as they would go to a Grammar School to learn Languages.[23]

It is this, in one sense paradoxical, dictum of the premier

23. J. Reynolds, *Works,* 1801, Vol. II, p. 86.

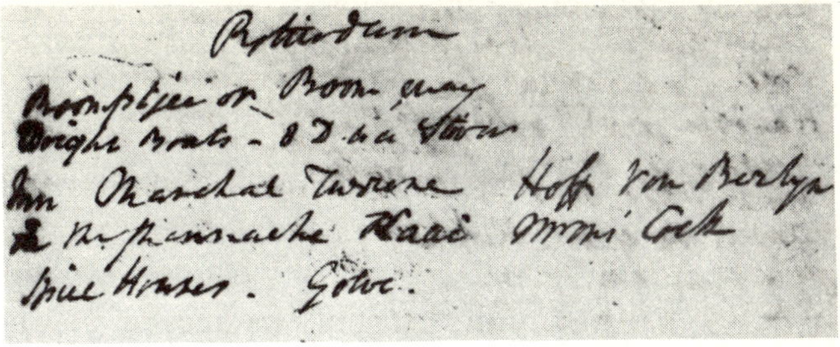

13. Sample page from Turner's travel-notes, here recording data about Rotterdam (*Itinerary Rhine Tour Sketchbook,* CLIX, p.14): *Boomptjes or Boom quay* (the famous tree-shaded main quay of Rotterdam).. *Doight Boits – 8D to a stiver* (cheap rowing-ferries and the fare in Dutch currency). *Inn Marchal Turrenne Hoff van Berlijn* (names of two hotels recognizable in later sketches). *In the Spannache Kaai Mons. Cock* (address of the Dutch collector Cock, with garbled version of *Spaansche Kaai*). Spiel Houses. Gowe (brothels, followed by the name of the little river on which Gouda is situated and thereby connected with Rotterdam).

champion of the Grand Style that has taken us to the heart of the matter in our present context. For it epitomizes the essential ambiguity of the forces that went into the shaping of Turner as a creative artist.

III

The Academicians's use of the terms "Grammar" and "Languages" links up with the *Examiner*'s "luminious" and with the engraver's "free" translation. Painting as language is an age-old metaphor, but in the years which elapsed between these three statements it was remarkably often used. Turner himself recorded of a Titian he saw in Paris in 1802 that the picture "admirably described" the Entombment.[24] But if "translation" may be taken as a key-concept of Turner's art in general,[25] here it should certainly be understood as both "vertical" translation and "horizontal", that is to say: from one period to another, and from one medium into another. Besides, if for him the vertical variety could never be personal enough, the horizontal could never be exact enough. An

24. *Louvre Sketchbook,* p. 31a.

25. John Gage, as quoted by N. Omer, Introduction to the catalogue of *Turner and the Poets,* Greater London Council Exhibition, Twickenham, 1975. p.9.

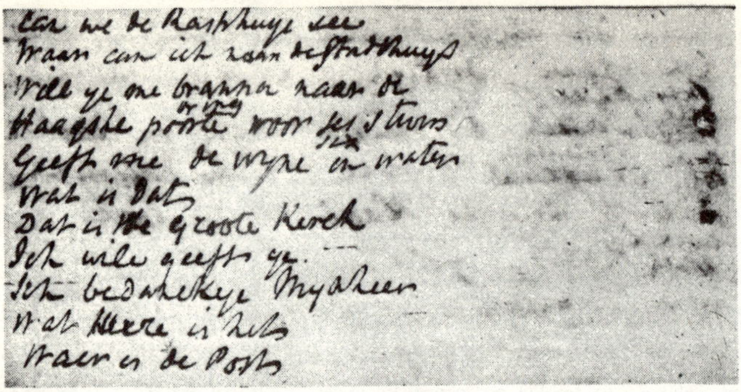

14. On the next page Turner noted useful phrases and points of interest, the spelling being half-phonetic and half-Dutch: ***Can we de Rasphuys see. Waar can ick naar de Stadhuys. Will ye me branna*** **(underneath:** ***bring)*** ***naar de Haagshe poorte voor ses*** **(underneath:** ***six)*** ***stivers. Geeft me de wijne en water. Wat is dat. Dat is de Groote Kirck. Ick will geeft ye. Ick bedackye Mijnheer. Wat Uure is het. Waer is de Post.***

example of the latter type can be shown in his dealings with engravers. This is his reply to Edward Goodall, one of his pupils subsequently to do much engraving after Turner's paintings, who had asked him how he should "render the reds":

> Sometimes translate it into black and at another time into white. If a bit of black gives the emphasis, so does red in my picture. And in the case of translating into white – put a grinning (*sic*) line into it that will make it attractive.[26]

In an earlier age, and specifically where the medium was verbal, the struggle for emancipation of the mother tongue as a means of communication would inevitably pass through a state of slavish, then challenging, and finally defiant imitations of the Ancients. Generations of aspiring poets had been obsessed with the idea that they must out-versify their models.

To the aspiring painters, though at a later date, the same applied. In fact by now, whenever the spirit moved them, the Wilsons, the Gainsboroughs, the Cromes, or the Constables in their landscapes would openly or covertly imitate. More often than not they would translate foreign and former expressions as literally as they could, not so much seeking imaginative equivalents in their

26. F. Goodall, *Reminiscenses,* 1902, p. 57. For "red as a tone" see the draft of Turner's second lecture, where he said: ". . .it is inevitably allowed that Engraving is or ought to be a translating of a Picture. . ."

own language as retelling conventional stories in a borrowed accent, an assimilated rhythm, and a tone to set the heart of the connoisseur at rest.

Turner, intellectually self-taught and professionally ambitious as he was, seems from an early age onwards to have felt that he should not retell popular themes from elsewhere in slurred prose or semi-articulate poetry. He did not make mechanical imitations; instead he over-reacted to works he admired and almost compulsively sought to outpaint his models – or for models to outpaint.

Where there did not as yet exist any recognizably British pictorial tradition,[27] the foreign background of these models was again two-fold. In the characteristically national interpretation of their landscape and in the elegant projection of its present facts into an idealized and generally bucolic past, the Italian – or Italianizing foreign – Masters were the norm. But they were the accepted alternative to the long history of Netherlandish influence. The strength of this influence, originally fostered in the Tudor and Caroline courts and now revived after many Dutch artists had once again settled in England during the reigns of Charles II and William III, was rooted in the special appeal of their fusion of technical mastery with an earthy observation of everyday life. What is more, ever since the seventeenth century the School's mood and subject-matter had been determined by the taste of a large and unsophisticated buyers' market at home which caused the details of most compositions to be shaped by the Dutch burgher's almost passionately urban materialism. This materialism, however, had been tempered by the Dutch farmer's and seaman's practical knowledge of the forces of nature, of the wind and the rain, and of the meaning of a changing cloud in the limitless expanse of the Dutch sky. And by being so tempered it had bestowed on itself a patrician nobility all of its own.

It was with this in his mind, no doubt, that Reynolds – who paid another visit to Holland within three years – had elaborated

27. In 1722 the later founder-member of the Royal Academy, Jonathan Richardson, was the first to call for a young artist of genius who should initiate an English School of painting to match the famous schools of the continent.

his "grammatical" advice to British painters and continued his journal as follows:

> We must be content to make up our ideas of perfection from the excellencies which are dispersed over the world. A poetical imagination, expression, character, or even correctness of drawing, are seldom united with that power of colouring which would set off those excellencies to the best advantage; and in this perhaps no School ever excelled the Dutch.[28]

In the development of Turner's styles what is really intriguing is not simply which features he took over and which he rejected, but where he surpassed the Old Masters, what became part of his personal idiom and when he spoke in a voice completely his own. This is where Reynolds's *XIIth Discourse* contains a revealing comment:

> The art of seeing Nature, or in other words, the art of using Models, is in reality the great object, the point to which all our studies are directed.[29]

Reynolds is here equating the direct perception of nature with a study of the Old Masters, and in particular the practice of copying them. His precept accounts for the fascination of a "close reading" of Turner's many Claudian derivations or his Poussin and Rosa imitations. That he should accept Reynolds's teaching so faithfully in his youth shows the humility of the man who today is so often represented as something of a potentate. Ultimately, however, does not the rigid linking together of "seeing nature" and "using models" account for the spell of those later pictures which when they were first exhibited were taken to represent nothing but the warring elements?

One aspect of the extra-ordinarily ambivalent attraction of the bourgeois art of Holland's Golden Age was that, contrary to eighteenth-century taste, historical subjects had constituted only a minor interest. In a country without a Court, if people were aware of their special role on the European stage – even after the hectic

28. Reynolds, *Works, loc. cit.*

29. Reynolds, *Discourses,* p. 217. The XIIth Discourse was delivered in 1784.

15. **A number of drawings in Turner's *Dort Sketchbook* show the Great Church from roughly the same angle as in the painting, "Dordrecht: the Dort Packet-boat from Rotterdam becalmed" (the "Large Dort"), but from different distances. This time Turner was particularly struck by cloud patterns. The sketches were taken from the landing-stage of the *Zwijndrechtse Veer*, the ferry sailing straight across to Zwijndrecht and referred to in the lower left: *Fery Boats.* The artist's notes, besides recording the costume of an absent female driver of a farmer's gig (*White Jacket Sleeves stroked Green W Bl Red, Cap Light Blue R B Stockings*), focussed on the light. Lower right reads: *Small (?) Scuyds rather prevalent/ Smoke Blue and the lightest of the whole/ on the covers from the L Scuydt –/ Water only yellow green.* At the bottom of the page he added: *Ray of light thro the Clouds to the right.***

period of their Eighty Years' War of Liberation from Spain – this awareness had not produced any Marlowe or Shakespeare-by-the-Zuiderzee; their outlet had been found in the translation of their expressive urges into a handful of pictorial genres whose connection with the realities – and illusions – of war and peace was emblematic at most. Among those genres was the naturalistic landscape, legitimized, after the 1620s especially, by an atmospheric intensity and serene inwardness as nowhere else.

Given his own ambivalent attitude to Court and nobility ever since he had escaped from the dark barbershop in Covent Garden with its curiously mixed clientèle, all this must have been very much in tune with some of Turner's most deep-seated feelings. No

16. On the next page Turner sketched the Dordrecht silhouette from the opposite bank of the river – here called Merwede – in a full-page drawing. Its atmosphere has the same serenity as the "Large Dort" which shows a number of parallel motifs, such as the stretch of dyke jutting out from the west bank of the *Noord*, with reeds and an angler's rowing-boat. The scene has been taken from the east bank of this river-branch which connects Dordrecht and Rotterdam, a little to the east from where the "Packet-boat" in the painting lies "becalmed" and hides the two windmills by her sails. The artist's note reads: *Dead calm. Water lighter/ in the Nort* (Turner's spelling of *Noord*). In front of the merchantman at anchor, middle left, is a ferry for carts and horses. Like many other drawings the sketch illustrates that Turner was content to sit and draw wherever ferries, packet-boats or post-chaises set him down.

matter how sincerely and wholeheartedly he wished to conform during his apprenticeship to the Academy's conservatism, "the fumes of history filled his brain, not its dry facts", as Martin Butlin has written.[30] What excited him in his reading was whatever was passionate and elemental. This he sought to render on canvas in terms of the emotional climate concerned, each event or situation being selected in the first place because of its dramatic associations and its intrinsic relevance to his life and his times. For if for a long time he painted to sell, it was perhaps in the end in a

30. Introduction to *Turner 1775-1851*, catalogue to the Bi-centenary Exhibition, 1975.

17. Turner, "Dordrecht: the Dort Packet-boat from Rotterdam becalmed", 1818 (Collection of Mr. and Mrs. Paul Mellon, Washington D.C.).

way only to sell his soul – a latter-day Faustus, unencumbered by any doctorate in divinity.

IV

Turner produced about eighteen directly Dutch-inspired paintings. In addition to these which can be distinguished by a Dutch reference in the title or a Dutch element at the heart of the conception, there are a large number of descendants whose parentage is more remotely Dutch or only conjecturally so. Both categories, needless to say, form the tip of the iceberg of which the nearly six hundred extant sketches from his Dutch tours constitute its long-hidden base.

When looking at the non-British elements in Turner's work as a whole, it is difficult to grasp the fact that he hardly travelled at all outside Britain until he was middle-aged. Nor is it easy to assess the extent of its implications. For British painters and poets, the chronology of their travels seems to have been a far more important factor in the development of their perception of nature than for their continental colleagues. Forced isolation from what was once the cradle of civilization and until recently the focus of all Tours, was instrumental both in their "discovery" of the homeland and in their idealization of a by then doubly distant Italy and Greece. And this, of course, runs parallel to the position of Italian art in the evolution of British taste. Turner, apart from his crucial trip to Paris and Switzerland during the shortlived Peace of Amiens in 1802, did not go abroad again until 1817 when, the blockade of France lifted since 1815, Europe had ceased to cower under the threat of Napoleon's armies. He was forty-two when he first toured the Netherlands and the Rhine provinces; instead of setting out a starry-eyed young artist on a voyage into the unknown, he had already lived a whole life.

Broadly speaking then, Turner's early attempts at "Dutch" painting had begun as the echoes of his acquaintance with Dutch art (and the Dutch scene) in British collections, especially in those of William Beckford and the Duke of Bridgewater, with each of whom he had stayed in 1799.[31] Next, there were the Ruysdael and Rembrandt "essays" which can be said to have started with the memoranda done in the Louvre in 1802. To this may be added his compositions with Dutch genre-scenes and atmospheric effects, in part belonging to his Van de Velde progeny such as "Ships bearing up for Anchorage" of 1802 or "The Sun rising through Vapour" of 1807 (to which he later appended "Dutch Fishermen cleaning and selling Fish"), and "pure" landscapes such as "The Forest of Bere" of 1808 and "Frosty Morning" of 1813.

Another group of "Dutch" paintings, begun before he had ever set foot on Dutch soil, starts with the politically-inspired "Boats carrying out Anchors and Cables to Dutch Men-of-War in 1665" which he painted in 1804, the year before Trafalgar. Then in the 1830s, when by French force and inner conflict the British-sponsored Kingdom of the Greater Netherlands was reduced to its present frontiers, his revived interest in Holland and what Holland had stood for manifested itself again. It did so in two ways. On the

31. Dutch paintings in the Bridgewater collection included important works by Rembrandt, Ruysdael, Cuyp, Van de Velde; in the Beckford collection works by Cuyp, Ruysdael, Hobbema and Van de Velde.

one hand, this time he quite openly went "Rembrandtish" and produced in addition to a curious "Rembrandt's Daughter" half a dozen Biblical and Shakespearian paintings; on the other hand, he returned to themes connected with the seventeenth-century Anglo-Dutch Wars. Of the latter category, "Helvoetsluys" and "The Prince of Orange landing at Torbay" are as typical as his "Jessica" and "Pilate" were of the former.

Turner's interest in maritime drama was of a special nature. Combined as it often was with political criticism in the guise of Romantic hero-worship, it also led him to paint four seapieces featuring the seventeenth century's most daring Dutch admirals Maarten Hartpertzoon Tromp and his son Cornelis.[32] To Turner – and judging from English-language biographies, prints and pamphlets, not to Turner alone – Cornelis Tromp, who like his father had been honoured with a baronetcy by Charles II, must have been a reckless and undisciplined but generous-hearted enemy leader with whom it was possible to feel an affinity across the ages. The connection of this theme with that of the spectacular Dutch raid up the Medway and subsequently with that of the arrival of "Dutch William" will be obvious. As groups, however, these pictures fall into a wider pattern. For together they merge into the large and less obviously "Dutch" category of essentially atmospheric paintings of storms and calms, and of the effect of either on men and their endeavours. By then the Romantic alchemy had transformed his materials almost beyond recognition; maritime drama from first turning epic had at last become cosmic.

This finally takes us to the profusion of landscape outlines, shipping clusters, and urban contours so eagerly captured for future reference on each of Turner's forays into Dutch territory. After 1817, besides passing through on several less documented occasions, he went again in 1825 and for the last time in 1840/41. Every sketchbook he brought back from these visits bears witness to his persistent interest in the unique *vie des formes* offered to the pictorially aware by the rivers, towns and countryside of

32. Cornelis Tromp was dubbed Van Tromp in Britain, like his father the renowned admiral whose (unauthenticated) portrait was in an English collection. This portrait, in Britain since the middle of the eighteenth century, was exhibited at the British Institution in 1821 (no. 112).

18. Rotterdam, Ooster Oude Hoofdpoort (Eastern Old Water Gate) (*Dort Sketchbook*, CLXII, 13a/14). Perhaps the most striking features of Turner's early Rotterdam sketches are the recurring instances where he clearly wants to record the curious combination of angular architecture and curvacious shipping, so typical of the Dutch urban scene. The big barge in the foreground is a *poon* with a carved rudder-head and a freshwater cask. Made fast to her starboard is a *boeier*, equally with rigging and spars left out. The barge on the left is a *tjalk*, moored against the Spaansche Kade or Kaai mentioned in the *Itinerary Rhine Tour Sketchbook*. The scene is taken from the Oude Haven, the river Meuse being beyond the gate-house. To the left of the Ooster Oude Hoofdpoort can be seen the Spanjaardsbrug, to the right the Jan Kuitenbrug with the Wester Oude Hoofdpoort. The poon's mast-top and gaff indicate the height of her rigging. The sculptured head on the rudder recurs in the Dort painting.

Holland. Land- and seascapes evidently conceived on his travels or composed with details culled from his stock of largely linear Dutch "capital", appear in his output of oils almost to the last. But the best indication of the inspirational power of these pictorial records can perhaps be found in a particular anecdote about his Chelsea cottage. This tells us that when hoisting himself on to the platform he had erected on the roof of his last home, he would point to the view inland and call it his "Italian prospect" and to the view down-river, declaring this his "Dutch prospect".[33]

33. F. Voss, *The Double Life of J. M. W. Turner*, 1951, p. 207.

IN SEARCH OF REALITY: TWO AMERICAN HEROES COMPARED

Just as one has come to speak of the Hemingway hero, so, I think, it has become possible to speak of the typical Bellow protagonist. Since both have succeeded in drawing and holding the attention of a large reading public, it may be interesting to examine what connects them and what makes them so different on the basis of a comparative analysis of the ideas to be found embodied in both these protagonists.

The main thing they have in common — also probably one of the main reasons for their popularity — is their need to solve the problem of identity in a society that no longer provides ready-made answers. What separates them is the way in which they try to reach this solution. This already becomes clear when we compare one of Hemingway's first books, *A Farewell to Arms* (1929), with Bellow's first work, *Dangling Man* (1944), novels which do not seem to be much alike except that it is war that determines the behaviour of the two main characters. What is most striking, however, is the difference between the protagonists' attitude towards war. In *A Farewell to Arms,* Frederic Henry's decision to take part in World War I is as personal as it is unequivocal: Europe beckons, adventure allures, but what his role as an American soldier on the Italian front is supposed to be remains obscure. He may tell Passini that he fights because 'there is a class that controls a country that is stupid and does not realize anything and never can', but what this argument means to himself in motivating his participation is demonstrated by his decision to opt out after he is nearly shot as a traitor during the Caporetto retreat. War to the early Hemingway hero simply meant change, excitement, foreign countries and peoples, and when at last the nearness of war forces him to an act of commitment, it lacks any moral or ideological appeal. All that remains is for the hero to attempt to save his own skin.

To the young man Joseph awaiting Army service, in Bellow's *Dangling Man,* war, too, is an incident, 'though the most important that has ever occurred', which latter qualification already indicates an important difference with Frederic Henry's approach. Yet also to Joseph it is in no essential way a crucial incident. War can destroy him physically, but, as he says, so can bacteria. Only in this respect does war concern him. Joseph himself is to follow his destiny in spite of the war, which conviction, however, saddles him with the awkward question whether he has a separate destiny. It is only at the end of the story that the answer to this crucial question is intimated. It is contained in Joseph's last words, after he has sent in his request to be taken into the armed services: 'I am in other hands, relieved of self-determination, freedom cancelled. Hurrah for regular hours! And for the supervision of the spirit! Long live regimentation!' These lines have often been interpreted as the ironic conclusion that mankind cannot long stand freedom, but equally valid is the interpretation that Joseph has said goodbye to his Ivory Tower existence as a sensitive intellectual and is ready to embrace the insensitive but vital realities of ordinary, everyday life. This may find corroboration in an earlier remark of his: 'What we really want is to stop living so exclusively and vainly for our own sake, impure and unknowing, turning inward and self-fastened.' This does not mean that Joseph's decision should be looked upon as the result of 'a personal morality and private will'. He himself denies this as being an impossibility. As he remarks: 'Alternatives, and particularly desirable alternatives, grow only on imaginary trees.' And as he continues: 'Yes, I shall shoot, I shall take lives; I shall be shot at, and my life may be taken. Certain blood will be given for half-certain reasons, as in all wars. *Somehow I cannot regard it as a wrong against myself*' (italics added). The enormous difference between *A Farewell to Arms* and *Dangling Man* in terms of the protagonists' attitude towards war is revealed in this last sentence. Frederic Henry did consider it as a personal wrong when 'certain blood' had to be given for 'half-certain reasons'. It caused him to opt out and to follow his own separate destiny. To Joseph the idea of a separate destiny has proved doubtful. As he reflects: '. . . to be pushed upon oneself put the very facts of simple existence in doubt.' He, the Bellow protagonist, realizes that his destiny is bound up with that of his fellow human beings in a much more complex and mysterious way than he can account for at this stage of his life. And this difference in attitude towards the problem of individuality will, as we shall see, continue to play an important role in determining the separate directions this quest for life will take for both the Hemingway and the Bellow protagonist. What continues to connect them is that both acknowledge that war, and violence in general, could teach them 'to sound creation'.

It is this 'sounding creation by violence' which eventually caused Hemingway to become absorbed in the professional man of action, and the development of his early hero into the later Hemingway hero. The sensitive, vulnerable man of 'open-eyed shock' of Hemingway's early fiction — Nick Adams, Jake Barnes, Frederic Henry —, pushed around and sickened by an overexposure to violence, turns himself into the man of action of his later fiction — Harry Morgan, Philip Rawlings, Robert Jordan, Richard Cantwell, Santiago —, the man able to keep his nerve under all circumstances, feeling at ease in the world where his self-reliance and physical competence save him from isolation and emotional disarray.

The reasons why Hemingway started to take an interest in the man of action, and subsequently 'became' one[1], are closely related to the particular problems the early Hemingway found himself confronted with, the principal one being how to cope adequately in an uncaring, indifferent universe with the phenomena of death and violence. The man of action, the professional, provided the answer, and since Hemingway's artistic work is an accurate reflection of his own personal problems and experiences, his fiction soon swarmed with matadors ('The Undefeated', *The Sun Also Rises*), prizefighters ('Fifty Grand'), sportsmen ('The Short Happy Life of Francis Macomber', 'The Snows of Kilimanjaro'), soldiers (*For Whom the Bell Tolls, Across the River and into the Trees*), and professional fishermen (*The Old Man and the Sea*). What Hemingway's solution of the problem of individuality actually boils down to is that he very soon started to yield to society's demands, instead of continuing to oppose them as he had done in his early fiction up to *Green Hills of Africa* (1935). Hemingway's later heroes, starting with Harry Morgan, begin to act in conformity with a conception of reality, accepted by society as the only one of real value; the reality, in fact, that war (aggression, violence) is the only yard-stick to measure one's manhood, and that death is to be ignored and denied the power to determine one's behaviour. The actions and reactions of the Hemingway hero become predictable and repetitive. He begins to lack what in Bellow's fiction, reflecting his 'sounding creation by violence', continues to provide one of the major driving forces activating his protagonists: the unwillingness to submit to any established conception of reality. This may not be too obvious in Bellow's second novel *The Victim* (1947), since the guilt and anxiety-ridden story of Leventhal, the Jew, who has taken upon his shoulders the moral burden of a world he never made, restricts itself to the problem of Jewish identity only, but in his third novel, *The Adventures of Augie March* (1953), the theme emerges in full scope and force. Man should remain available to all of life's possibilities, and he should stubbornly elude as Richard Chase has put it 'all the identities proferred to one

[1] For a detailed analysis see my *Ernest Hemingway: The Artist As Man of Action* (Assen: Van Gorcum, 1972).

by the world, by one's past, by one's friends.' In *Augie March,* the Bellow protagonist assumes the identity respectively of a proletarian boy on his picaresque way up the American social ladder, a thief, an apprentice to the world of shady American business, an adopted son, a tramp, a lover, a student and would-be intellectual at the University of Chicago, a Trotskyite of sorts, an eagle tamer, and a merchant seaman. 'A man's character is his fate,' Augie remarks at the beginning of his long quest for life, and if this is true one can understand why Augie's character in this third novel of Bellow's remains elusive, refuses 'to become'. Augie's availability to all of life's possibilities, his refusal to submit to versions of reality imposed upon him by other people (his brother Simon's, Einhorn's, Mrs Renling's, the Magnuses', Thea Fenchel's), ends in anarchy, a riotous accumulation of countless characters and incidents, energetic but shapeless, unrelated, without a central organizing principle, so it seems. At the end Augie exclaims: 'Why I am a sort of Columbus of those near-at-hand and believe you can come to them in this immediate *terra incognita* that spreads out in every gaze.' But though the real Columbus may not have had the slightest idea what he was going to find, he did have some solid reasons why he was going to explore it, which can hardly be said of Augie. The question why he should want to come to those near-at-hand when he keeps refusing to join or help them, remains unanswered. One can explore as many realities as one can imagine, but if it is done for the sake of exploration only, then Bellow's third novel, despite exciting reading, ultimately does pose Maxwell Geismar's question of what we can really make of it all.

Seize the Day (1956), Bellow's next novel, serves as a kind of counterpoint to *Augie March.* There are those who do want to submit to other people's conceptions of reality, but even fail in this. Finishing college, becoming a Hollywood star, a salesman, a stock-market speculator, a familyman raising children, are all versions of reality that are highly regarded in American society. Tommy Wilhelm, the protagonist of *Seize the Day,* tries them all and fails miserably. To succeed in this kind of society one should at least possess some of the cold, narcissistic self-centredness of a Dr Adler, Tommy's father, a successful retired doctor, only intent on his own comfort and ashamed of his son who has turned out to be a social misfit; or one should have the qualities of a Dr Tamkin, investor, alleged psychiatrist, mystic and philosopher of sorts, but in reality merely a confidence man, who cheats Tommy out of his last eight hundred dollars. Just as Dr Adler (the name is already suggestive) may be conceived as symbolizing an invalidated social and cultural genteelism, so Dr. Tamkin ('attempting, tampering?') can be looked upon as a representative product of modern mass society in which everything is available ready-made to everybody except a set of norms to provide values surpassing crass materialism.

At the end of the story Tommy is jostled by a group of mourners into a funeral parlour. There, standing by the coffin of a nameless stranger, who might have been not only himself, but also Dr. Adler, who has rejected his love, or Dr. Tamkin, who has taken advantage of his feelings of dependence, he starts weeping uncontrollably, emptying himself, it seems, of all those versions of reality he had vainly chased, ready 'to become' again.

Seizing the day has proved an unworkable principle for Tommy Wilhelm. In this novel, which is short of perfect, Bellow achieves all his artistic aims, because for once he has not allowed his exuberantly rich talents to run away with him, which can hardly be said of his next novel, *Henderson, the Rain King* (1959). Yet this book shows an important development of Bellow's main themes, connecting it not only again with Hemingway's work, but also indicating where both writers part ways in their solution of the problem of individuality. Although the character of Henderson may, at first glance, not seem to have much in common with Bellow's previous protagonists, the problems he has to face are pretty much the same. A scion of a well-known, old and rich family, Henderson, a huge hulk of a man, weighing two hundred and thirty pounds, is six feet and four inches tall, moody, tyrannical, and, as he himself admits, probably mad. He marries a girl of his own social class, has children, divorces her after twenty years of marriage, fights bravely in World War II, though actually too old for active duty, marries again, starts a successful pig farm just to spite a Jewish army friend, and leaves at the age of fifty-five for a trip to Africa, because 'things got worse and worse and worse', because he 'could not suppress a voice that spoke in his heart and said, I want, I want, I want', and because he senses that in Africa he might find things 'which were of old' and which might make his body and spirit whole again. Together with a single native guide, Henderson travels afoot into the interior of Africa, to leave 'certain things' behind on account of the mess he had made of everything and to burn all the bad out of himself. Society has beaten him as it had beaten Tommy Wilhelm, but the fault might not be entirely his, but also that of his particular society.

The first tribe of Africans, the Arnewi, Henderson and his guide Romilayu, encounter in the heart of Africa have a serious problem: their cows are starving because some irrational custom forbids them to water the beasts from a cistern abounding with frogs that have mysteriously appeared from nowhere. Henderson expects help from the Arnewi for his own problems, which are also irrational, so with his superior technological know-how he insists on helping them to solve theirs. But the explosion of the bomb Henderson constructs from rifle shells and his flashlight, not only destroys the frogs but the cistern as well, depriving the Arnewi of their only water supply. Henderson's contact with society, even such an old and elementary one as that of the primitive Arnewi, has again resulted in disaster. Mortified and heart-broken he decides to move on still deeper into Africa, to make one last attempt at exonerating himself and to find out what the mysterious message *grun-tu-molani* (man-want-to-live), delivered to him by the old queen of the Arnewi, as an extension, so it seems, of his own 'I want', could actually signify.

It is among the even more savage and primitive tribe of the Wariri that Henderson gets his second chance to redeem all his former failures, and to find the answers he is looking for. In his eagerness to help, to serve, he succeeds, with a tremendous effort, in moving the statue of the goddess Mummah for the Wariri, the only condition to be fulfilled to make it rain, after which feat he, 'Henderson of the U.S.A., Captain Henderson, Purple Heart, veteran of North Africa, Sicily, Monte Cassino, etc., a giant shadow, a man of flesh and blood, restless seeker, pitiful and rude, a stubborn old lush with broken bridgework, threatening death and suicide', is driven round, naked, by a bunch of savage black women as their new Rain King, until the clouds burst and he is allowed to collapse from mere exhaustion and anguish.

The episode of Henderson's stay among the Wariri undoubtedly contains some of the wildest and richest writing of burlesque that has appeared in twentieth-century fiction, but it is King Dahfu, that fantastic black prince of the African wilds, with his expert knowledge of some of the most seminal Western philosophies, who shows Henderson that *grun-tu-molani* may be much but that it is not enough. It is more important to know how to live, in any shape or form, a problem Dahfu thought could be solved once the belief in the transformation of human material, on the principle that the flesh is influenced by the mind and the mind influenced by the flesh, was strong enough. Nature, according to Dahfu, is a deep imitator, and 'as man is the prince of organisms he is the master of adaptations. He is the artist of suggestions. He himself is his principal work of art, in the body, working in the flesh . . .'. And since mankind as a whole is tired of itself (that is, of its present form of individualism which has only caused him misery and failure), it might need 'a shot in the arm from animal nature.' Man, for instance, could absorb lion qualities, as Dahfu himself has experienced by his close association with the lion he keeps caged under his palace, and his proposal to carry out this experiment with Henderson enthralls Henderson, who cannot help thinking of his own close association with pigs as an explanation of his unsatisfactory way of existence. However, Henderson's fear of the nearness of Dahfu's lion is too great, although Dahfu assures him that fear is necessary since 'as a moulding force it comes second only to nature itself.' The lion can change Henderson, and resurrect the rudiments of high character long-buried in him. He could be noble, and, as he has come to know, without 'high conduct' there can be nothing but misery. Before submitting himself to Dahfu's extraordinary experiment Henderson has one last objection. Why should he try to act the lion, who is a hundred percent beast; why shouldn't he copy Dahfu himself? But Henderson should first empty himself completely, be the beast utterly for one moment, and recover his humanity later. Henderson gives in, and *is* the beast, having claws, and hair and teeth, and roaring until he is bursting with noise, but there remains one last thing: his human longing. Dahfu consoles him: 'The career of our species is evidence that one imagination after another grows literal. . . . Imagination! It converts to actual. It sustains, it alters, it redeems! What Homo Sapiens imagines, he may slowly convert himself to. . . .'

But Henderson realizes that he will never make a lion; he is the work of a too powerful and original 'although blockaded imagination'. Yet his enacting the lion has not been quite in vain. It has, after all, proved to be his major experience through which he has been able to empty himself, stripping himself bare to his essential self. He is now willing to overcome his old self, even if he has to force himself into a part, deceive himself a while, 'until it began to take'.

The end of Bellow's extraordinary tale finds Henderson running round his airplane on the cold, silent, Arctic airfield of Newfoundland, a stopover on his way to America, with a Persian orphan in his arms and a lion cub as his sole piece of luggage. His experiences among the Wariri have 'unpigged' him, his failure to absorb lion qualities together with the death of King Dahfu, killed by the lion assumed to incarnate Dahfu's father, have 'unlioned' him. Remembering an almost-forgotten close association with an old bear with whom he had worked in an amusement park when he was a boy of sixteen, Henderson suddenly realizes that he had probably never come to the pigs and lions as 'a tabula rasa'. Something already deep was inscribed on him, and remembering the profound nature of his 'enbearment', he also realizes that whatever gains he made 'were always due to love and nothing else'. Without love, no change, seems a somewhat platitudinous conclusion after some three hundred pages of exciting, original fiction. But Henderson through his long preposterously clown-like sufferings has personally earned it as the only means of off-setting the cold, cosmic inhumanity he had once discovered in the head of an octopus. And it leaves him free to choose his identity on a human basis. Henderson, the Rain King, is at the end of his tortuous Odyssey ready to enter medical school at the age of fifty-five to give concrete form to his new conception of 'high conduct'.

In his fifth novel, Bellow has succeeded in dramatizing freshly within the context of his own preoccupations (the utter confusion of reality and identity in a formless and normless America) a number of well-known philosophical ideas.[1] The personal twist he gives them at the end may come as a surprise, but it anticipates what becomes even more clear in his later works that Bellow's moral position as an artist is firmly on the side of humanity.

Some critics have discovered in Henderson a parody of Hemingway, but nothing could really be further from the truth. Hemingway, too, went to the beasts to get 'a shot in the arm from nature'. His close association with bulls actually developed into a vision of life, in which courage as a moral force is conceived as being able to effect transcendence through the concomitant form of ecstasy when man faces or takes death. This vision soon began to act as his sole frame of reference within which his creative work was conceived, forcing him, as we have already remarked before, to grow more and more absorbed in the man of action, who alone, by virtue of his particular qualities, is able to derive the maximum of meaning from this vision. This frame of reference was at Hemingway's disposal when he set out for Africa, and consequently the protagonists of his work based on his own African experiences (*Green Hills of Africa*, and two long stories) can be conceived as reflecting one particular conception of reality, that of the man of action, the later Hemingway hero, although the case is a little more complicated in the stories, 'The Short Happy Life of Francis Macomber', and 'The Snows of Kiliman-

[1] Marcus Klein in his fine article 'A Discipline of Nobility: Saul Bellow's Fiction' (*Saul Bellow and his Critics,* ed. Irving Malin, 1967) has convincingly shown a parallel between Henderson's story and Nietzsche's *Also Sprach Zarathustra.*

jaro', since in these stories the transition from the early Hemingway hero, the Nick Adams character, to the later Hemingway hero, the Harry Morgan character, finds dramatization.[1]

So the identity of the Hemingway hero begins to find concrete form in his African fiction, a process that is completed in his subsequent work starting with *To Have and Have Not,* and what this means becomes clear when we compare the middle-aged version of the Bellow protagonist, Henderson, with the middle-aged version of the Hemingway hero, Richard Cantwell of *Across the River and into the Trees.* Like Henderson, Cantwell also has his number of divorced wives to deal with, like Henderson, he is also a veteran of most of the important battles of World War II, and like Henderson, he is a giant shadow, a man of flesh and blood, pitiful and rude, a stubborn old 'lush', threatening death and suicide. But where he differs from Henderson is that he has ceased being 'a restless seeker'. Cantwell has long ceased 'becoming', he is a 'Be-er', a professional soldier, acting in conformity with his particular version of reality. His availability to life's possibilities has long vanished, his responses to life's phenomena no longer offer surprises; they have become predictable and repetitive. Even the threat of death, and the Colonel expects to die any moment from a heart-attack, is unable to effect any change in the Colonel's habitual responses, and this reveals itself most clearly when we examine what could have made the novel a significant human document: his attempts to make up the balance of his life in settling accounts with his war experiences. By recounting his war reminiscences he may purge his bitterness, but it never leads to any greater awareness of himself and the enormous events in which he himself had played such an active and honourable part. His responses remain entirely emotional and are never qualified by reflection and evaluation. There is consequently no soul-searching of any significance, and our main impression of Cantwell's interminable monologue, which takes up the book's entire central section between the brief evocation of the duckshoot at the beginning and at the end of the novel, is one of emptiness and poverty of ideas, entirely in conformity with the cliché version of reality of the professional soldier as an overbearing, presumptuous, empty-minded bully.

Henderson, on the other hand, the later version of the Bellow protagonist, still refuses to become a 'Be-er', which does not mean

[1] For a detailed analysis I refer again to *Ernest Hemingway: The Artist as Man of Action,* p. 129 ff.

that he does not want to. But his availability to life's possibilities is still not exhausted: at the end of the novel he is ready for yet another version of reality: that of the medical profession, providing him with the opportunity to give concrete form to what the greater awareness of his inner-most needs, brought about by his African adventures, had made clear to him: the necessity of 'high conduct' to end his misery and failures. Bellow's work continues to offer the surprises and freshness of genuine creation, as his novel *Herzog,* following *Henderson, the Rain King,* again proves.

In *Herzog,* we meet the Bellow protagonist as the professional man, not as a doctor, but as a university professor of history. The opportunities for his conducting his life in accordance with the principle of 'high conduct' are plentiful. But Herzog wouldn't have had some of the peculiarities of the typical Bellow character, if he had not mismanaged everything. When the book opens Herzog is not only slightly mad, like his predecessor Henderson, but his life, too, has turned out to be a complete ruin. He has not only failed as a husband, lover, and father, but also as a scholar. Not only his first but also his second marriage has broken up, and his great work on Romanticism, which was to stun the scholarly world, has come to nothing. In a frenzied attempt to get a grip on himself and to find explanations for his present state, he lives his life again in crowding reminiscences of his childhood, adolescence, and manhood, invoked by his feverish condition during his aimless travels between Chicago, New York, Boston, and his country place in the Berkshires, while he jots down unsent letters to his family, friends, wives, mistresses, fellow-scholars, statesmen and famous philosophers, dead and alive. His frantic search transcends his individual case and assumes the nature of an existential exploration of the human condition in general. In accordance with his principle of high conduct Herzog wants to contribute his share to the improvement of humanity's lot, but it is his abject failure to do so, that poses the central question in the book: the question of his employment of other human beings and their employment of him. Which one is true, which one reveals the essence of the human condition? Is it his employment by the reality instructors, the Shapiros, the Himmelsteins, the Gersbachs, the Madeleines, the Dr Edvigs, who had swindled, conned, manipulated him, taking his savings, driven him into debt? People who had all betrayed his trust, evoking thereby a vision of 'mankind as a lot of cannibals, running in packs, gibbering, bewailing its own murders, pressing out the living world as dead excrement', and creating the impression that one must sacrifice one's poor individuality to a truth which is only true in so far as it brings down 'disgrace and dreariness upon human beings', so that 'if it shows anything except evil it is illusion'. Or is it their employment by him, Herzog, childish, confused and high-minded Herzog, with an amorous heart and moral impulses, soft-headed and impractical, 'ambitious only mentally', the natural dupe of people like his second wife Madeleine, ruthless and calculating, or his 'best' friend, Valentine Gersbach, the histrionic, hypocritical megalomaniac, practical and ambitious only materially? Is it his version of reality, the reality of people who like Herzog himself try, however clumsily, 'to live out marvellous qualities vaguely comprehended', that expresses the essence of the human condition? Even if the qualities of faithfulness, generosity, love, manifest themselves, as a rule, only as 'hearts quaking with cheap and feeble charity or oozing potato love'? At least they don't represent 'a class of people profoundly dangerous to the rest', by whom must not be understood 'the ordinary criminals', but 'the people seeking power'. Herzog's whole agonizing soul-searching actually revolves round this problem, weighing the pros and cons of which view really defines human nature and adds most to life-enhancing possibilities in a spiritually confused age, where modern science teaches that it might be best to impose a moratorium on definitions of human nature.

The end of the story finds Herzog back in his country place in Ludeyville. What his long journey as 'the suffering joker' has taught him is to live with ambiguities, according to the psychiatrists a sure sign of restored health. There is the ambiguity of having a human life but also an inhuman life; of having sentiment while at the same time behaving brutally; of knowing that 'consciousness, when it doesn't clearly understand what to live for, what to die for, can only abuse and ridicule itself', and that he, Herzog, has been doing exactly this, because 'his face is too blind, his mood too limited, his instincts too narrow'. There is finally the ambiguity of realizing that personal life is a humiliation, and to be an individual contemptible, but that without 'the inspired condition' of the individual, without the something that produces 'intensity, a holy feeling', human beings can no longer be called human. It is this intensity that may mean something, a sign of 'moral realities', 'a proof of eternity'. Herzog no longer makes any argument about it. As he remarks at the end: 'I am pretty well satisfied to be, to be just as it is willed, and as long as I may remain in occupancy'. Herzog has finally accepted his own conception of reality as true. Remaining human may mean being abused, duped, but instead of paying back in kind, thus diminishing the chances of keeping the spark of humanity alive, one 'must be trying to keep tight the tensions without which human beings can no longer be called human'. One should want them in human form, even if one's definition of human nature is based on such vaguely comprehended qualities as faithfulness, generosity, love.

The difference between the later Bellow protagonist and the later Hemingway hero again becomes clear when we compare, in terms of the respective versions of reality on which they act, Herzog with one of Hemingway's later abused and duped protagonists, Harry Morgan of *To Have and Have Not*. Harry Morgan, too, has been abused, duped, and betrayed by the people he has put his trust in. But his responses to this treatment are entirely in conformity with the kind of reality from which it issues: the reality of mankind as a race of cannibals, the reality that if life shows anything except evil it is illusion. Morgan retaliates in accordance with this reality, and we follow him on his lonely, reckless course to destruction and death, cheating and murdering as he has been cheated and abused. Harry Morgan conforms. The presence of violence and death in *To Have and Have Not* are no longer questioned but taken for granted. They have ceased functioning as dramatic motives determining the situations from which Harry could derive his values as a human being. Harry Morgan, like Cantwell, is a 'Be-er', and his actions and reactions, too, have become predictable. There is no development through greater awareness of his condition. He remains a product of his environment, and his death is an accident, and not the inevitable tragic outcome of opposing views of life. At the end of *Herzog*, the Bellow protagonist also has finally 'become', but not because he has conformed, but because he has reached greater awareness by recognizing the anomalies that make up the human condition, an impression which finds corroboration in Bellow's latest novel, *Mr Sammler's Planet* (1969). In *Mr Sammler* the discoveries of Herzog are affirmed, but this time not as a result of 'explanation', which is for 'the mental masses', for 'adult education', but as the result of 'distinguishing', a higher activity. To give this affirmation even greater weight, the distinguishing is done by an old man, a Polish Jew, an intellectual and ex-journalist, who in the Old World lived through the worst degradations man can inflict on man, who has survived the greatest massacre in history, and who now spends his remaining years in the New World, in an uneasy position of dependency on a number of cranky women and a rich nephew, Dr. Gruner, a well-known surgeon. All Sammler wants after these experiences is 'with God, to be free from the bondage of the ordinary and the finite', to be perfectly disinterested, for 'what besides the spirit should a man care who has come back from the grave'? He likes to think of himself as *hors d'usage*, not a man of the times, not necessarily human, with little regard for most creatures or earlier forms of himself. But he soon realizes that 'in the human setting, along with every one else, among particulars of ordinary life, he *was* human', and that consequently he has to act as a human being, saddling him again, like all the earlier Bellow protagonists, with the old question of how to define human nature and its underlying reality. Is it the reality of mankind as cannibals, pressing out the living world as dead excrement, as Mr Sammler has every reason to believe? Is its truth such that if it shows anything except evil it is illusion, as Mr Sammler, too, has every reason to believe? On his daily bus ride through New York he sees a black pickpocket at work, shamelessly robbing and terrorizing the defenceless old and weak. He informs the police, despite the fact that the huge negro is on his tail. When later the negro is viciously beaten up by his son-in-law Eisen, Mr Sammler protects him, saving him from being killed. When his nephew Elya Gruner, whom he loves and esteems, is dying he tries to persuade Gruner's daughter Angela, a worthless sex-ridden creature, to make to her father some sign of repentance for her dissipated empty life, so that he may die in peace, well knowing that he, Sammler, may jeopardize his own chances of continuing financial support from the Gruners. When his own daughter, Shula, a confused and eccentric girl, steals Dr Lal's manuscript about the moon, a work she considers of vital importance for the study about H. G. Wells she wants her father to complete, Mr Sammler is very upset and does everything in his power to restore the work to Dr Lal. When she next discovers in Gruner's house the money he has earned from illegal operations, and wants to keep it for her father to live on after Dr Gruner's death, he compels her to restore the money to Gruner's lawyer. Life's 'low tricks, its doggish hind-sniffing charms', keep Sammler involved, forcing him to act as he does, and enabling his creator Bellow to gather through his protagonist the findings of his life-long preoccupations and to mould them into a vision of life which not only sheds new light on his earlier fiction but which also finally contains Bellow's 'message' to mankind.

In most of the forms of personal existence 'there is little scope for the great powers of nature in the individual, the abundant, generous powers. In business, in professions, in labor; as a member of the public, as an inhabitant of the cities. . .; as experiencer of compulsions; as endurer of strain; as father, husband obliging society by performing his quota of actions — the individual seems to feel these powers less, less and less.' It seems that the individual 'wants a divorce from all the states that he knows' (*Augie March, Henderson, the Rain King*). Man as an individual seems to want to get rid of himself, since 'this liberation into individualism' after the long epochs of namelessness, has brought him nothing but misery and failure (*Dangling Man, Seize the Day*). The conclusion Mr Sammler arrives at is that 'individualism is of no interest whatever if it does not extend truth', if it is not 'an instrument for obtaining truth'. But when do things seem to be true? To Mr Sammler, when he was blinded in Poland, when he froze in Zamosht, when he starved in the tomb, when he saw the swollen shapes of the dead Arabs in the Sinai Desert, that is, when he found himself, like the Hemingway hero, in circumstances of extreme danger, facing violence and death. But whereas it enabled the Hemingway hero through the concomitant state of ecstasy to get rid of that part of his individualism which caused misery and failure in society, it was Sammler's experience that there is something in man which he feels is important to continue, something that has to go on: the spirit, however 'cheated, outraged, defiled, corrupted, fragmented, injured', but still the spirit. It is the spirit that lends man his human qualities, which cannot develop if one accepts as the one and only reality the vision of mankind as 'a lot of cannibals'. Man may be a killer, but he has also a moral nature. The anomaly can be resolved by insanity only, unless one accepts the inevitability of imitation. The ancients had this right, as Mr Sammler reflects. Greatness without models? Inconceivable! Everybody may be human only in some degree; only the capacity to be human may be natural. Therefore, make it the object of imitation to reach and release the high qualities, and to try 'to live with a civil heart, with disinterested charity, with a sense of the mystic potency of humankind, with an inclination to believe in archetypes of goodness'. For 'a desire for virtue was no accident' (*Henderson, Herzog*). These are the terms of the only contract man can conclude to enable the spirit to grow, as, for instance, Sammler's nephew, Dr Gruner, 'through all the confusion and degraded clowning of his life through which we are speeding', had known instinctively; as 'in his innermost heart, each man knows'. As Sammler knows. As all know, 'for that is the truth of it — that we all know, God, that we know, that we know, we know, know'.

It is these concluding lines of the novel, reading like an incantation, which not only lend symbolic significance to the presence of H. G. Wells, the indirect cause of Sammler's philosophical exchange with Dr. Lal, in which he expounds the essence of his view of life, but which also explain Sammler's reluctance to ever start his study about this utterly disillusioned, one-time optimistic proclaimer of human progress.

Just as at the end of *Henderson, the Rain King*, the question might seem justified whether this particular 'message' of Mr Sammler's actually contains anything extraordinary, or startling, or new. Again the answer must be that, coming from a man with Sammler's experiences, it could be described in exactly these terms by virtue of its desperately courageous stance in the face of the overwhelming evidence that points to the untenable nature of the *Weltanschauung* behind it.

Like Bellow's *Mr Sammler's Planet*, Hemingway's last important work, *The Old Man and the Sea* (1952), can also be said to contain *his* final message to mankind. In *The Old Man* we find once more the typical Hemingway situation, though this time stripped to its bare bones. The social context in which the story is placed is virtually nil and it is free of all the entanglements of modern life. The reason why we find Santiago alone with the big fish is that with Santiago we have moved into the realm of myth-making, where personal and social factors or forces (early experiences, wounds, wars, revolutions) have lost their significance as determinants in the hero's activities. Santiago does not embody in the first place the characteristics of a specific individual, but those of the ideal Hemingway hero, grown to mythological dimensions. This development was inevitable. The solution of the problem of individuality is that the 'Becomer' becomes a 'Be-er'. When a man has become a 'Be-er', he can grow only in one way: in size, up to the point where he has placed himself outside the ordinary human situation. In Santiago, the 'Be-er', in the appearance of the later Hemingway hero, has detached himself completely from the social forces that could still effect changes in him. For Santiago to protest that, at his age, he should have to fight a big fish in a small boat on the open ocean is simply inconceivable. It is therefore understandable that the final statement on the human condition as contained in *The Old Man and the Sea* offers no surprises. That man has to assert his manhood in the face of insuperable obstacles is not only predictable but also repetitive in the Hemingway canon. What does appear from the story of Santiago, however, is that a fundamental untruthfulness has crept in. The anomaly that man is a killer, but also possesses a moral nature, is never really solved. Hemingway himself tried to solve it by postulating that the truly great killer must have a sense of honour and a sense of glory, terms only to be met by the initiated, the select, the elite, but hardly by those who constitute the majority of a modern mass society, where the anomaly generally manifests itself as a great confusion of values, leading invariably to the most fantastic forms of sanctimony, of which the customary imploration of the Lord's blessing on the works of man's destruction may be said to serve as the classic example. The trouble with the novels of Hemingway's last period, starting with *Across the River and into the Trees,* is that he has allowed this sanctimony to intrude by suggesting a symbolic resemblance between his protagonists and the Christ-figure. In *The Old Man* especially, the references are so numerous that accident may safely be excluded. Yet, Santiago, as the last Hemingway hero, is as unfit for this symbolic casing in which he is forced, as the great marlin is for his skiff. A few instances, exemplifying where the blurring of the values that underlie the original Hemingway vision occurs, must suffice. There is no real Christian humility in the Old Man, despite the assertion that he had attained it without knowing it. 'How many people will he feed, he thought. But are they worthy to eat him? No, of course not. There is no one worthy of eating him from the manner of his behaviour and his great dignity.' No one is worthy to eat him, but the Old Man thinks himself worthy enough to kill him. He says, it is true, that he is only better than the fish through trickery, but at the same time he acknowledges that he kills him chiefly for pride to show the fish what kind of man he is. It is not the teaching of Christ that gives him confidence, but his remembering his own feats of prowess and strength. When he confesses to his love of the flying fish, the delicate robber birds, the green turtles and hank bills, evoking the image of that other Christian friend of animals, Francis of Assisi, the 'complete malignancy' with which he hits the sharks, and his calling the Portuguese man-of-war a 'great whore', strike odd notes. When he confesses to his feeling of Brotherhood, it is a Brotherhood of the worthy and the noble, far from universal. As the Old Man tells the boy: 'We are different', meaning we are the 'initiated' versus 'the others'. At the end of his ordeal Santiago is filled with regret and sorrow that he has killed the great fish, and considers its killing in the good Christian tradition as sin, but his attitude towards the killing during the fight is similar to that of the bullfighter, that is, the act of killing has a significance that rises beyond that of practical value.

What we see, then, is confusion in the values that motivate the Old Man. The original Hemingway vision does not contain Christian elements. By introducing them Hemingway severely undercuts its truthfulness. The version of reality which now appears to underlie his *Weltanschauung* resembles to an alarming extent the one his early protagonists so strongly reacted against, the reality in which the anomaly of man as killer and as having a moral nature is either ignored or buried under layers of half-hearted compromises, leading inevitably to hypocrisy and sanctimony. The Hemingway hero's conformity to a version of reality he originally rejected has become complete.

What conclusions can finally be reached on the basis of this comparative analysis? In Hemingway's work the individual, in trying to solve the anomaly of man as killer and as having a moral nature, places himself outside the community of men. Man as a killer can find transcendence through the concomitant state of ecstasy when facing or taking death. The one condition that has to be fulfilled for him to realize himself, to feel one with the great forces of the universe, is that he has a sense of honour and of glory. Consequently he can only belong to a small group of the intitiated, isolating him from the majority of mankind. Moreover, he is now unable to change any more. Hemingway's attempts to bridge the gap between his protagonist and the community by allowing man's moral nature to intrude in the shape of Christian elements results in exactly the same kind of fundamental untruthfulness he has tried to escape from. The solution of the problem of individuality in having it determined by man's relations with the universe only, that is, with the abstract ideas of death and love, has proved unworkable. It either ends in complete isolation, or in untruthfulness.

In Bellow's work the individual, in trying to solve the anomaly, has placed himself firmly within the community of men. His actions are primarily determined by his relations with his fellow human beings, not with abstract ideas. Man as a killer is recognized as blocking the road to change, to his availability to all of life's possibilities. Only the conception of man as having a moral nature offers an opportunity to break through the deadlock in which man finds himself at this stage of his evolution. 'The liberation into individualism' can only follow this direction, if it is to retain a human form, despite the fact that it will continue to bring man misery and failure.

Amsterdam J. Bakker

A WAY WITH *PARADISE LOST*

It is often claimed that Milton's *Paradise Lost* should be read 'historically'. In order even to begin to appreciate a poem so stuffed with Seventeenth Century religious and scientific notions, and making such theological claims on the reader's attention, apart from the almost equally disconcerting epic pretensions of its length and style, it is said that we should deliberately abandon our Twentieth Century attitudes or prejudices and attempt to adopt rather the prejudices of Milton's earliest readers. By soaking ourselves in the period we should shape ourselves to be ideal members of Milton's original 'fit audience . . . Though few'. The best known exponent of this view was C. S. Lewis who in *A Preface to Paradise Lost* (OUP, 1942) argued that

> You must, so far as in you lies, become an Achaean chief while reading Homer, a medieval knight while reading Malory, and an Eighteenth-Century Londoner while reading Johnson. Only thus will you be able to judge the work 'in the same spirit that its author writ' and to avoid chimerical criticism (p. 63).

Now without embracing what Lewis castigated as 'the fallacy of the Unchanging Human Heart' (which, one agrees with him, is likely to leave only a miserably boring abstraction) it is easy enough to see that Lewis's way is quite as silly and impossible. For a start such a view totally underestimates the effects of physical environment upon the reader and overlooks the imaginative conditioning that clothes, furnishing and food have upon one's sense of what it is like to live at any period. In Lewis's own example we have the comical picture of 'an Achaean chief' actually sitting down to *read* Homer; and the fact that we do *read* Homer or *Beowulf* or Chaucer (even Dickens) makes the effect of the work somewhat different for us than for an earlier audience who heard it recited or chanted or just simply read aloud (with or without rhythmic or musical accompaniment). This is a comparatively trivial objection, but the smell or ambience of different places at different times should never be forgotten and is impossible to recapture. More substantially one must weigh in with a reminder of what might be called 'the historical fallacy' which is the mistaken notion that the past can be truly retrieved. In other words in order to read *Paradise Lost* as a Seventeenth Century reader one would have to believe that it is possible to recreate an authentic Seventeenth Century mental world, which completely overlooks that our imaginative grasp of that world is entirely dependent on later piecemeal reconstruction by Eighteenth, Nineteenth and Twentieth Century historians. Our sense of what it was like to live in the Seventeenth Century hardly corresponds at all to the actual experience of anybody who lived at the time. Our view is selective, and we can hardly even judge what we have left out, but that would not matter so much (for after all our Twentieth Century experience and views of our own lives are selective too) if our selective picture of the Seventeenth Century were not selective in Twentieth Century ways that cannot correspond to the limited view of any real Seventeenth Century person. Then, of course, the question arises of what kind of Seventeenth Century reader we should attempt to become: in what decade, in what part of what decade, should one choose to be born? What would be the ideal age to adopt as one of the first purchasers and readers of *Paradise Lost* hot from the press in 1667? Where should one choose to be born? Into what social class? Perhaps more crucially, what shade of theological opinion should one hold? What exactly should one have thought of the course of the Civil War and the recent Restoration? How much education should one have had? How much experience of the wide world?

Above all the idea of equipping oneself to be a reputable historical reader appears more nonsensical when one considers that no one in Milton's own time would have gone around claiming to be a typical reader. The self-consciousness needed for the part would inevitably spoil the illusion. And most devastatingly, this very notion of assuming an historical rôle to read Milton is a very Twentieth Century attitude revealing a developed historical sense quite foreign to the Seventeenth Century itself. One can hardly imagine Milton himself taking the part of a Greek chieftain to read Homer or of a Roman senator to read Virgil. Just as in the Elizabethan theatre and later, historical plays were performed in contemporary costume with barely a gesture in recognition of historical authenticity, so too Medieval, Elizabethan, Jacobean readers and succeeding generations read its literature unhistorically, for its contemporary value to the reader. Books were read not because they were historically or culturally good for you, but because they had present relevance; not because they had antique virtue, but because they were still alive, an attitude supported by the favourite Horatian formula of 'instruction and delight'. We can only live in the present: all our past, as we are able to imagine it, is our present and does not exist independently of what we make of it now. The claim that one should read *Paradise Lost* historically is a declaration of defeat and shows little faith in the energy and validity of the work to stand up to and sustain a Twentieth Century mind and imagination. It reveals a failure to believe in the reader's power to recognise in the art of the past truths and realities which continue to inform, support, transform, transfigure modern appetites and necessities. A book three hundred years old is not worth reading because it was worth reading three hundred years ago but because it is worth reading now, three hundred years later. Its value is not antiquarian but existential: by it, through it, we learn better to perceive ourselves in our present age.

Here one needs to enter a large reservation by saying that this does not exclude the traditional claims of scholarship, but rightly understood should set scholarship in its proper place, which is a more exalted place than academic routine normally allows; for scholarship should be seen rather in the light of love than in the shade of science. Having fallen in love with the person for my sake, I am naturally inspired to study the loved one for her own sake. Having grasped what the work of art can give us, we should be naturally led to give it as much of our attention, of mind and emotion, as we are able to. Having received and having been informed and cultured by the object we love we desire spontaneously to cultivate it; and successful cultivation always requires knowledge of the kind of plant it is, how it grows, how it grew, and what are the best conditions for its growth. Scholarship like poetry should come 'as naturally as the Leaves to a tree' or 'it had better not come at all'. So from love we learn the need to see the work in detail and see it as a whole for its own sake; we learn to study it out of respect for its own nature, which if we are lucky in love will serve to increase our own imaginative involvement with the work, and even with the world, imperfectly reconstructed as it must be, which created the work. Love creates scholarship, and scholarship intensifies, complexifies and subtilizes our love.

This prompts the question: why should one love *Paradise Lost?* It is clear that large parts of Milton's poem are unlovable to most modern readers, and probably have been rarely loved by anybody at any time, possibly not even by Milton himself. If we do genuinely fall in love with substantial parts of the poem, however, we may become more charitable to the less lovable sections. At least we can then afford not to love them without feeling guilty about it. Here we are usefully brought to the 'concept of availability' discussed with particular reference to *Paradise Lost* in Philip Hobsbaum's *A Theory of Communication* (Macmillan, 1970):

> just as all of his experience is not available even to the most gifted creative writer, so all of a writer's work is not available to even the most interested reader . . . there is a gamut of availability, ranging down from works which are ever-present classics, part of our life stream, to those which cannot, properly speak-

> ing, be read at all . . . Obviously there is an element of re-creation in any response to literature; what varies is the amount of personality involved, the amount of work, that is to say, done by the reader. And this, in its turn, derives from the quality and completeness of the stimulus. There is a distinction to be made between responding to a pattern and filling it in from the proffered outlines. In the former case the work is available; responses are similar among different readers because their reaction has been determined by what has been communicated. But work that is incompletely available will not determine reaction at all, except among those who happen to share the author's sympathies and prejudices (pp. 48-9).

It would not be difficult to re-phrase this concept of availability in terms of my analogy of falling in love; what is more difficult, if not impossible, is to describe why some poems or some parts of poems are more lovable, more available, than others, and eventually Mr Hobsbaum's 'theory of communication' proves to be no more convincing than anybody else's. The best one can do is to thrash around hopefully with such phrases as meaningfulness, imaginative reality, felt life, psychological significance and the like until one is actually face to face again with the poem or passage itself and one can really begin to say why those lines, and those, and those, are indeed available and capable of eliciting a loving response. Certainly it is true that many parts of *Paradise Lost* are not available in this sense, nor ever have been, and all the scholarship in the world will never make them live. To some extent we may still need them in order to better understand what is still alive and available to love. And here we should realize the difference between different kinds of understanding, which provisionally for want of better terms, we might call imaginative and intellectual understanding. Both may depend upon the study of footnotes and background, but in one case the knowledge we acquire helps us to deepen and extend our love, in the other case background obstinately remains background and the poetry for all the supporting information we have obtained stays dead. We may need the inert knowledge, even the dead poetry, to strengthen our hold on what is alive, which in turn may cast an aura of life on the moribund; but we still ought to recognize how artificial that tranferred and borrowed life is.

Now no one has ever denied that large parts of *Paradise Lost* are still available: Philip Hobsbaum makes such a claim for books I, II, IV, IX and the conclusion of book XII, 'bearing in mind, however, that all except the last carry an expendable amount of waste matter' (*op.cit.* p. 264, note 20). With this minimum claim most lovers of

Paradise Lost would agree, in many cases wanting to add at least the invocations to books III and VII, as well as selected passages from other parts of the poem, including the transformation of Satan and the other fallen angels to serpents in book X and Adam's lament which follows in the same book, and . . . And so on, one can go on adding favourite bits and pieces of all that is lovable and still available in the poem, although one might have to admit that some of these later additions may be available in a way slightly different from those chosen first; appealing not quite to the same depth, perhaps, and demanding (or deserving?) not quite the same level of engagement. As A. J. A. Waldock says of Satan's grotesque transformation scene in book X (lines 504 ff.):

> It is a scene we would not give up for worlds, but to treat such a scene (as would seem to be usually done) as if it were in sober verity the conclusion and climax of a valid development is surely to lapse into critical absurdity. To attempt to link such a scene as this with what happens in the first two books of *Paradise Lost* is to try to bring incommensurables together, for the kind of art exemplified in this passage and the kind of art with which the presentment of Satan began have simply no meeting-point. They are different realms of discourse *(Paradise Lost and Its Critics*, Cambridge paperback edition, 1961, p. 92).

Undoubtedly the major reason for the Twentieth Century reader's sense of the growing unavailability of more and more of *Paradise Lost,* our increased awareness of the erosion of meaning in the poem over the centuries, is directly due to the shift in the status of theology. One notices how often apologists for Milton's work find it necessary to claim exemption from the class of doubters of its poetic greatness because they are Christians, and are fortunately still able to feel some identity with a fair amount, if not all, of Milton's theological beliefs. Conversely it is evident from the last sentence of the passage from Philip Hobsbaum's book that he seems to think that Christians are hardly acceptable at all as trustworthy critics of *Paradise Lost*, indeed because they are likely to share too many of Milton's own sympathies and prejudices, which inclines them to fill in too much that is not there in the poem. But theology may be an exploded science, and may be regarded as no more than one kind of philosophy among many others, yet one should not assume that all theology is lost, nor that all of Milton's theology is unavailable to the non-Christian reader. And for the rest of this essay I want to take the theme of 'the Paradox of the Fortunate Fall' (the '*felix culpa*' theme) as it appears in *Paradise Lost* and through it try to show at least one important aspect of what it means to claim that Milton's poem is still alive for us and still able to help us live, whether or not we are Puritans and Christians struggling desperately to return to the Seventeenth Century, or simply willing to admit that we are the products, bearing all the expected psychological marks, of our own century to which we are tied.

The Paradox of the Fortunate Fall is dramatized in book XII of *Paradise Lost*, when after having been told the future, mainly unhappy, story of mankind following the Fall, Adam is assured of man's final Redemption. An account of the Second Coming and the Final Judgement, when Christ shall reward

> His faithful, and receave them into bliss,
> Whether in Heav'n or Earth, for then the Earth
> Shall all be Paradise, farr happier place
> Then this of *Eden*, and farr happier daies.
> (ll. 462-465)

leads Adam to proclaim:

> O goodness infinite, goodness immense!
> That all this good of evil shall produce,
> And evil turn to good; more wonderful
> Then that which by creation first brought forth
> Light out of darkness! full of doubt I stand,
> Whether I should repent me now of sin
> By mee done and occasiond, or rejoyce
> Much more, that much more good thereof shall spring,
> To God more glory, more good will to Men
> From God, and over wrauth Grace shall abound.
> (ll. 469-478)

This causes A. O. Lovejoy, whose famous article on 'Milton and the Paradox of the Fortunate Fall' (first published 1937, reprinted in his *Essays in the History of Ideas*, The Johns Hopkins Press, 1948) was the first to trace the tradition of the idea, to remark that it is as if Adam was expressing 'a serious doubt whether his primal sin — the intrinsic enormity and ruinous consequences of which had elsewhere been so copiously dilated upon — was not, after all, rather a ground for self-congratulation' (p. 277). As Professor Lovejoy goes on to show, this curious paradox and the theological problems that arise from it were not at all new to Milton's poem and he cites instances from Ambrose, Leo I, Gregory the Great, St Augustine and the Middle Ages onwards, and quotes the Easter Even hymn, the *Exultet*, which is the classic expression of the idea: '*O certe necessarium Adae peccatum, quod Christi morte deletum est! O felix culpa, quae talem ac tantum meruit habere redemptorem!*' Later in *Tragedy and the Paradox of the Fortunate Fall* (Routledge, 1953) Herbert Weisinger discussed the origins of the idea in the myth and ritual of the ancient Near East, its development in Hebrew and Christian thought, and its continued power to move us in tragic drama. However, before going on to say something about Weisinger's thesis, one should note that in two respects Professor Lovejoy is misleading in his discussion of the place of the paradox in *Paradise Lost.* He ends his essay with the following observations:

> Though the hint of antinomianism latent in it had made many writers to whom (the paradox) was probably familiar avoid expressing it, it had nevertheless a recognized and natural place in the treatment of the topic in Christian theology — that of the culmination of the redemptive process in human history — which was also for Milton the culminating theme in his poem. Yet it undeniably placed the story of the Fall, which was the subject of the poem announced at the outset, in a somewhat ambiguous light; when it was borne in mind, man's first disobedience could not seem the deplorable thing which, for the purpose of the poet — and of the theologian — it was important to make it appear. The only solution was to keep the two themes separate. In the part of the narrative dealing primarily with the Fall, the thought that it was after all a *felix culpa* must not be permitted explicitly to intrude; that was to be reserved for the conclusion, where it could heighten the happy final consummation by making the earlier and unhappy episodes in the story appear as instrumental to that consummation, and, indeed, as its necessary conditions (p. 295).

But his reference here to keeping the two themes of the Fall and the final Redemption separate, in the first place overlooks the interweaving of the promise of Redemption with the disobedience and its consequence in the opening lines of *Paradise Lost.* Secondly, Professor Lovejoy seems not to have noticed that the *felix culpa* passage at the end of the poem matches a declaration by Satan in book I of his determination to bring about a contrary conclusion:

> If then his Providence
> Out of our evil seek to bring forth good,
> Our labour must be to pervert that end,

And out of good still to find means of evil;
(ll. 162-5)

These lines not only contain an idea itself not far removed from the Paradox of the Fortunate Fall (162-3), but turn the paradox upside down in Satan's expressed intention to pervert God's plan for mankind. Re-reading this earlier passage then in the light of Adam's exclamation of gratitude we cannot help being aware of the ironic reversal which faces Satan in the end and which supplies man with a demonstration of God's love which is totally unexpected to Adam, though not to the reader, and gives an appropriately buoyant lift to the final lines of the poem that to some extent counterpoints their overt narrative content. As Alastair Fowler comments 'Addison was right . . . to remark that at the end of the poem Adam is left triumphant in the depth of misery, while Satan is miserable in the height of his triumph. Some paradox is inherent in the story.' (*The Poems of Milton*, Longmans Annotated English Poets, 1968, p. 1050). But this is a paradox the reader is prepared for: rather than the two themes being kept separate, they are intertwined at the outset; made to balance in the speeches of Satan and Adam in the first and last books; and in the eventual opposed fates of Satan and Adam ironically linked. Adam fails in order to triumph, Satan triumphs only to fail. Or as the paradox is expressed by one of the devotional writers quoted by Professor Lovejoy: " 'We should be lost (*perdus*) if we had not been lost' " (St Francis de Sales, himself quoting Themistocles).

One of the ways of explaining the fascination of the *felix culpa* theme as a means of entering into a worthwhile relationship with *Paradise Lost* is to understand it as an example of a theological notion that has immensely satisfying psychological validity. However the first chapter of Herbert Weisinger's book in which he discusses 'The Psychology of the Paradox of the Fortunate Fall' is somewhat peremptory and disappointing for the reasons indicated by Anton Ehrenzweig in his own discussion of 'The Theme of the Dying God':

> Weisinger showed that the Classical Greek tragedy descends directly from the Neolithic ritual of the dying god. The hero of tragedy has to perish in order to triumph. Weisinger himself offers another rationalistic interpretation of the theme which he calls the 'fortunate fall'. He feels it rests on a need to maintain man's free will and self-determination in the face of overwhelming external forces. Psycho-analysis knows well enough how poignant our narcissistic mortification can become if our unconscious wish for omnipotence and immortality is

> thwarted by the limitations of reality. All wisdom we can muster is needed to accept the fact of our personal death. Indeed Freud himself . . . suggests that the 'dying god' theme could be explained by a piece of wise philosophizing on the necessity of facing death as a fact. But this explanation is perhaps too restricted for so universal a motif of the creative imagination. As far as I know, it was left to Marion Milner, a psycho-analyst with unusual artistic sensitivity, to explore the motif through her own artistic sensibilities and to interpret it as a reflection of the creative process itself . . . . (*The Hidden Order of Art*, Paladin paperback, 1970, p. 188).

This last sentence leads Ehrenzweig, supported by Mrs Milner's work, to suggest that the 'dying god' theme, linked with the Paradox of the Fortunate Fall, is the minimum content of any successful work of art as it expresses the ability of the ego to go through psychological breakdown, and reconstitute itself more richly as a result. In Ehrenzweig's own words: 'Death and rebirth mirror the ego's dedifferentiation and re-differentiation. This double rhythm can be seen as an interaction between basic life and death instincts active within the creative ego' (p. 190). Hence the happy Fall: better not to have fallen, but had man not fallen then he would not have had the opportunity to experience the splendour and joy of the Redemption, or of Art and Poetry in general, and *Paradise Lost* in particular. 'We should be lost if we had not been lost'. We would not survive as human beings, let alone as artists, if we did not experience perpetually the whole cycle of periodic depression or breakdown at various levels and reconstitution or recreation, by which mental awareness is enriched and the harmony of the ego ensured.

Theology may in this way be released from its claims as a science dealing with verifiable truths, and treated, like all philosophical systems, in its different concerns and aspects as an illuminating fiction. And certainly Milton's theology has sufficient imaginative pressure not only in the *felix culpa* theme to sustain such interest. All philosophies, all theologies are fictions, essentially expanded metaphors, since in our earthbound language, in our post-lapsarian language, we can only talk about God indirectly, symbolically, through metaphor. This has led some philosophers to despair of talking about God at all: the final point of Wittgenstein's *Tractatus Logico-Philosophicus* — 'Wovon man nicht sprechen kann, darüber muss man schweigen'. But although the task is impossible, just as Milton's task was impossible in *Paradise Lost,* one can talk about God all the same, through poetry: for poetry is forever conjured out of impossibility and the better part of theology is poetry. And it is Blake and Wordsworth who pre-eminently help us to read Milton's theology as poetry of the psyche. Blake's epics *Milton* and *Jerusalem*, like much else in his work, are a deliberate attempt, among other concerns, to re-write Milton's epic in terms of psychic reality. At its simplest, and it does not need to be expressed as simply as this, the struggle between Satan and God may be viewed psychologically as the conflict between the id or the libido or energy and the super-ego or conscience or restraint. One may refer here to the relevance of A. J. A. Waldock's remark in *Paradise Lost and Its Critics* (p. 93) that Milton's Hell differs from other theological (and literary) Hells in that each of them except the Hell of *Paradise Lost* is a terminus, the end of the road for the damned. But this is explainable if one understands that Milton's Hell as it represents the unconscious must allow access to the conscious mind or the ego, which makes even more cogent Blake's famous saying in *The Marriage of Heaven and Hell* that

> The reason Milton wrote in fetters when he wrote of Angels & God, and at liberty when of Devils & Hell, is because he was a true Poet and of the Devil's party without knowing it.
> (Blake, *Complete Writings* ed. Keynes, OUP, p. 150).

In and through Blake's work it is possible to interiorize almost the whole of *Paradise Lost:* the universal struggle of the poem happens in the psyche of every individual. There too the Redemption takes place preceded by the Temptation and Fall. Milton himself gives justification for this kind of psychological interpretation of his work in at least two respects: firstly, by introducing his own person so dramatically and poignantly into the poem in the invocations to books I, III, VII and IX, which in themselves are revealing accounts of the creative process and Milton's awareness of the different levels of his own mind that parallel the structure of the universe where his epic is being enacted. It is as if his personal drama and the drama of his persons share one interior. This is particularly apparent with the introduction of the Orphic theme in book VII 32-39, which psychologically ties Milton's fears for himself (Orpheus as the dying, torn and scattered god or king being the image of psychic self-destruction that needs to be re-gathered to ensure re-creation or Redemption) to Adam's downward path to disobedience and fall. Indeed this very allusion makes clear in the poem the bond between the theme of the Dying God and the Paradox of the Fortunate Fall. Moreover these invocations relate the progress of Milton's own epic task in carrying through his poem and the psychological burden entailed (in a sense Milton is his own here looking forward to his own redemption at the completion of his poem) with the development of narrative events within the epic. Secondly, Milton himself at various points in the poem seems to view Adam and Eve as allegorical figures within a symbolical psycho-drama, with Adam representing *intellectus* or *mens* and Eve *ratio* or *anima* (see Alastair Fowler's footnote to *Paradise Lost* IX 335, *The Poems of Milton, op. cit.* p. 874). If this interpretation is accepted then the Fall of Man may be justly seen amongst other things as an account of the loss of mental integration indicative of a psychic split. And this might also be regarded as the natural consequence of the growing self-consciousness which is explicitly conveyed by the narrative of *Paradise Lost* in Adam and Eve's response to one another and to God after the Fall, as well as being implicit in the allegorical psychological presentation. Satan is dramatized as a solipsist from the beginning of the poem (especially in his great address to the sun in book IV) and Adam and Eve move towards solipsism at the end of the poem: 'thou ... shalt possess/ A paradise within thee, happier farr' (XII 585-7).

It is their obsession with the means of obtaining, possessing and maintaining this internal paradise that leads the Romantic poets to reflect and develop the solipsistic theme of Milton's poem. Wordsworth like Blake was concerned to write an epic of the individual mind that would challenge direct comparison with *Paradise Lost*. In one of the few parts of *The Recluse* to be written, which he used in the 'Preface' to *The Excursion*, Wordsworth invoked the same muse as Milton, Urania, but at once set about establishing the differences between his poem and *Paradise Lost*:

For I must tread on shadowy ground, must sink
Deep — and, aloft ascending, breathe in worlds
To which the heaven of heavens is but a veil.
All strength — all terror, single or in bands,
That ever was put forth in personal form —
Jehovah — with his thunder, and the choir
Of shouting Angels, and the empyreal thrones —
I pass them unalarmed. Not Chaos, not
The darkest pit of lowest Erebus,
Nor aught of blinder vacancy, scooped out
By help of dreams — can breed such fear and awe
As fall upon us often when we look
Into our Minds, into the Mind of Man —
My haunt, and the main region of my song.

(*The Poetical Works of William Wordsworth* ed. de Selincourt and Darbishire, OUP, Vol. 5, pp. 3-4, ll. 28-41).

Wordsworth's interiorized psychological quest could not be more cogently announced than in these lines: what Milton had done for the universe, Wordsworth intended to do for the individual mind. For the Romantics the Poet was seen as the creative aspect of Everyman writ large; and as a man fulfilling his essentially creative nature, a nature which needs to be creative, a maker of symbols and of language and of formal structures, if it is to survive at all, the Poet represents man's nature most completely and at its best. So Wordsworth's interest in 'The Growth of a Poet's Mind' (the stated subject of *The Prelude*) rises from his concern with the circumstances of man's fallen nature that compels him to redeem himself by making new wholes, new paradises, which give external form to the interior quest for psychic unity.

In a sense Wordsworth's task was redundant since Milton had written the definitive version of the Fall of Man that yet looks forward to Man's Redemption understood in either religious or psychological terms. And ever since the first appearance of *Paradise Lost* great poets and small have written variations on Milton's theme. Milton's poem is of enormous importance in giving a universal mythical form to internal psychic reality; and it may be regarded as a projection into an objective whole coherent enough to be grasped imaginatively of a universal state or condition of mind. *Paradise Lost* is the ground fiction of all our states of mind. Those parts of the poem which do not support this figuration (like the War in Heaven which is not only poetic nonsense but psychological nonsense too) have long since faded. As it emerges from our consideration of the *felix culpa* theme the Fall of Adam is the Fall of Everyman and is a necessary Fall: all poetry, all art, even tragic art, signifying 'the happy final consummation' of the Fall.

C. C. Barfoot

AN UNCOMMON LANGUAGE: CROSSING WITH WHITMAN

S. Betsky-Zweig

> O learn to read what silent love hath writ,
> To hear with eyes belongs to love's fine wit.
> Shakespeare, Sonnet 23

England and the United States may, as the tired witticism has it, be separated by a common language but they have nevertheless long been connected in the visual arts and in literature. In 1799 Benjamin West, the American expatriate painter who was president of the Royal Academy of Art, presented Joseph Turner with his Associate's diploma. In 1802 West declared the election of Turner as a full Royal Academician. Later the dedication of Turner's greatest supporter, John Ruskin, would make his art known in the United States West had left. In 1845 and earlier Americans had purchased Turner paintings, drawings, etchings and reproductions.[1] Yet Turner's impact, by way of Ruskin, rather than through first-hand experience of his art, can be felt in this summarizing paragraph:

> By Ruskin's death in 1900, *Modern Painters* had been read in part or in full by tens of thousands of Americans. Each reader had at least seen the name Turner, and many must have fully understood the author's impression of the artist's stature. Because of the book's phenomenal popularity, and because of new methods of publication and distribution, it is likely that no painter has been so rapidly introduced to so many people in the entire history of Western art. Americans welcomed the introduction to Turner, but few pursued an understanding of the new acquaintance. Most of those who did found him to have left a record of exceptional, erratic talent, not quite in keeping with their artistic goals.[2]

1. The first Turner oil painting to come to America, *Staffa, Fingal's Cave*, was bought by Col. James Lenox in 1845. The same collector purchased *Fort Vimieux* in 1850. Both canvasses were given to the Lenox Library which became the New York Public Library. M. Butlin and E. Joll, *The Paintings of J.M.W. Turner*, London, 1977, pp. 180 and 175.
2. Joseph R. Goldyne, Introduction and Text, *J.M.W. Turner, Works*

Fig. 6: Rembrandt, *Faustus.*

counteract the unfair competition of Johannes Jansonius who had started publishing unauthorized editions of Blaeu's *Het Licht der Zeevaert*. And perhaps, some twenty years after Bacon had first spread the idea of progress through science, a reference to divine inspiration seemed no longer necessary. But in 1608 it must have seemed a prudent move to invoke the light of Heaven when publishing the latest findings of astronomical research. P.C. Hooft well understood the idea of Blaeu's symbolism when in his laudatory poem on the verso of the frontispiece of the *Licht der Zeevaert* he concluded that the book teaches the order of the heavens and "through its light the light of Heaven is set aflame".

London — Margarita Russell

These words could apply to the most critically disturbing and greatest of America's nineteenth-century poets, Walt Whitman. He too was and is accused of not adhering to generally accepted goals and like Turner must be looked at long and hard by each generation of audiences. Is it so surprising, then, to find that even when both men were alive the younger writer, still a journalist and not yet known by his shortened name, probably read about Turner and quite clearly, as this reading of one of his poems merely suggests, may have seen some of his work?

> Ruskin's American debut came in late July 1847 when the first American edition of *Modern Painters I* appeared under the imprint of Wiley and Putnam. None of the first American reviewers seems to have known the author's identity (Emerson, who read *Modern Painters* in October 1847, on board ship bound for England, wrote home to his wife that "if any one wishes to know [it] was written by a young man named Ruskin.") The effusive lines young Walter Whitman dashed off for the *Brooklyn Daily Eagle* of 22 July 1847 indicate only that the first volume was just appearing, for Whitman's notice gives no evidence that he had read the book.[3]

Similarities between the poet Whitman and the painter Turner were observed by the intelligent American business man James Jackson Jarvis in the 1860's. Jarvis was a friend of Charles Eliot Norton who had earlier bought many Turner drawings, "fed" to him by Ruskin, and which he exhibited in 1874.[4] Norton's introductions to artists in Europe led Jarvis to become a cultivated dilettante and critic, able to value early Italian art as well as that of his own time. Although he found Turner limited by his "lack of a religious sense" he could write that "Turner is too profoundly original to have successful disciples. The benefit he does art is to manifest its capacities in a new and popular direction". When Jarvis published these comments in 1869 in *Art Thoughts: Experiences and Observations of an American Amateur in Europe* he might

on Paper from American Collections, Berkeley, California, University Art Museum, 30 September-23 November, 1975, p. 36. My great debt to Mr. Nichol Clark of the Washington, D.C. National Gallery of Art for help in tracing American connections with Turner is most warmly acknowledged.

3. Roger B. Stein, *John Ruskin and Aesthetic Thought in America, 1840-1900*, Harvard, 1967, pp. 41-42.

4. W.D. Peat, *Turner in America*, The Art Association of Indianapolis, John Herron Art Museum, November 12-December 25, 1955, n.p.

have been thinking of his compatriot Whitman rather than of the English painter. J.R. Goldyne finds this kind of critical acuity important for the purposes of art history as well: "It is significant for an understanding of the state of American art criticism in the 1860's that Jarvis proclaimed Turned to be '... the most varied and thorough master of landscape' in the same tome which could recognize Courbet as the 'strongest, the truest, and most satisfying of the realists ...' and compare him with Walt Whitman."[5]

The Turner as seen through nineteenth-century eyes, whether American or Ruskin's, was particularly compatible with certain shifts in American taste.[6] Roger B. Stein has pointed to the movement in the arts from the sensuous to the moral, to a stress on nature (American art critics are only now, in our own day, extensively studying nineteenth-century U.S. landscape painting), to the importance of the individual "seer" as exemplified by Emerson's American Scholar. Art and religion and nature were being seen as one, and Turner and later Whitman are part of this necessarily general statement. What must not be forgotten, then or in our time, are the continuing arguments about the effectiveness and stature of either man — although Turner has finally reached almost full acceptance. *The North American Review* could write of Ruskin in 1848 that his views on art were harmful, ignored the past, and committed the fallacy of "truth to nature". The article sounds familiar to our ears.

Because the criticisms of Turner and Ruskin were also levelled against Whitman and because they are still being used it is interesting to examine with some care one poem I believe is solidly

5. Goldyne, pp. 31-32.

6. Goldyne, pp. 33-35, discusses the American collectors and artists who saw Turner's work, particularly in England, and how they reacted to it. Some Turners were owned by Americans and especially his graphic work was widely distributed and studied. It was not only popular but also used didactically: how to compose, draw, and see the possibilities of landscape. This was true mostly in the case of Turner's *Liber Studiorum*. When we find (thanks to Nichol Clark) that the Reverend E.L. Magoon, who also owned a Ruskin watercolour, exhibited his Turners in Troy and Buffalo, New York, in 1862 and 1863, we must assume Turners were shown before that in major centres. *Bacharach on the Rhine*, a watercolour belonging to Rev. Magoon, was shown along with B. Frodsham's Turners, *Young England, Young Ireland* and *Young Scotland.*

constructed and fine in the many ways we ask of good poetry. The process of scanning this poem cannot confine it within a painting's frame but it can point to felicities we recognize as successful art.

In the first two lines of Whitman's "Crossing Brooklyn Ferry" a surprising movement to painterly conventions occurs. A poet who works mostly with the oral devices of chant, recitation, repetition, the long breath, Whitman here focusses his eye on a canvas rather than his ear on a cataloguing song. Spaces, perspective, colour, working through a central metaphor, are his materials. He changed the original 1856 title, "Sun-Down Poem", to "Crossing Brooklyn Ferry", perhaps as he saw more clearly the visual, physical implications of the ferry ride. From land across water to land again: a half hour before sunset a boat carries the speaker-observer. Beginning as an apparently straightforward romantic confrontation with nature,[7] addressed directly, the meeting shifts to the shores of urbanism, industry, crowds, all connected by the crossing of the man-made ferry:

> Flood-tide below me! I see you face to face!
> Clouds of the west — sun there half an hour high — I see you also face
> to face.

Whitman addresses himself to a simultaneous viewing of water, sky, clouds, seen as his eye faces each element. The water is moving, growing in "flood-tide" and the ferry moves through the water. Space is manipulated by the poet's eye. It sees each phenomenon where it belongs. Using his own eye as point of view he remains centred in the canvas while his vision encompasses and records the disparate pieces. Perspective is refined, distanced or exploded, foregrounded, brought not only right under his eyes but also into his head, to disappear in lines of meditation upon what spaces have revealed. Movement occurs on several levels: water

7. Butlin and Joll (pp. 180-181) describe the genesis of *Staffa, Fingal's Cave.* First exhibited with a quotation from Scott's *Lord of the Isles*, it was while visiting Scott for consultation about an illustrated edition of his *Poetical Works* that Turner made the difficult trip to Staffa and Fingal's Cave "which, since its accidental discovery ... in 1772, had become a place of pilgrimage for those concerned in the romantic movement ..." His sketches "show that, in fact, Turner's main interest was in the sea voyage rather than in Fingal's Cave itself".

flowing, boat sailing, head bending to look down, head raised to look up, sun sinking to meet all these levels, to illuminate them, then to disappear for one more day into the last words of the poem, into "eternity" and "soul".

The voice may sound like — and of course is — the Whitman voice of conversational intimacy rising and falling as it plays against large exhortations. But in this poem the voice adds a dimension not usually present in Whitman's other works. It is as if, for once, Whitman had found a painter's vision and a painter's tools — here almost a Turner's — to thicken, point up, stroke his language into unexpected precisions. The use of light and colour and the reflecting, mirroring water between two urban shapes is "face to face" with, say, a Turner painting of a city fire as seen from a distance or a closely observed waterscape.[8]

Whitman's unusual juxtaposition of voice and eye here (rather than odour or sensation or touch) is strengthened by his title. The action and scenery of crossing from one crowded shore to another, surrounded by fellow passengers, near sunset, turn into a metaphor for time, for historical connectedness, for the artist's immortality. As Whitman crosses the water he can float from birth to death. The metaphor enables him also to float forward into a future where we live so that he can address us "face to face" and paint us into his picture.

For once (Lawrence's criticism of him) Whitman does not "merge" with his subject. "Crowds of men and women attired in the usual costumes, how curious you are to me!" The others and the self keep their places on the canvas instead of blurring into one figure. This compositional tact saves the poem from Whitman's convoluted I-am-you-and-you-are-me. We are left free to take our small part on the canvas because we are "disintegrated" rather than mixed in at once. "The simple, compact, well-joined scheme, myself disintegrated, every one disintegrated yet part of

8. Sanford Robinson Gifford, an American painter of the Hudson River School, records in his unpublished letters (Smithsonian Institution Archives) experiences in looking at Turners in London in 1855. He writes of *The Burning of the House of Parliament* and *The Grand Canal of Venice,* especially of the latter: "... splendid in light and gorgeous in color ... There is great *infinity* as well as great indefiniteness in the forms ... The whole picture is very light and brilliant ... The other picture [*The Burning*], is also very splendid in light and color" (Goldyne, p. 28).

the scheme ... " sounds direct enough but just as we have read "The similitudes of the past and those of the future ..." and begin to shrink from Whitman's over-friendly merging of time and of differences, we find "The glories strung like beads on my smallest sights and hearings" freeing us from the over-familiarity. There is no religious allusion in these "beads"; they are ordinary beads adorning the senses, eye and ear. They are "strung" so their sound and their appearance become "glories"; the bead-string stretches into the walk in the street and the passage over the river. Because these are small compact glories slipping and clicking like beads on to a thread we accept where the walk, then the ferry trip over the river, lead us as the string grows:

> The current rushing so swiftly and swimming with me far away,
> The others that are to follow me, the ties between me and them,
> The certainty of others, the life, love, sight, hearing of others.

The beads are strung, the knot completed. We have been led to the ferry gates and will share with Whitman his "smallest sights and hearings" since the "glories" are tightly held by the ties between people, the ties between past and future, the ties of the current encircling the bead of the world.

Why this disintegration into "smallest" beads? What is the "scheme", the composition into which Whitman wants to draw us?

> A hundred years hence, or ever so many hundred years hence, others will see them,
> Will enjoy the sunset, the pouring-in of the flood-tide, the falling-back to the sea of the ebb-tide.

The short string, the short passage, the short time needed for this ferry crossing are long enough for Whitman to have drawn us in and then drawn us further, behind the guard rails. For twenty lines we have escaped his wider brush. Now he changes to brushes of broader width; we are no longer those others who will also enjoy "the shipping of Manhattan north and west, and the height of Brooklyn to the south and the east", the islands, the sun, the tide. Now we are identified completely with Whitman. He apparently has a permanent ticket for the Brooklyn Ferry, and in reading the rest of the poem we must decide whether we will share it with him, as he insists we should, or stay on shore.

We are swayed perhaps to accompany Whitman by his ability to shove objects around, magically, as a painter does, on a static canvas. Movement and non-movement are achieved by careful placing of colour and mass, light and dark, so water flows as figures stand still. Yet all the time those figures are moving, crossing between air, sky, sun, cloud, water, land. Fixed on a moving boat we cross while immobile. The self-contained flat picture surface can hold this kind of contradictory movement, as in a Turner painting. And time and water can seem to move, can seem to stand still, can flood and ebb. "Just as you stand and lean on the rail, yet hurry with the swift current, I stood yet was hurried." Better this kind of merging and identification than the coyness of "Song of Myself's" "If you want me again look for me under your boot-soles." The hurrying and standing are created in "Crossing Brooklyn Ferry" by the contradiction of shared passengership. The final line of "Song of Myself", "I stop somewhere waiting for you", makes the poet stationary and the reader the mover, the traveller. On the ferry, poet and fellow passengers record the precise visual scene. The eye does the work of the walker of other poems; the brush flows with the eye.

> I too many and many a time cross'd the river of old,
> Watched the Twelfth-month sea-gulls, saw them high in the air floating with motionless wings oscillating their bodies,
> Saw how the glistening yellow lit up parts of their bodies and left the rest in strong shadow,
> Saw the slow-wheeling circles and the gradual edging toward the south,
> Saw the reflection of the summer sky in the water,
> Had my eyes dazzled by the shimmering track of beams,
> Look'd at the fine centrifugal spokes of light round the shape of my head in the sunlit water,
> Look'd at the haze on the hills southward and south-westward,
> Look'd on the vapor as it flew in fleeces tinged with violet ...[9]

Whitman's overabundance: the eye has recalled the years of sketching and the canvas has multiplied into a gallery. If we now read the paintings as they are displayed we realize (as Whitman prophesies in this poem) that "others" have read them before us.

9. The Turner oil purchased by the New Yorker Col. Lenox in 1850, *Fort Vimieux*, was exhibited in London in 1831. One review at the time, in the *Library of the Fine Arts*, notes "the firing of red-hot shot, the sun of a bloody hue 'low, deep and wan', the forlorn and frightened gull" (Butlin and Joll, p. 175).

The gulls become Eliot's plovers and Stevens' Sunday pigeons. Even Hopkins, who admired Whitman, let a windhover fly. But the eye remains the conduit for words in Whitman's poem: in the sun-dazzle of the water, vision reflects the poet haloed by "spokes of light". The light picks out the surrounding scene, and "haze", "vapor" and "fleece" become the solid impressions of the marine-working world. The brush stroke pushes the halo into position as just one more visual fact as it highlights now "the vessels arriving", the people aboard, the white sails of schooners and sloops, the ships at anchor and the sailors "at work in the rigging or out astride the spars" while the smallest, abstracted detail is visible: "The round masts, the swinging motion of the hulls, the slender serpentine pennants ..."

Movement increases as the sun sets lower and as the ferry approaches the shore.[10] The world is turning gray, the poet looks even more closely, says what is still available to sight. So a Turner left his canvas darkening, the salient points still bright, quick, intense. The scene must be put down quickly, the words rushing, the paint touched with speed.

> The large and small steamers in motion, the pilots in their pilot-houses,
> The white wake left by the passage, the quick tremulous whirl of the wheels,
> The flags of all nations, the falling of them at sunset,
> The scallop-edged waves in the twilight, the ladled cups, the frolicsome crests and glistening,
> The stretch afar growing dimmer and dimmer, the gray walls of the granite storehouses by the docks,
> On the river the shadowy group, the big steam-tug closely flank'd on each side by the barges, the hay-boat, the belated lighter,
> On the neighboring shore the fires from the foundry chimneys burning high and glaringly into the night,
> Casting their flicker of black contrasted with wild red and yellow light over the tops of houses, and down into the clefts of streets.[11]

10. Butlin and Joll, p. 175, comment on *Fort Vimieux* that "the cool yellows and greys of the Tate sketch have been transformed in the exhibited picture by the fiery sunset ..."

11. The Butlin and Joll descriptions of the first two "American" Turner oils include many reviewers' comments on their colour. Of *Staffa, Fingal's Cave* (1832) they write: "In general, Turner was praised for the poetic effect with which he invested the subject and for keeping his 'love

This canvas seems finished as the light moves on the urban scene. A long time would elapse before artists paid similar attention to the industrial landscape.

The artist steps back from his easel in sections four and five, considers the picture's permanence in contrast to his mortality. Immortality is possible through the work of art, he hopes. But better to state it openly: "What is it then between us?" Place and time will not break the connection between artist and his future audience; all "... had been struck from the float forever held in solution", the sea, the waters of the womb have cast all ashore to receive "identity by my body", to live as individuals afloat even when severed from the amniotic fluids. The Brooklyn ferry as navel cord?

If it is true, as Whitman claims, that "what I should be I knew I should be of my body", then what connects us with him across the years? Our bodies may be similar enough, but in section six Whitman reminds us of deeper parallels. The physical alertness of the poem's preceding sections moves into the darker sunset of emotional, specifically biographical landscape. All of us "struck from the float" know the castaway's struggles. The light probes inward, picking out details of despair, self-doubt, a sense of evil, a fear of failure. The canvas turns black.

> It is not upon you alone the dark patches fall,
> The dark threw its patches down upon me also,
> The best I had done seem'd to me blank and suspicious,
> My great thoughts as I supposed them, were they not in reality meagre?
> Nor is it you alone who know what it is to be evil,
> I am he who knew what it was to be evil,
> I too knitted the old knot of contrariety ...

Between birth and death, between shore and shore, the "dark patches" appear; in knitting "the old knot" he (and we)

> Blabb'd, blushed, resented, lied, stole, grudg'd,
> Had guile, anger, lust, hot wishes I dared not speak,
> Was wayward, vain, greedy, shallow, sly, cowardly, malignant,
> The wolf, the snake; the hog, not wanting in me,
> The cheating look, the frivolous word, the adulterous wish, not wanting,

---

of yellow, red and blue in this instance subordinate', as the *Morning Herald* put it on 7 May" (pp. 180-181).

> Refusals, hates, postponements, meanness, laziness, none of these wanting,
> Was one with the rest, the days and haps of the rest ...

"The rest"? Whitman's palette slides from black patches to the "rest", the human beings, the figures emerging from dark memory, recalls that he had friends, loved openly or anonymously, "Lived the same life with the rest, the same old laughing, gnawing, sleeping," a line where "gnawing" as a verbal for eating repeats the force of the earlier lines. Painting this self-portrait he believes we too recognize in our own mirrors, he notes his dramatic stance and comments in words familiar in our therapeutic circles:

> Play'd the part that still looks back on the actor or actress,
> The same old role, the role that is what we make it, as great as we like,
> Or as small as we like, or both great and small.

Whitman alters his point of view, following the word "small" and his picture of the "dark patches" staining all of us, in our inherited or self-made roles: "Closer yet I approach you." With his eyes now on us, his future readers, he asks "Who knows, for all the distance, but I am as good as looking at you now, for all you cannot see me?" The view foreshortened, time condensed, our eyes become the poet's eyes as he describes in section eight his love of Manhattan, river, ships, gulls, the gods who clasp his hand, call to him. All converge into the ties he feels with us. We sidle away, perhaps, from the poet's importunities. How dare he move from his admiration for "mast-hemm'd Manhattan" to the claim that all we see with him from the ferry's deck "pours my meaning into you?" How dare he query:

> We understand then do we not?
> What I promis'd without mentioning it, have you not accepted?
> What the study could not teach — what the preaching could not accomplish is accomplish'd, is it not?

Whitman dares because, first, his tone is intimate, cajoling and slyly colloquial; a speaking voice more memorable as it soon changes into a public fortissimo. Second, we can so far accept his painting as it unrolled from the opening recognition of tide, sun, clouds across the water, a painting about water in one hundred lines. It is not as comfortable or easy or general an acceptance as Whitman would have us believe. This is part of the crux of literary judgement; has Whitman written a good enough poem to get away with this Americanized (Emersonian?) version of Wordsworth's stress on nature and man in place of study and preaching? An examination of the concluding section may help us decide.

The painting almost ready for vernissage, Whitman commands us to look at it again, pausing himself between exhortation and review to add some finishing touches. He has created an entire world out of an ordinary commuters' voyage, endowed it with a grandeur previously saved for Mt Blanc, for global travellers. From Turner we have learned to see the essence of nature, careful representation as exploded into the shape behind the shape, the colour behind the colour, until sea and sky move into presences, into the simplest and most complex of swathes of paint. Turner's later landscapes are living flesh as Cezanne's apples are landscapes. Whitman has to use words. Disappointing us at first with "Gorgeous clouds of the sunset! drench with your splendor me, or the men and women generations after me!" he shouts out his orders until he recovers the painter's method: "Receive the summer sky, you water, and faithfully hold it till all downcast eyes have time to take it from you." As the sun sets and the sky darkens, the water under the ferry still reflects the colour our eyes perceive, the water itself acting as recording canvas. Whitman makes the connection strong and physical.

Whitman's vision of the "fine spokes of light" around his head (first mentioned in l. 33), now diverging in the water, is exact.[12] He adds "or any one's head" so that we all cast our haloes into the democratizing current. He calls for the ships' flags "of all nations" to be lowered and, divested of nimbus and flying pennants, we reach the shore: "Burn high your fires, foundry chimneys! cast black shadows at night-fall! cast red and yellow light over the tops of the houses!" The final pigments are applied to that Whitman poem most involved with pure colour.

12. It is in Turner's *Staffa* that a nimbus appears, foretelling rain rather than sainthood. Like Whitman, he was always eager to learn of the latest scientific studies related to his work, and Butlin and Joll, p. 181, record that "the way Turner has painted the setting sun surrounded by a nimbus, which does not appear in any of the sketches, may derive from his meeting with the Edinburgh physician, Sir David Brewster, in 1831 ... At this time, Brewster and his circle were investigating such natural phenomena". Turner wrote of this in his letter to Lenox in New York.

We are reading a poet not a painter — and a poet not especially fond of the brief sketch except as part of a larger work. Whitman's final lines are those of a truly verbal artist, those lines which could be inscribed (as Turner liked to do) under the frame enclosing "Crossing Brooklyn Ferry". The spectator is not trusted. The physical imagery of the ferry trip must be extended into yet more explicit (or unnecessary?) meanings. The journey may have brought us from Brooklyn to Manhattan or vice versa; from birth, from afternoon maturity, to life still burning in the night. We can acquiesce with Whitman's elimination of chronology so that he now stands with us waiting for the boat to dock, more than a hundred years later. We concede to him the right and even the power to write a poem about writing a poem about all of us writing the poem with him. Can we concede as well to his concluding lines?

Whitman calls to the very "thingness" of the art, "Appearances, now or henceforth, indicate what you are." Behind the paper, behind the canvas, must be the real thing. But Whitman knows there are layers upon layers and only the mad would strike behind the mask. So "You necessary film, continue to envelop the soul" and let "our divinest aromas" be hung about our bodies; let the cities and harbours and freight "bring your shows"; let these and the ample rivers expand, an expansion "than which none else is perhaps more spiritual". Appearances and growth are both necessary and divine — nature and industry subsumed in one dream, one hope. Whitman adds a practical order with the kind of common sense about society he showed in his prose works: "Keep your places, objects than which none else is more lasting." We know appearances only through objects or vision of objects; each thing in its place.

"Crossing Brooklyn Ferry" praises the objects of this world, the "dumb, beautiful ministers" making the physical journey symbolic, rich, detailed, possible:

> We use you, and do not cast you aside — we plant you permanently
> within us,
> We fathom you not — we love you — there is perfection in you also,
> You furnish your parts toward eternity,
> Great or small, you furnish your parts toward the soul.

The problem of evaluation, already mentioned, is troublesome in Whitman's case. It has become increasingly clear how much his poetry not only freed but influenced those who followed, from

Pound and Eliot and Stevens and Williams to almost every poet around the world and up to the present. How sound or helpful his influence has been is a question deserving further study. If we admit here also the delicate but very real question of personal taste (shudders at "the barbaric yawp", at the garrulity, at the repetitious cataloguings should be taken seriously) we might come to a balanced judgement of this poem. Within the Whitman canon it stands with "A Child Went Forth" and parts of "Song of Myself" as coherent, moving, strong in its controlling imagery. The Brooklyn Ferry is the artist's Ship of Death as well as the Ship of Life and it carries us past all shores.

To make these claims for a Whitman poem is especially difficult for a reason applicable to few other poets generally called major or important; there are in print few of the detailed, careful readings we have come to expect of poems worthy our attention. It is as if generations of readers, critics, scholars have decided, when faced by the unorthodox line-length, poem-length and incantatory sound of a Whitman poem, to rest upon generalized apreciations or depreciations.[13] This has been an attempt to see if a Whitman poem could, as much as space permits, be read with the closeness we have the professional good manners to use for other poems as we judge them.

Whitman paints a ferry boat sailing and reminds us:

13. How easy it would be to mediate between differing Whitman scholar-critics if the story told of Turner's solution to Col. Lenox's complaint that the *Staffa* painting was "indistinct" could apply to a poem. Butlin and Joll (p. 181) examine the "Turnerian mythology" of Turner's supposed reply "You should tell him [Lenox] that indistinctness is my *forte*". The original letter (1845) proves this transcription inaccurate; Turner said "Indistinctness is my fault". The passage describing Turner's solution to his "fault" in the New York picture is worth citing in full:

> In fact, there is good reason to believe that at any rate part of the indistinctness of which Lenox complained was due to the varnish having bloomed on the journey. Turner advised wiping the surface with a silk handkerchief and this appears to have done the trick. Eventually, however, Lenox came to admire the picture greatly, and five years later added a second Turner oil ... to his collection.

Poor Whitman had only the silk of the grass, "... the handkerchief of the Lord,/ A scented gift and remembrancer designedly dropt,/ Bearing the owner's name someway in the corners, that we may see and remark, and say *Whose*?" ("Song of Myself").

You furnish your parts toward eternity,
Great or small, you furnish your parts toward the soul.

It should be clear now with what carefulness the poem has led us to this lovely declaration of our life's journey beyond landfall. D.H. Lawrence asked in "The Ship of Death": "And can a man his own quietus make/with a bare bodkin?" His answer was "No", close to Whitman's sense of the permanence of objects, the necessity on "the longest journey" to call aloud, simply and unashamedly. Lawrence says:

Oh build your ship of death, your little ark
and furnish it with food, with little cakes, and wine
for the dark flight down oblivion.[14]

"Crossing Brooklyn Ferry" can speak to us as it did to Lawrence, through the years, just as Whitman prophesied it would.

Leiden S. Betsky-Zweig

14. Many poets have paid their tributes to Whitman. Closest to D.H. Lawrence and to "Crossing Brooklyn Ferry" is Allen Ginsberg's "A Supermarket in California", which ends:

> Ah, dear father, graybeard, lonely old courage-teacher, what America did you have when Charon quit poling his ferry and you got out on a smoking bank and stood watching the boat disappear on the blade waters of Lethe?

THE GREATNESS OF *THE BOSTONIANS*

> "Since *The Bostonians* I find myself holding the 'critical world' at large in singular contempt."

It surely nowadays requires considerable justification to publish yet another article on Henry James. My own excuse is the unequivocal conviction expressed in my title. My first reading of *The Bostonians,* in 1940,was an extraordinarily vivid experience. The impact of the book was immediate and startling – the high intelligence, the wit, the vivacity and tempo, the simplicity of plot and elegance of structure. It seemed to me then, as it seems to me now after repeated re-readings, to be one of those "absolute" novels, examples of the art that are complete in themselves, novels which resist any misplaced efforts to read anything into them from outside, novels like *Persuasion, Silas Marner, The Scarlet Letter* and *Typhoon.* The only difference is that *The Bostonians* is 200,000 words long. I have since read most of James's other novels, early, middle, and late, but that initial impression of the outstanding quality of *The Bostonians* remains. If James is to be considered as a master of the art of the novel, then *The Bostonians* can bear the weight of examination as his major achievement, as an outstanding example of all that one means by the novel as a creative art form. But when I plough through the mass of criticism on Henry James, I am disheartened, but not surprized, to find that such favourable and confident views are not generally held.[1]

1. The omission of *The Bostonians* from the New York collected edition was no accident. The novel was totally unamenable to the kind of revision to which James was addicted at that time. Apart from its inclusion in Macmillan's collected edition in 1921-23, it was never reprinted for fifty-nine years. (I have not been able to find in the British Library the Dial Press edition of 1945, with P. Rahv's introduction. Matthiessen's edition appeared in 1947, and John Lehmann's Chiltern Library edition, with Trilling's introduction, in 1952. Since then, it has been easily accessible, and is currently in print in the Penguin Modern Classics; the references in the text are to this edition.)

With the exception of F. R. Leavis,[2] even the admirers of *The Bostonians* do not seem to admire it for what it is, but rather as a social, political and cultural document. Lionel Trilling, in his introduction to the 1952 edition, quite rightly draws attention to the fact that when the story of *The Bostonians* was conceived in 1883, James had just paid two visits to America, and had lost both his father and mother within the year. Memories of the Cambridge and Boston of his youth were obviously especially strong at the time. But the kind of construction Trilling puts upon the facts is wildly out of tune with the nature of the book. For Trilling, *The Bostonians*

> is a story of the parental house divided against itself, of the keystone falling from the arch, of the sacred mothers refusing their commission and the sacred fathers endangered.

The characters are described in the same psychological and anthropological jargon

> Basil Ransom . . . is akin to Yeats, Lawrence and Eliot in that he experiences his cultural fears in the most personal way possible, translating them into sexual fear, the apprehension of the loss of manhood . . . The very name of Olive Chancellor might suggest a deteriorated Minerva, presiding in homosexual chastity over the Athens of the New World . . . Verena is conceived as a sort of Iphigenia in Tauris, forced to preside as the priestess of the sacrifice of humanity . . . Dr Tarrant is a kind of shaman, gloomily doing sexual service of some dim, grim kind to deprived Boston ladies; and Matthias Pardon, the newspaper man, is the castrate priest of the huge idol of publicity.

Trilling seems to be anxious to reduce *The Bostonians* to a text for J. G. Frazer or Malinowski.

Irving Howe's introduction to the Modern Library Edition (1956)[3] shows a greater willingness to discuss *The Bostonians* as a

2. It is worth pointing out that it was forty years ago, and eleven years before *The Great Tradition,* that Leavis first stressed the importance of the early James and the achievement of *Washington Square, The Portrait of a Lady,* and *The Bostonians*: "All three have the abundant, full-blooded life of well-nourished organisms", *Scrutiny,* V (1937), 398-417.

3. Subsequently incorporated in Howe's *Politics and the Novel,* New York 1957.

novel. Howe offers comparisons with *The Europeans* and stresses the relationship with Hawthorne's *Blithedale Romance*;[4] he speaks of "surface vivacity", "marvellously dry wit", "a free and happy release of aggressive feelings", and "the broadest touches of burlesque". But although Howe reveals a feeling for the literary qualities of the novel, and, incidentally, puts his finger on the weakness of Trilling's approach, he sees the essence of the book as "a struggle between competing ideologies". Howe certainly wants to praise *The Bostonians,* but he gives the highest praise for its quality as a critique of industrial capitalism:

> All that we have since associated with industrial society was moving into sight – call it depersonalization or *anomie,* the sapping of individuality or the loss of tradition. James could not quite meet the problem through a frontal attack, but in *The Bostonians* he approaches it in his own way. He did not specify the social coordinates, the fundamental causes, of the problem, but he dramatized and elaborated it with a critical sharpness that no American novelist has yet surpassed.

For a Marxist literary critic, and Irving Howe is surely one of the most literate, sensitive and intelligent, this is the highest praise. But it is praise for qualities which are only peripheral to *The Bostonians,* if they are there at all.

The appreciative criticism of *The Bostonians* is, however, far outweighed by the unappreciative. A few representative samples will suffice. J. W. Beach, in *The Method of Henry James* (1918, reissued by the author 1954), describes the story as follows:

> The reader is called upon for the greatest patience . . . Basil wins out; and in his triumph, I suppose, we are shown the triumph of commonsense, or of natural law. The demonstration is not very convincing. And the process is often dull . . . a potentially melodramatic conclusion does not drown the memory of a story dragged out to a tiresome length.

S. Gorley Putt, in *A Reader's Guide to Henry James* (1966), speaks astoundingly of the "strained grey quality of the prose, re-

4. Marius Bewley's pioneering article, comparing *The Bostonians* with *The Blithedale Romance,* first appeared in *Scrutiny,* XVI (1949), before being incorporated in *The Complex Fate,* London 1952.

lieved by some amazing set pieces of character drawing", and describes the finale as

> those harrowing closing chapters of the novel where the strain breaks out at last in shrill hysteria like the shriek of an unlubricated engine . . . It is all competently done, but on what a disappointing level . . .

But it is the judgements of Leon Edel, the leading authority on Henry James, that should carry the most weight. In *Henry James, the Middle Years* (1963), Edel lays great stress on the fact that *The Bostonians* was originally planned as a six-part serial and that, in the course of writing, it more than doubled its length. After speaking of its "oppressive detail", and "a kind of uncontrollable prolixity everywhere", Edel attempts a kind of half-hearted judicial judgment:

> The modern reader may squirm over some of the *longueurs*; yet today the book's social documentation has an historical interest, and the writing is never without its charm. It is a novel which contains memorable scenes and memorable characters. However, it must be accounted a failure in comparison with Henry's best work – even though its place in American literature is significant.

Edel follows this with a psycho-biographical explanation:

> The personal venom in *The Bostonians* and its underlying feelings indicate the turn taken by Henry's imagination after his departure from America. In accommodating himself to his new London life, he was in some deep underworld of emotion, reliving ancient and morbid states. This, we might speculate, lay at the bottom of his inability to discipline the material of his novel, and his tendency to drag it out far beyond its prescribed length.

If James's most celebrated admirer can damn *The Bostonians* with such faint praise, what need is there to go on to invoke such anti-Jacobites as Maxwell Geismar?

The foregoing quotations give some idea of the variety, the weight and, perhaps above all, the tone, of the critical opinion on *The Bostonians.* To assert, in the face of such a cloud of witnesses, the proposition that *The Bostonians* is a very great example of the

Henry James, age 42 or 43, at the time of writing *The Bostonians.*

novelist's art, is to raise the fundamental issue of what the novel is all about. In what follows, I shall try to answer a number of simple questions. Firstly, what was James's attitude when he set about writing *The Bostonians* – what, to coin a phrase, was his artistic stance? Secondly, what is the social background of the novel, what is the plot, and what is the structure? Thirdly, how is the novel carried through, how is it "done"? And finally, what is the place of *The Bostonians* in James's *oeuvre*?

In the five years between 1876 and 1881 James had produced five major novels (*Roderick Hudson, The American, The Europeans, Washington Square,* and *The Portrait of a Lady*), a considerable number of short stories and novellas (including *Daisy Miller*), a major critical biography (*Hawthorne*), and a sizeable amount of literary journalism. After the completion of *The Portrait,* four years were to elapse before James started work on his next major novel, *The Bostonians.* Those four years involved a period of conscious stocktaking and a determination to concentrate his artistic powers and assert them in some new direction.[5] Within the same period James had twice re-visited America, and had lost not only his mother and father, but also his brother Wilky, whose health had been undermined by his military service in the Civil War. It was not until April 1883 that James drafted his first plan of *The Bostonians* in a letter to his American publisher James Osgood,[6] and it was a year later that he got down to work on it. The first instalment appeared in the *Century Magazine*[7] in November 1884,

5. See F. O. Matthiessen and K. B. Murdock, eds., *The Notebooks of Henry James,* New York 1947, p. 23 sq.

6. Carl J. Weber, *The Rise and Fall of James Ripley Osgood,* Waterville, Maine 1959, gives an excellent account of Osgood's importance in transatlantic publishing. The substance of James's letter to Osgood is in *The Notebooks* pp. 46-49. Osgood went bankrupt during the serialization of *The Bostonians,* and James lost money on his contract for the novel. Nevertheless, we must agree with Mark Twain that "Osgood was a lovely fellow".

7. The *Century Magazine* was a continuation of *Scribner's Magazine.* The English edition was published by F. Warne and Co. James had met the editor, R. W. Gilder, in 1883, and had published several short stories in it already. Unlike Dickens and Thackeray, James had no special strategies for serial publication. But in this case there was not much point anyway: the assistant editor, L. F. Tooker, fed the manuscript into the magazine like lumps of

and was published side by side with instalments from Howells's *The Rise of Silas Lapham,* selections from *Huckleberry Finn,* and a series on "Battles and leaders of the Civil War".

Now in June 1883 there appeared in the *Century* a review by James of the correspondence of Carlyle and Emerson which had been published by Osgood in the same year. Like Arnold's *Culture and Anarchy,* and Mill on Bentham and Coleridge, the Carlyle-Emerson correspondence is one of the seminal paradigms of the culture of the age. In his review,[8] James is obviously struck by the dramatic possibilities of the unlikely friendship between Emerson, the blandly optimistic progressive, and Carlyle, the rancorous, cantankerous reactionary: "what disparities of tone, of manner, of inspiration! ". James carefully qualifies Emerson's sweetness and serenity:

> he had a high and noble conception of good, without having, as it would appear, a definite conception of evil . . . He has not a grain of current contempt . . . the salt is wanting in his taste of things . . . Emerson speaks of his friends too much as if they were disembodied spirits. One doesn't see the colour on the cheeks of them and the coats on their back.

And of course Carlyle provides a dramatic contrast:

> he has fearfully little amenity. . . he has a vivid conception of evil without a corresponding conception of good . . . he is like a man hovering on the edge of insanity – hanging over a black gulf and wearing the reflection of its bottomless deeps in his face . . . Pessimism, cynicism, usually imply a certain amount of indifference and resignation; but in Carlyle these forces were nothing if not querulous and vocal.

cheese – in three instances breaking off in the middle of a chapter. Needless to say, the egregious Tooker did not think much of *The Bostonians*, and much preferred Howells's *Silas Lapham.* (cf. Arthur King and A.F.Stewart, *The House of Warne*, London 1965, p. 11; Samuel F. Chew, *Fruit among the Leaves.* New York 1950, p. 91 sq.; Caroline Ticknor, *Glimpses of Authors,* London n.d., ch. 19; L. F. Tooker, *Joys and Tribulations of an Editor,* London 1922, ch. 10; Herbert F. Smith and M. Peinovich, "*The Bostonians*: creation and revision". *Bulletin of the New York Public Library,* LXXIII [1969], 298-308.)

8. Reprinted in L. Edel, ed., *The American Essays of Henry James,* New York 1956.

A year after the publication of *The Bostonians,* James reviewed Cabot's *Memoir* of Emerson.[9] Two points are important in this review. Firstly, James recalls seeing Emerson on the platform of the Boston Music Hall on New Year's Day 1863, reading the "Boston Hymn" to celebrate Lincoln's proclamation freeing the Southern slaves. Secondly, James is struck by the remark that Emerson could see nothing in Dante, Shelley, Aristophanes, Don Quixote, Jane Austen and Dickens, and that he thought Hawthorne's novels "unworthy of him". James comments:

> There were points as to which Emerson's conception of right could be violated, but he had no great sense of wrong – a strangely limited one, indeed, for a moralist – no sense of the dark, the foul, the base. There were certain complications in life which he never suspected. One asks oneself whether that is why he did not care for Dante and Shelley and Aristophanes and Dickens, their works containing a considerable reflection of human perversity. But that still leaves the indifference to Cervantes and Miss Austen unaccounted for.

James's two essays on Carlyle and Emerson can provide a clue to what I have called his artistic stance in *The Bostonians.* Firstly, the Emerson-Carlyle polarity is the model for the fundamental polarity in the novel between an idealistic optimism and an aggressive, masterful pessimism. The setting, of course, of James's polarities is on a very, very minor scale and in a highly particularized milieu. The Emersonian element is represented by a circle of post-bellum Boston reformers who range from the fatuous to the sleazy. Its most charming representative is old Miss Birdseye:

> this frumpy little missionary was the last link in a tradition, and when she would be called away the heroic age of New England life – the age of plain living and high thinking, of pure ideals and earnest effort, of moral passion and noble experiment – would effectually be closed . . . the only thing that was still actual for Miss Birdseye was the elevation of the species by the reading of Emerson . . . (p. 157).

The Carlylean element is represented by the hero, Basil Ransom, a

9. Reprinted in *Partial Portraits* (1888) and in Edel's *The American Essays of Henry James.*

dispossessed and impoverished Southerner, who has Carlyle's conservatism, pessimism and bitterness, without Carlyle's mania, imagination or humour. Ransom

> was very conceited, for he was much addicted to judging his age. He thought it talkative, querulous, hysterical, maudlin, full of false ideas, of unhealthy germs, of extravagant, dissipated habits, for which a great reckoning was in store. He was an immense admirer of the late Thomas Carlyle, and was very suspicious of the encroachments of modern democracy (p. 164).

In fact, *The Bostonians* represents the novelist's way of getting the Emerson-Carlyle antithesis down to the manageable proportions of art. And that leads to the clue provided by James's review of the Emerson *Memoir,* in which he stressed Emerson's "confession of insensibility" to creative literary art. James set too much store by amenity to say out loud with Blake "he who generalizes is an ass", but that is what he is really saying in his novel. In *The Bostonians* he is showing the philosopher how the novelist deals with humanity through the particular instance, through the local, specific and individual. And also how the novelist, unlike the philosopher, can look at humanity from a variety of points of view, or through a number of filters. For although James could explain to himself the reasons for Emerson's indifference to Dante, Shelley, Aristophanes and Dickens, he could not account for, or, one suspects, forgive, Emerson's indifference to Cervantes and Jane Austen. Emerson was indifferent to Cervantes's sense of human absurdity and pathos, and indifferent to Jane Austen's power of controlled, astringent irony. In *The Bostonians* James seems to be almost consciously asserting the very special power and force of the novelist's vision of life: on the one hand intensifying the understanding of the individual by locating him in a highly particularized environment; and on the other hand extending, as it were, the picture of life by a multiplicity of viewpoint in which irony, and even sarcasm and farce, are not incompatible with humour and pathos. In the language of the turf, *The Bostonians* is sired by Cervantes out of Jane Austen, with Dickens and Hawthorne not very far away in the stud book.

Now whatever *The Bostonians* is about, it is not, in any general sense, about Bostonians or Boston. James makes it abundantly clear that "the Bostonians" was simply the label that the hero, Basil Ransom, gives to Olive Chancellor and her protégée Verena Tarrant.[10] It is a very particular section of Boston with which the novel deals. Olive lives on Charles Street to be sure, with a view of Back Bay, and with a culture that included German philosophy and George Eliot, and her wealth would certainly have given her access to a circle of Boston society that was somewhat higher than the one she chose to inhabit. Even so, at its highest level

> this little society was rather suburban and miscellaneous; it was prolific in ladies who trotted about, early and late, with books from the Athenaeum nursed behind their muff, or little nosegays of exquisite flowers that they were carrying as presents to each other (p. 154).

But when Mrs Farrinder of Roxbury [11], the polished exponent of women's rights, thinks of using Olive to break into Boston "society", Olive recoils. She "knew her place in the Boston hierarchy, and it was not what Mrs Farrinder supposed" (p. 31). Olive had no aspirations for Beacon Street Society; she had deliberately chosen as her ambience the slightly seedy and faintly malodorous world of Boston's South End:

> The ladies, who were much the more numerous, wore their bonnets, like Miss Chancellor; the men were in the garb of toil, many of them in weary-looking overcoats. Two or three had retained their overshoes, and as you approached them the odour of the india-rubber was perceptible . . . Most of them had an anxious, haggard look, though there were sundry exceptions – half a dozen placid, florid faces . . . Ransom was conscious of all these middle-aged feminine eyes, conscious of curls, rather limp, that depended from dusky bonnets, of heads poked forward, as if with a waiting, listening, familiar habit, of no one being very bright or gay . . . (p. 29 and p. 44).

10. James's jocular letter of 6 March 1884 to T. S. Perry, in which he says that the novel is "a remorseless exploitation of Boston. Look out on Marlborough Street; I am especially hard on the far end" (V. Harlow, *T. S. Perry*, Durham N.C., 1950, p. 316), has to be weighed against the very explicit statements in the novel itself, particularly Chapters 35 and 39.

11. The point of Mrs Farrinder's living at Roxbury is that it was the erstwhile location of Brook Farm, the transcendentalist phalanstery.

"But there would be too much to say just here were this incurable eccentric to let himself go."

Henry James in America 1905 (1)

When Verena and Olive move to fashionable circles in New York, it is only as an unusual "performance", something to enliven Mrs Burrage's Wednesday afternoon salon. The world of "the Bostonians" was never meant to have a representative quality; it is of the very essence of the plot that the social background should be odd, curious and peripheral. It is most certainly not the world of the Boston Brahmins – if anything, it is the world of the Boston Harijans.

The plot is of an elemental simplicity. Basil Ransom, a tall, dark, handsome but impoverished Southerner, of reactionary opinions, is attracted to Verena Tarrant. She is the beautiful and innocent child of a fatuous mother of old Abolitionist stock, and a highly dubious father who earns a precarious living as a mesmeric healer, and who has been in his time a fraudulent spiritualist and table-rapper.[12] He has trained his daughter Verena to perform as an extempore "trance speaker", and the girl has been taken up by Olive Chancellor, the shy, spinsterish intellectual, who uses Verena to spread the doctrine of feminine emancipation to the underprivileged of Boston's South End. Olive senses almost immediately the threat to herself of Basil's interest in Verena. Other young men are also attracted to Verena, and two of them propose: the bumptious newspaper reporter Matthias Pardon, and the charming, wealthy, but ineffectual Harvard man, Henry Burrage. But Verena keeps both of them off without much difficulty. Some time after their first meeting, Basil revisits Boston and secretly meets Verena, and from that point onwards she finds herself naturally attracted towards him. The rest of the story is concerned with the overcoming of her repugnance to his reactionary ideas (which is not really very difficult), and with the overcoming of her sense of loyalty to the possessive Olive. There is an idyllic wooing and a triumphant conquest. Basil Ransom is the Kingly Redeemer of the captive maiden.

The plot is as simple, as natural, and as normative as that. There are no complex moral issues; there is indeed no moral issue or moral struggle at all. For Verena to abandon her progressive social "ideas" in order to marry the reactionary Ransom is no real prob-

12. For the factual background, see Howard Kerr, *Mediums and Spirit Rappers and Roaring Radicals,* Urbana, Ill., 1972, Ch. 8.

lem for her. James makes Verena's intellectual innocence quite clear from the outset; her attachment to the "cause" is quite devoid of any deep intellectual passion. As for Verena's attachment to Olive, James never intended his readers to suppose that there should ever be any validity or permanence in that. Verena's surrender to Basil is obviously acutely painful, indeed tragic, for Olive, and painful for Verena herself inasmuch as she does not like to have to hurt Olive. But that is never intended to be a debatable "issue"; the novel does not pose any question of whether Verena should or whether she shouldn't. It is only our modern critics with socially and psychologically progressive attitudes who invest the plot with complexities.

The structure of the novel is equally clear and straightforward. The first twelve chapters are devoted to Basil Ransom's visit to Boston to meet his cousin Olive Chancellor, and to his first sight of Verena Tarrant at Miss Birdseye's feminist meeting. Chapters 13 to 20 are concerned with Olive's acquisition of Verena. Chapters 21 to 25 describe Basil's lodgings in New York, his temporary entanglement with Olive's sister, Mrs Luna, and his surreptitious visit to Verena in Boston. In Chapters 26 to 34, Verena and Olive visit New York, Basil attends Verena's performance at Mrs Burrage's salon and makes his intentions quite clear to Verena in an excursion to Central Park. Verena realizes that she loves him, and retreats back to Boston with Olive. There is a lapse of time during which Olive takes Verena to Europe and perfects her as an instrument of the feminist cause. Chapters 35 to 39 are located at Marmion,[13] the seaside resort at Cape Cod, where Verena and Olive have come to prepare for Verena's great public appearance at the Boston Music Hall; where Miss Birdseye, attended by the faithful Dr Mary Prance, has come to die; and where Basil has come "to take possession of Verena Tarrant". Basil courts Verena for a long summer month; Miss Birdseye dies; and Olive spirits Verena away from Basil. Finally, Chapters 40 to 42 move back to Boston, to the great meeting at the Boston Music Hall, and to Basil triumphantly carrying off Verena before she has made her speech.

13. The real place is Marion. The editor of the *Century Magazine*, R. W. Gilder, had a summer cottage there, which James had visited in 1883 (R. W. Gilder, *Letters*, London 1910, p. 139, and L. Edel, *Henry James, The Conquest of London*, London 1962, p. 505).

One is compelled to offer some such pedestrian account of the divisions of the book, because of the charges of weakness of structure that have been made against it.[14] The trouble is that the critics are possessed of two external and irrelevant pieces of information: that the book in its final form was twice its originally planned length; and that James himself confessed to considerable difficulty in writing the middle portion. The answer is, of course, "never trust the artist, trust the tale". An objective reading of the book itself reveals no difficulties with the structure; it is quite straightforward and obvious. One of the frequent criticisms is the detail of the descriptions and the slowness of the action. Much has been made of the fact that James takes 40,000 words to describe the first twenty-four hours of the story. Such an objection would hardly be tactful in the presence of an admirer of Joyce's *Ulysses,* a novel which describes twenty-four hours in considerably more wordage and with considerably less lucidity. James uses the richly descriptive technique of the opening chapters of *The Bostonians* to establish the very special and specific social ambience of the story, and also to establish the very special and unusual ironic tone. Word-counts of the openings of other great novels, *The Scarlet Letter* or *Middlemarch* for instance, would reveal a comparably high ratio of words written to time passed. And no one has ever commented adversely on the superb opening of *The Portrait of a Lady,* which uses 24,000 words to describe the first day of the heroine's arrival in England.

As for James's own admission that he had difficulties with the middle of the story, the concrete achievement belies the author's doubts. The centre of the novel is much more than a bridge between the opening and the finale. It provides the essential developments of the characters. The idealistic and highly moral Olive literally buys Verena from her parents; she is cunning enough to resile from demanding a vow of celibacy from Verena; she is quite ready to throw her sister, Mrs Luna, at Basil, and when that gambit fails, she is even prepared to negotiate with Mrs Burrage to obtain young Henry Burrage as a complaisant husband for Verena.

14. A. Habegger, "The Disunity of *The Bostonians*", *Nineteenth Century Fiction,* XXIV (1969), 193-209. Irving Howe says that *The Bostonians* "falters about halfway".

Henry James in America 1905 (2)

(All this is from a passionate anti-slavery advocate.) A nice ironic touch is the suggestion of the odious journalist Matthias Pardon that Verena should be exploited with a big public debut:

> he wanted something on another scale, something so big that people would have to go round it if they wanted to get past. Then lowering his voice a little, he mentioned what it was: a lecture in the Music Hall, at fifty cents a ticket, without her father, right there on her own basis (p. 111).

At such an early stage in her manipulation of Verena, that is the last thing the fastidious Olive would want, yet that is what she ultimately comes to – including even the inevitable lecture agent, Mr Filer (the defiler).

The middle part of the book also deals with Basil Ransom's temptations. He toys with the idea of accepting the role of complaisant husband to Olive's wealthy widowed sister, Mrs Luna; her money would give him the necessary backing for the propagation of his reactionary ideas. But when confronted with the presence of Verena at Mrs Burrage's salon, Basil rejects the importunities of Mrs Luna; his ideas are certainly important to him, but his natural attraction to Verena is more important. The long and loving description of Basil's shabby lodgings on the corner of Second Avenue gives us proleptically an idea of the sort of life Verena is going to lead. And Basil's passionate declaration of his repellent ideas to Verena, in the course of a delightful outing in Central Park, makes it quite clear to Verena, as well as to the reader, precisely what she is ultimately going to let herself in for:

> Once Verena was fairly launched the spirit of the day took possession of her; she was glad to have come, she forgot about Olive, enjoyed the sense of wandering in the great city with a remarkable young man who would take beautiful care of her . . . But little by little she grew weary and rather sad . . . she had yet never dreamed of such a wholesale arraignment as Mr Ransom's, so much bitterness as she saw lurking beneath his exaggerations, his misrepresentations . . . her reflections softly battled with each other as she listened, in the warm, still air, touched with the far-away hum of the immense city, to his deep, sweet, distinct voice, expressing monstrous opinions with exotic cadences and mild, familiar laughs, which, as he leaned towards her, almost tickled her cheek and ear . . . One must lead

> one's own life; it was impossible to lead the life of another, especially when that other was so different, so arbitrary and unscrupulous (pp. 282, 283, 285, 285-6).

That scene in Central Park is essential to the structure of the book and enables James to achieve the finale with the utmost economy and force. When, on the very last page of the story, Basil rushes Verena out through the portals of the Boston Music Hall, she knows exactly what it is going to be like "to lead the life of another".

In insisting on the simplicity, normality and inevitability of the plot and structure of *The Bostonians,* one runs the risk of producing a rather reductive impression of the whole. But the book is rammed with life; it is both sharply ironic and yet vivacious and high-spirited. The quality of the novel lies in "the doing", from sentence to sentence and from page to page. A textbook example, too long for quotation, of James's sheer linguistic virtuosity, can be found in the subtle differences between Verena's two feminist speeches (in Chapters 7 and 28); the first is under her father's influence, and the second is after eighteen months of Olive's tutelage. Plenty of critical attention has been given to the sarcastic portraits of the Bostonian milieu; it needs to be pointed out that these are impressions in the minds of individual characters, honed up occasionally by authorial intrusion.[15] Basil the Southerner is not the only hostile witness to the Boston scene. It should perhaps be remembered that the over-quoted description of Miss Birdseye – "she was heroic, she was sublime, the whole moral history of Boston was reflected in her displaced spectacles" – is in fact a valuation by Olive Chancellor. The venomous portrait of Mrs Tarrant is also Olive's, spiced with her jealousy of Verena's mother:

> Mrs Tarrant, with her soft corpulence, looked to her guest very

15. In revising the text of the serial for publication in book form, James took pains to eliminate a considerable number of authorial intrusions, so the ones that were left, were left very deliberately. In their discussion of other textual alterations, Smith and Peinovich (see note 7) make the interesting point that "the book is more offensive to the refined sensibilities than is the serial". Far from softening the irony and sarcasm, in response to hostile criticism, James in fact sharpened it up.

bleached and tumid; her complexion had a kind of withered glaze; her hair, very scanty, was drawn off her forehead *à la Chinoise*; she had no eyebrows, and her eyes seemed to stare, like those of a figure of wax (p. 98).

All the value judgements in the novel are local and situational, and are filtered seemingly effortlessly through the characters, in a way that recalls Jane Austen rather than James's later "technique".

As an almost breathtaking instance of what one can only call James's "wit", a combination of seriousness and vivacity, one may point to the moment where Olive goes to tea with the Tarrants and finds Verena flirting with Matthias Pardon and the two Harvard men. She is so upset that she takes Verena out onto the back porch in the cold winter evening, to make her promise never to marry:

"... But promise me one thing, and I shall be – oh, so tender!"

"What a strange place for promises," said Verena, with a shiver, looking about her into the night.

"Yes, I am dreadful, I know it. But promise." And Olive drew the girl nearer to her, flinging over her with one hand the fold of a cloak that hung ample upon her own meagre person, and holding her there with the other, while she looked at her, suppliant but half hesitating. "Promise! " she repeated.

"Is it something terrible? "

"Never to listen to one of them, never to be bribed –"

At this moment the house-door was opened again, and the light of the hall projected itself across the little piazza. Matthias Pardon stood in the aperture, and Tarrant and his wife, with the two other visitors, appeared to have come forward as well, to see what detained Verena.

"You seem to have started a kind of lecture out here," Mr Pardon said. "You ladies had better look out, or you'll freeze together! " (p. 117)

And S. Gorley Putt talks of "the strained grey quality of the prose"! He must have been wearing sun-glasses when he read *The Bostonians.* It is passages like the above that demonstrate the immeasurable advantages of the pre-Freudian and pre-permissive novelist.

For high comedy, a few extracts may suffice from Basil's dialogue with Miss Birdseye on the jolting Boston tram. Basil introduces himself, with all his Southern charm, as having been at Miss Birdseye's party:

> ". . . I came with Miss Chancellor, who is a kind of relation of mine, and you were very good to me."
>
> "What did I do? " asked Miss Birdseye, candidly (p. 185).

Miss Birdseye complains that she cannot sleep:

> "You ought to come down South," the young man suggested. "In that languid air you would doze deliciously! "
>
> "Well, I don't want to be languid," said Miss Birdseye. "Besides, I have been down South, in the old times, and I can't say they let me sleep very much; they were always round after me! " (p. 186)

Miss Birdseye says that after carrying the Bible to the negroes, she is now carrying the Statute-book to unemancipated womanhood:

> Ransom found himself liking Miss Birdseye very much, and it was quite without hypocrisy or a tinge too much of the local quality in his speech that he said: "Wherever you go, madam, it will matter little what you carry. You will always carry your goodness."
>
> For a minute she made no response. Then she murmured: "That's the way Olive Chancellor told me you talked." (p. 186)

"Murmured" makes Miss Birdseye's reply modest as well as candid. "Said" would have made it simply rude. Miss Birdseye senses an affinity between Basil and Verena:

> "I wonder very much that Miss Tarrant didn't affect you that evening! "
>
> "Ah, but she did! " Ransom said, with alacrity. "I thought her very charming! "
>
> "Didn't you think her very reasonable? "
>
> "God forbid, madam! I consider women have no business to be reasonable."
>
> His companion turned upon him, slowly and mildly, and each of her glasses, in her aspect of reproach, had the glitter of an enormous tear. "Do you regard us, then, simply as lovely baubles? " (p. 187)

The "lovely baubles" comes as the climax to the preceding succession of sparks and flashes. The dialogue creates the terms and the background by which it is to be understood. It is incredible to find that in a book called *The Comic Sense of Henry James* (by R. Poirier) there is no place for *The Bostonians* at all.

The deathbed scene of Miss Birdseye, so often referred to as if it were merely a sort of compensation for James's earlier ironic treatment of her at the beginning of the book, is anything but charming or sweetly sentimental. It exemplifies a kind of artistic intelligence that is clearly superior to Dickens; for pathos and good humour it suggests Cervantes; and for the tragedy of cross-purposes it is as fine as anything in Conrad. Miss Birdseye addresses Verena:

> "Oh, I haven't effected very much; I have only cared and hoped. You will do more than I have ever done – you and Olive Chancellor, because you are young and bright, brighter than I ever was; and besides, everything has got started."
>
> "Well, you've got started, Miss Birdseye," Doctor Prance remarked, with raised eyebrows, protesting drily but kindly . .
>
> "We will think of you always, and your name will be sacred to us, and that will teach us singleness and devotion," Verena went on . . .
>
> "Well, it's the thing you and Olive have given your lives to that has absorbed me most, of late years. I did want to see justice done – to us. I haven't seen it, but you will. And Olive will. And Mr Ransom will – and he will be proud to have helped."
>
> "Oh, mercy, mercy! " cried Verena, burying her head in Miss Birdseye's lap.
>
> "You are not mistaken if you think I desire above all things that your weakness, your generosity, should be protected," Ransom said, rather ambiguously, but with pointed respectfulness. "I shall remember you as an example of what women are capable of," he added; and he had no subsequent compunctions for the speech, for he thought poor Miss Birdseye, for all her absence of profile, essentially feminine.
>
> A kind of frantic moan from Olive Chancellor responded to these words, which had evidently struck her as an insolent sarcasm . . . (pp. 345-6).

James uses the interplay of already established characters to create the poise and balance of the scene: the innocent generosity of

Verena, the placid optimism of Miss Birdseye, the aseptic realism of Dr Prance, the Southern courtesy of Basil, and the passionate agony of Olive.

The grand finale has been called melodramatic, but such an epithet is purely reductive. James had retained, after twenty years, a vivid impression of his attendance at the Boston Music Hall to witness Emerson reading the Boston Hymn. The excitement of the concluding episode of the novel is fixed by a detailed description of the ground-plan of the Hall: the thronged auditorium, the stairway leading up to the platform from below, the waiting-room under the platform, and the solid Boston policeman in the little vestibule, barring access to the waiting-room. The time-scheme, recalling the final hour of Marlowe's Dr Faustus, is equally detailed: the minutes are counted up to and beyond 8 p.m., the advertized time of the lecture. It is only after the scene is set, and the clocks are in motion, that Basil Ransom bursts into the waiting-room:

> What he wanted, in this light, flamed before him and challenged all his manhood, tossing his determination to a height from which not only Doctor Tarrant, and Mr Filer, and Olive, over there, in her sightless, soundless shame, but the great expectant hall as well, and the mighty multitude, in suspense, keeping quiet from minute to minute and holding the breath of its anger – from which all these things looked small, surmountable, and of the moment only. He didn't quite understand, as yet, however; he saw that Verena had not refused, but temporized, that the spell upon her – thanks to which he should still be able to rescue her – had been the knowledge that he was near.
>
> "Come away, come away," he murmured, quickly, putting out his two hands to her.
>
> She took one of them, as if to plead, not to consent. "Oh, let me off, let me off – for *her,* for the others! It's too terrible, it's impossible! "
>
> "What I want to know is why Mr Ransom isn't in the hands of the police! " wailed Mrs Tarrant, from her sofa.
>
> "I have been, madam, for the last quarter of an hour." Ransom felt more and more that he could manage it, if he only kept cool . . .
>
> "There's one thing I want to know: are we going to spend

> half an hour talking over our domestic affairs? " Mr Filer demanded, wiping his indignant countenance. "Is Miss Tarrant going to lecture, or ain't she going to lecture? If she ain't, she'll please to show cause why. Is she aware that every quarter of a second, at the present instant, is worth about five hundred dollars? " . . .
>
> Olive meanwhile was literally praying to her kinsman. "Let her appear this once, just this once: not to ruin, not to shame! Haven't you any pity; do you want me to be hooted? It's only for an hour. Haven't you any soul? " . . .
>
> Mr Filer was now pouring forth his nature in objurgations and oaths, and brandishing before the culprits – Verena and Ransom – the extreme penalty of the law. Mrs Tarrant had burst into violent hysterics, while Selah revolved vaguely about the room and declared that it seemed as if the better day was going to be put off for quite a while. "Don't you see how good, how sweet they are – giving us all this time? Don't you think that when they behave like that – without a sound, for five minutes – they ought to be rewarded? " Verena asked, smiling divinely, at Ransom. Nothing could have been more tender, more exquisite, than the way she put her appeal upon the grounds of simple charity, kindness to the great good-natured, childish public.
>
> "Miss Chancellor may reward them in any way she likes. Give them back their money and a little present to each".
>
> "Money and presents? I should like to shoot you, sir! " yelled Mr Filer . . . (pp. 382, 381, 383, 384).

The excitement and tension for Basil is real: "he felt more and more that he could manage it" (note too "he should still be able to rescue her", rather than "he would"). The tragic desperation of Olive is real, in the incoherence of "not to ruin, not to shame". The hesitation, confusion and innocence of Verena is real. But there can be no melodrama in the presence of the perspiring Mr Filer: "if she ain't going to lecture, she'll please to show cause why." Indeed, as one reads in its entirety the final section of the book, one cannot but recall I. A. Richards's aphorisms on poetry: that the poet is the man who never says *less* than two things at once, and that the essence of great poetry is that it provides the reconciliation of opposites. In *The Bostonians*, James achieves his finest, and most ambitious, example of the novel as dramatic poem.

The Princess Casamassima followed shortly after *The Bostonians*, and the two novels are often bracketed together. Nothing could be more unfair to *The Bostonians.* James was creatively exhausted, and *The Princess Casamassima* shows all the symptoms. The plot is frankly implausible: in a rash moment of enthusiasm the hero makes a promise to devote himself wholly to the anarchist cause, but by the time he is called upon to fulfil his promise he has come to admire the qualities of the established order. There is no pressure of inevitability at all. To acquaint the hero with the amenities of civilization, James is even forced to the clumsy expedient of having the hero's mistress rent a country house for a couple of months and later of sending him on a brisk package tour of the Continent. The structure of the novel is very precarious, and the descriptive settings are not integrated into the story – compare the Greenwich Park scene in *The Princess Casamassima* and the Central Park scene in *The Bostonians.* The poverty of invention is reflected in the fact that, for his *femme fatale,* James has to resuscitate the Princess, complete with duenna, from his earlier novel *Roderick Hudson,* written ten years previously.

The public failure of *The Bostonians* marked a turning point in James's career. In his later novels, James was preoccupied with particular aspects of technique in a way which seems to have precluded an ability to sustain the other aspects. He was preoccupied with the "dramatic" in a way which precluded the scenic; he was preoccupied with the "plot", as the vehicle for problems of moral choice, in a way which precluded the physical description of the characters. Never again did he achieve that rich and varied organic texture, that liveliness as an index of life, which is the hallmark of the greatness of *The Bostonians.*

Nijmegen T. A. Birrell

OTELLO AND *OTHELLO* - THE MODERNITY OF VERDI'S SHAKESPEARE

Boito's libretto for Verdi's *Otello* has always been considered as one of the finest texts ever written for an opera. It is admittedly less polished than the *Falstaff* libretto, but the history of opera gives ample evidence that comic librettos are easier to write than tragic ones. The history of Verdi's and Boito's collaboration is sufficiently known. The original draft of the text was in Verdi's hands early in 1880; the composition of the music was finished in 1885; scoring and revising took another year. During that period Verdi participated in the creation of the final version of the text most actively. Although it had not been easy to persuade him to tackle *Otello,* (the music publisher Ricordi had to draw heavily on his expense account), there is no doubt that the subject excited a strong interest in the composer once he was under way. The interest showed itself especially in the numerous alterations which Verdi suggested to Boito's original draft. They resulted in many minor changes and in the addition of some of the most striking scenes: the love duet in Act I, the choral serenade in Act II and Desdemona's scene in the final act. (1) In all these one recognizes, of course, Verdi's theatrical instinct. However, the precise delineation of Verdi's share in the ultimate libretto is of hardly more than academic interest. Much more interesting is the fact that the libretto seems to anticipate a characteristically 'modern' interpretation of the play in a number of important respects, whereas in others it seems to be firmly rooted in the conventional nineteenth-century attitude. The ambiguity that characterizes the libretto to a reader acquainted with twentieth-century Shakespeare criticism can, I believe, be shown to be related to certain musico-stylistic features of the opera.

Consider Boito's first act. It opens with the storm that begins Shakespeare's second act. Thus Boito achieves at once a splendid operatic opening of truly Shakespearean flavour, and 'unity of place' — it is as if he had taken to heart Johnson's remark: 'Had the scene opened in Cyprus, and the preceding incidents been occasionally related, there had been little wanting to a drama of the most exact

[1] See Winton Dean, 'Shakespeare and Opera' in P. Hartnoll, ed., *Shakespeare in Music: A Collection of Essays* (London 1964), to which I am in many respects indebted. It was partly, however, out of dissatisfaction with Winton Dean's article 'Verdi's Otello' in *Shakespeare Survey 21* (ed. K. Muir, Cambridge 1968) that the present essay was written.

and scrupulous regularity.' (2) But the decision to start the opera in Cyprus — a decision that was only taken after long deliberations between Verdi and Boito — resulted in the loss of a number of important issues that Shakespeare deals with in the first act. Thus Brabantio and his peers disappear altogether; the theme of 'magic' is reduced to a single and meaningless reference in Boito's III, ii, and the racial aspects involved in Othello's relationship to the Venetian community are largely suppressed. Most importantly, however, we lose in the opera the picture of that community which Shakespeare paints in the first act. He achieves a sharp and profound analysis of a bourgeois, decadent society, the moral climate of which provides Iago with his principal motivation:

> Preferment goes by Letter and affection,
> Not by the old gradation, where each second
> Stood heir to the first . . . (I, i).

It is a society in which 'honesty' and 'honour' have become dissociated, and it is again Iago who astutely diagnoses the disease:

> As I am an honest man, I thought you had received
> a bodily wound; there is more offence in that
> than in reputation . . . (II, iii).

It is a society lacking in what Shakespeare called 'degree' in *Troilus and Cressida.* It is of such a society that Desdemona is a child, and by its defective moral standards she is, in Shakespeare's conception, inevitably limited. She is, in the first act, carefully placed in a social and moral *milieu,* and although she is in a technical sense innocent, Othello's long speech in I, iii about his social calls at Brabantio's house, where he used to impress Desdemona with stories about his adventures, to which she would respond with 'a hint', leaves little doubt about the kind of moral atmosphere in which Desdemona naturally feels at home. Desdemona, like certain other Shakespearean heroines — Hermione in *The Winter's Tale* comes to mind — was profoundly misunderstood by the typical nineteenth-century reader

[2] See Samuel Johnson, the 1765 edition of *The Plays of William Shakespeare; Othello*, General Note.

Another effect of the disappearance of the first act is that the problem of the 'double time scheme' is even more sharply focused in the opera than in the play. See on this M. R. Ridley's introduction to the Arden *Othello,* 7th ed. (London 1958, repr. 1967, pp. lxvii ff.) The quotations in this essay are all from this edition.

and all too easily idolized as an angelic creature of pure innocence. Shakespeare's real Desdemona is, of course, nothing of the sort. Her tragedy in the play is not that, as a creature of immaculate purity, she falls victim to the forces of sheer evil — such being the stock nineteenth-century view —, but that, though innocent of adultery, she falls victim to forces at work within the society of which she herself is a product, the society that shaped her and that she herself helps to shape.

In losing Shakespeare's first act, the opera loses Shakespeare's placing of Desdemona in social and moral terms. The loss is not compensated for. In the character of Desdemona, Verdi and Boito seem to have indulged in the typically nineteenth-century sentimental dream of virtue and love embodied in a pure woman. We must remember that neither Verdi nor Boito were able to read Shakespeare in the original, so that their tendency to italianize and sentimentalize Desdemona may have been partly caused by the translation they read. The conventionality of the character comes out, I believe, most embarrassingly in the aura of holiness with which she is surrounded. Desdemona's *Ave Maria* may serve a purpose as a dramatic counterpart to Iago's *Credo* (which, of course, was Boito's invention), the moment nevertheless emphasizes the limitations of Boito's and Verdi's conception of her character as compared with Shakespeare's.

The *Ave-Maria* may also serve to typify the musical style of Desdemona's representation in the opera. Nobody will question the beauty of Desdemona's music, but it is nevertheless marked by a certain thinness of invention, a rarefaction that seems to indicate a comparatively low level of vitality. Hanslick, in his famous 1887 review of the opera, registered a similar impression: 'Verdi's Desdemona — really 'pallida morte futura', like Vergil's Dido — touches us more deeply with her farewell song than the more composed Desdemona of Rossini; but as a piece of music, Verdi's 'Song of the Willow' is definitely inferior to Rossini's' (3). Desdemona's pallor as a dramatic character is matched by the pallor of her music. It is not, of course, inferior music, but its inspiration is limited by the same factors that limit the dramatic conception of the character. She is, in E. M. Forster's term, a 'flat' character, and this is the sense in which her music is 'flat'. It is the sort of music that evokes in the listener only one response, however strong the response may be (4).

[3] Eduard Hanslick, 'Verdi's *Otello*', in *Music Criticisms 1846-1899* (ed. & tr. H. Pleasants, London 1951).
[4] E. M. Forster, *Aspects of the Novel*, Ch.4 (London 1927).

Interestingly enough, the music of the lovers in *Falstaff*, which is not unlike Desdemona's from a musical point of view, does not strike us as in this way deficient. But those lovers are *really* innocent, nor is the dramatic situation at all one that calls for profound characterization.

It is in its attitude to Desdemona, then, that the opera exhibits a characteristic nineteenth-century limitation. However, this should not be taken to imply that this view of Desdemona, and in fact of the whole play, is entirely obsolete. In *Shakespeare Survey 21*, devoted to *Othello*, Dame Helen Gardner has an extremely interesting but not impartial article on *Othello* criticism since Bradley, in which she aligns herself with those modern critics (such as John Holloway in *The Story of the Night*) who are essentially in agreement with Bradley in their appreciation of the play. It seems entirely characteristic of the intellectual paralysis with which Desdemona can strike even the best critics that Helen Gardner bases her argument on what is, in the last analysis, a sentimental attitude towards her: 'Her presence in the play flatly contradicts the supposed insights of Iago'. Well, it does not, if the play is properly read. Winton Dean is clearly of the same mind: 'Desdemona's part has a tender lyricism that would melt a heart of stone'. In talking about Desdemona, such critics employ arguments and metaphors which indicate that the critical faculty has been blocked. Their predicament is still essentially the same as Verdi's and Boito's.

There are, however, other important functions of Shakespeare's first act to which Verdi and Boito have responded more creatively. These concern the character of Othello himself, and the quality of his relationship with Desdemona. If Desdemona, in the characteristic response of the nineteenth-century reader, appears as the pure woman of 'angelic sweetness' in Hazlitt's phrase, or as 'the eternal womanly in its most lovely and adorable form' in Bradley's, Othello figures conventionally as 'the noble hero'. It was T. S. Eliot who initiated the typically 'modern' response to Othello in his 1927 essay 'Shakespeare and the Stoicism of Seneca'. He quotes Othello's final speech and comments: 'What Othello seems to be doing in making this speech is *cheering himself up*.' Eliot's observation has found its way into modern Shakespeare criticism in various guises: F. R. Leavis, in his essay on the play in *The Common Pursuit*, speaks of 'heroic self-dramatization'; D. A. Traversi uses the same term in *An Approach to Shakespeare*; G. Wilson Knight, in *The Wheel of Fire*, speaks of an 'exaggerated, false rhetoric'. Any modern reading of the play interprets Iago's lines about Othello in the very first scene of the play in this light:

> But he, as loving his own pride and purposes,
> Evades them, with a bombast circumstance,
> Horribly stuff'd with epithets of war.

Thus the 'noble hero' is from the first moment clearly placed in the evaluation of Iago's cruel, jealous, but always intelligently judging perceptions. Othello's rhetorical self-glorification has become an essential factor in twentieth-century discussions about the play.

It seems that Verdi and Boito have taken great care that the important hints about this aspect of Othello's character contained in the first act should not be lost in the opera. From his first appearance on, Verdi's Otello is presented as a noble hero with precisely the flaw that Eliot was the first to note in 'official' Shakespeare criticism. The *Esultate* arioso in the first scene could not be better characterized than by the term 'self-glorification'. There is the slightly hysterical tone that marks Otello's music throughout the opera. More specifically, the melodic line at the end of the arioso recalls the typical music of Verdi's middle-period heroes. The regressive quality of the music seems to fall in with the moral and psychological regression that is implied in the concept of self-dramatization. It is in particular such melodic turns as the one found here that contrast sharply, in their peculiarly Verdian earthiness, with the rarefied music of Desdemona's utterances. Thus the two characters are clearly distinguished by purely musical means. But while the Desdemona music is regressive in the psychological sense, making for a simplified response on the listener's part to match the composer's simplified attitude to the issues involved, that of Otello is regressive in an artistic way, involving a deliberate handling of the moral implications of a musical style, and thus evokes in the listener a complex response. In the case of Otello, the quality of the music seems to imply a moral judgement that we have recognized as characteristically modern.

In good opera, music is always used to characterize, although it is not often very clear how this is done. Verdi's Otello would seem to provide a particularly interesting case of musical characterization: it is achieved by means of deliberate and carefully controlled reverting to a 'heroic' type of music that one associates spontaneously with middle-period Verdi, but which *Otello* and *Falstaff* are generally supposed to have transcended. (It is the technique of Strauss's *Ariadne auf Naxos*, but executed with immensely greater subtlety and with a moral seriousness of which Strauss was incapable.) The recognition of the heroic element in Otello's music should tell us a great deal about the unique sort of maturity achieved in this opera, and about the way in which the maturity has been reached. It results from a powerful intellectual control over musical styles, and a willingness on Verdi's part to re-interpret his own musical past critically. As we will have occasion to argue, there can be little doubt that the confrontation with Wagner was one of the factors that prompted this self-examination.

Of course, the libretto itself provided Verdi with a most suitable occasion to re-examine his musical past in terms of the moral issues that his and Boito's enlightened response to Shakespeare's play had disclosed for them. Otello is a military man, and so the 'heroic' aspects of his nature receive strong support from conventional military musical formulae. The 'epithets of war' mostly sound in the orchestra, but strongly affect the melodic line of the voice part. Thus, in the love duet of the first act, Desdemona's transports are interrupted by a characteristic outburst of military self-glorification from Otello. In II, v, there is another such outburst, founded on a passage in Shakespeare that is absolutely central to an adequate understanding of the play:

> I had been happy if the general camp,
> Pioners, and all, had tasted her sweet body,
> So I had nothing known: O now for ever
> Farewell the plumed troop, and the big wars,
> That makes ambition virtue; O farewell
> Farewell the neighing steed, and the shrill trump,
> The spirit-stirring drum, the ear-piercing fife;
> The royal banner, and all quality,
> Pride, pomp and circumstance of glorious war! (III, iii)

What this speech conveys is Otello's incapacity to represent to himself his feelings about Desdemona's supposed adultery otherwise than in the form of a lament on the loss of his military glory. Again the music here is that of Verdi's middle-period heroes; there is a ring of 'false rhetoric' in it that stresses the quality of Otello's deepest feelings — 'Rea contro me!' The scene follows Shakespeare very closely, and culminates in the oath-taking passage, where the musical line of the voice parts almost becomes a parody of what we tend to think of as 'real Verdi', the orchestra sounding 'epithets of war' all the time. In this passage, where the 'heroic' music reaches its culmination, the tune is technically of a familiar type: the *Risorgi-*

mento marching-hymn, implanted on a dramatic situation no less conventional: the revenge-scene. The unmistakably parodying effect which the music here acquires derives from the ambiguities of the situation: the heroic music of political idealism is here applied to a private cause and the revenge sworn is revenge for a crime that was never committed (5).

In this way Verdi may be said to use music creatively in precisely the same way that Shakespeare uses language: this is 'music in action'. In a carefully controlled way musical language and character are associated in order to achieve critical insight not only into character but into musical language as well. How close the opera's conception of Otello is to Shakespeare's conception of Othello appears from the astonishing intelligence with which the libretto concentrates on what is most important in the play. We have argued that the musical depiction of the heroine reflects the limitations of certain nineteenth-century stock responses, although the frequently noted quotation from the 'Agnus Dei' of the *Requiem* on Desdemona's words *Tu gli perdona* may be an indication that Verdi proceeded with full consciousness even in the musical characterization of his heroine. Where Otello is concerned, however, the opera's characterization is 'in the best modern way'. Thus in II, iv the libretto carefully mentions the factors that lead to Othello's undoing: different social and cultural background, age and colour. Note also how the love duet uses all the important material from Shakespeare's I, iii, and culminates in a passage that reproduces Shakespeare verbally:

> E tu m'amavi per le mie sventure
> Ed io t'amavo per la tua pietà. (I, ii)
>
> She lov'd me for the dangers I had pass'd,
> And I lov'd her that she did pity them. (I, iii)

In any modern interpretation of the play, these lines summarize the peculiar quality of the love-relationship between Othello and Desdemona. They contain, in a nutshell, Othello's self-dramatization as well as Desdemona's immature and romantic infatuation, which is not wholly free from a certain perversity that her upbringing and social background might have favoured.

One of the most impressive musical climaxes of the opera is built on these lines, just before the 'kiss motive' is first heard in the orchestra. It is this motive that functions as the musical correlative

[5] See B. Szabolcsi, *A History of Melody*, p. 179 (English transl. London, 1965).

of the complex issues involved in the relationship between Othello and Desdemona. These pages have always been held up as evidence by those who consider *Otello* as an opera written under the immediate influence of Wagner. The whole love-duet strikes a recent critic as '. . . distilled Wagner: the essence without the long-windedness' (6). This description admirably fits the kiss motive itself; Verdi's traditional sequential structuring is here replaced by a chromatic shift over a very short compass. The question of Wagner's influence on Verdi is of course a difficult one. Perhaps modern critics tend to play down the issue too easily because the differences between the two composers have become so obvious. But we must not forget that to nineteenth-century ears the similarities must have been much more obvious and significant. Tchaikovsky, for instance, who was by no means uncritical towards Wagner, felt that from *Aida* onwards Verdi's development had been beneficially affected by the German composer (7). This was surely a striking observation, since it was — and still is — the custom either to deplore Wagner's influence on Verdi, or else to ignore it. The kiss motive, however, seems to pose a problem which neither of these approaches can fully grasp. Its suitability is not in question here, nor its inherent beauty, but we should envisage the possibility that, precisely because of its Wagnerian leanings, the passage represents one more example of 'conscious' music-making which, like the 'heroic' Otello music or the *Requiem*-quotation, considers itself critically at the very moment when it operates. This music asks questions about itself, that is, about its moral implications. Just as Verdi can pose moral problems by reverting to an earlier musical style of his own, problems relating to the implications of the heroic attitude, so he can pose moral problems by reverting to a musical style of expression that is essentially alien to his artistic genius, and which evokes the tremendous musical as well as moral question of Wagner. It is not simply a question of Verdi being influenced by Wagner, but of Verdi being urged to greater moral seriousness by the Wagnerian challenge, and by implication rejecting the Wagnerian conception of love.

For the kiss motive is not properly what its usual appellation suggests. It is first of all the motive of Otello's and Desdemona's peculiar relationship. Its true function is not apparent until the end of the opera. The last two scenes gather up the various strands of

[6] C. Osborne, *The Complete Operas of Verdi*, p. 423 (London 1969).
[7] Peter J. Tschaikowski, *Erinnerungen und Musikkritiken*, pp. 189 ff. (Leipzig, 1945).

Verdi's musical structure: the dialogue between the lovers opens with the kiss motive; the heroic music comes back in the final scene with a muffled sound, converted into a funeral march for a military hero. The libretto does not reproduce Shakespeare's famous final speech at this point, but it recalls what Otello had sung in II, v:

> Ecco la fine del mio cammin. . .
> Oh! Gloria! Otello fu. . . .
>
> (Behold the end of my journey. . . .
> Oh, glory! Othello's day is done. . .)

This is dramatically as fine as Shakespeare's final speech, and its moral effect is the same. The funeral march does indeed sound for a military hero: Otello, on Desdemona's death-bed, is lamenting himself. Then the kiss motive blazes forth to reveal its full ambiguity. It is the motive of a love that is basically self-love, of a destructive love that is unable to pass beyond itself and can find consummation only in death. One does not want to labour the point, but in this scene Shakespeare, Wagner and Freud seem to have joined efforts to create an effect that Verdi must have recognized as eminently dramatic, yet the full implications of which he experienced as foreign to his moral nature. By adopting a meta-musical style of composition, he could at once do justice to his intellectual understanding of the issues at stake, and at the same time convey his moral detachment from them in an almost literary manner. If Shakespeare provided Verdi with an opportunity of understanding and conveying the implications of a love that in the last analysis consists of 'cheering oneself up', his own musical past on the one hand and the tremendous contemporary experience of Wagner on the other furnished him with the musical means of expressing his mature understanding of the issues in sound. The kiss motive is the most, and perhaps the only, unmistakably Wagnerian passage in Verdi's work. To understand that he did not come to deal with Wagner until the moment when the latter's full moral significance had become perceptible, and that the perception led to rejection at the very same moment, is to appreciate properly the stature of Verdi's mature genius.

The modernity of Verdi's *Otello* consists, then, in its growing away from the conventional contemporary interpretation of the play towards an understanding of its deepest issues that we easily recognize as our own. It is only in its treatment of Desdemona that the opera remains a period piece. In musical terms, its modernity is most clearly apparent in its use of meta-musical techniques. *Otello* is the opera in which Verdi definitively and decisively came to grips with Wagner. He had failed to do so in *Aida,* and the fact that he showed himself annoyed when the critics called *Aida* Wagnerian proves, not so much that *Aida* is not Wagnerian, but that its Wagnerianism was not yet fully conscious. In *Otello* the challenge could no longer be avoided. The Wagnerian example here serves an unmistakable function in the total musical pattern. In doing so it judges not only the quality of Otello's love for Desdemona, but also the musical style, and implicitly the moral philosophy, to which it refers. Verdi's 'Liebestod', while undoubtedly provoked by Wagner, thus presents the most profound reply to Wagner that any composer has ever been able to make.

Verdi's opera was originally planned to be called *Iago.* Iago is the third major character whom twentieth-century criticism has made to appear in a new light. The nineteenth century saw him as a satanic figure, the embodiment of sheer evil. Thus he provided a convenient contrast to Desdemona, the embodiment of pure virtue. Seen in these terms, Iago can only contribute to an oversimplified interpretation of the tragedy. Modern critics have stressed Iago as representing the forces of *will* and *intellect.* In reality, Iago is clearly defined by his role in the picture of Venetian society that Shakespeare offers. He appears basically as a cynic with a curiously logical mind. His cynicism is not really unjustified: he is the most perceptive diagnostician of his environment. Given the sort of society that he lives in, he plays an indispensable role. The greatness of his conception resides in the fact that, utterly unconscientious, he is yet the conscience of his society. If Othello represents a form of love that is unable to extend beyond itself, Iago represents a state of mind unable to appreciate what is beyond its ratiocinative capacity. The typical form in which he expresses himself is that of the rationalistic argument or syllogism, in which words are treated as if they were algebraic symbols:

> I must show out a flag, and sign of love,
> Which is indeed but sign... (I, i).
>
> I follow him to serve my turn upon him:
> We cannot all be masters, nor all masters
> Cannot be truly followed... (I, i).
>
> Men should be what they seem,
> Or those that be not, would they might seem none. (III, iii)

Iago's music in *Otello* is almost wholly confined to arioso parlando. The contrast with Otello's more conventional ariatic style emphasizes Iago's cold cunning and intelligent arguing. Yet we have stressed that Otello's ariatic style must not be taken at face value; similarly, an evaluation of Iago's music should take into account the moments in the opera when Iago assumes a more traditionally melodic style of expression, most notably in the oath-scene, where he is imitating Otello, and in the account of Cassio's dream shortly before, where he is insinuating, and where the reassuringly familiar Verdian melody is, after all, the musical correlative of his elaborate lying. Such passages show that Iago also plays a role in the metamusical pattern constituted by the whole opera. His more conventional 'satanic' nature is foregrounded in the drinking-scene, but we must pay Boito and Verdi the tribute of having understood Iago's part in the tragedy better than any such term as 'satanic' can suggest. The true test for this is, of course, his *Credo,* which Verdi is reported to have welcomed as 'most powerful and wholly Shakespearean'. Winton Dean has expressed doubts about this judgement, and Boito's poetry here is certainly not up to Shakespeare's standard. The excuses for the *Credo* are obvious: Iago had to have a showpiece aria, and dramatically the *Credo* is balanced by Desdemona's *Ave Maria,* so that the conventional contrast between Desdemona's holiness and Iago's satanism receives structural support. But it is at least uncertain whether all this suffices to explain Verdi's enthusiasm. The most important passage in the *Credo* has an immediate relevance to Iago's function as diagnostician of the social framework in which Shakespeare so firmly sets him:

> Credo che il giusto è un istrion beffardo
> E nel viso e nel cuor,
> Che tutto è in lui bugiardo.
>
> (I believe that an honest man is a mocking actor,
> Both in face and heart,
> That everything in him is a lie.)

Compare with this Iago's speech on reputation in Shakespeare's II, iii, and the relevance of the *Credo* text, apart from its shock-effects as romantic blasphemy, becomes visible (8). Statements like this one are constantly proved right by Iago's surroundings on the purely

[8] Much the same point is made by W. H. Auden in his essay 'The Joker in the Pack' in *The Dyer's Hand* (London 1963).

rationalistic level, which is the level to which his vision is limited. Iago knows how important it is to keep up the show of honesty, but he also knows that in his society honour does not pay. Thus, in Verdi no less than in Shakespeare, Iago's primary function is not to represent pure evil of a metaphysical sort, but to represent the destructive force of the intellect divorced from the moral faculty. If in Verdi this is not so apparent as in Shakespeare, and the picture remains blurred by remnants of the more conventional nineteenth-century view of Iago, we must attribute this to the loss of the first act. Characteristically, however, the libretto copies from the first act a major indication of Iago's public function in the play: his motivation by a desire for promotion is alluded to in the first scene of the opera.

There are a great many more interesting features of the libretto than we have touched upon. For instance, the reduction of Emilia to a mere servant is again related to the disappearance of the first act. In the play, Emilia is narrowly associated with Desdemona's social background, on which she offers certain important comments that reflect Iago's own, though qualified by her more humane temper. Also, in the play she provides Iago with one more motivation: his suspicion of Othello's misconduct with her. She is therefore an important factor of the social study the play offers. Of this, nothing is left in the opera.

Emilia's most important passages in the play follow closely on the willow song at the end of the fourth act. Boito's addition to the willow song, which is not, of course, intended to replace the conversation between Emilia and Desdemona, is nevertheless of great interest:

> Egli era nato per la sua gloria,
> Io per amar...
>
> (He was born for his glory,
> I for love...).

The words stress the tragic apartness of the two lovers. At the same time they remind us how 'modern' the opera's conception of Otello is, by isolating him in his self-glorification, and how limited that of Desdemona, by sentimentalizing her attitude to love.

Nijmegen W. Bronzwaer

A PLEA FOR INTERTRANSLATION: NOTES ON THE CYCLOPS CHAPTER OF *ULYSSES*

The unusual narrative structure of the Cyclops chapter must have puzzled many a common reader and fascinated or intrigued many a critic, but both categories are at least in a position to be able to talk or to write about it. Translators, however, are deprived of this kind of outlet. They cannot afford to discuss any possible interpretations of the text that may occur to them, they just have to make up their minds, for it is the interpretation they will put upon the text of the original that is going to shape their translation of it.

An analysis of the Cyclops chapter shows that it consists, basically, of first-person narrative, interrupted from time to time by interpolations, passages of varying length and written in diverse styles, which seem to come from nowhere in particular. These are interruptions on the printed page only, for after each of them the narrative is resumed as though there had not been any break at all. Part of the narrative flow but clearly different in time perspective, are the anonymous narrator's cynical comments. This narrator's identity is not going to be disclosed, he will remain nameless throughout the chapter and so will his silent listener. He seems to have a knack of picking up any bit of gossip to be heard in Dublin and he is always prepared to pass the information on to anybody who may be induced to stand him a drink, although the reader should not take what he says at face value.

Both men, narrator and listener, are sitting in some pub, maybe a few hours after the events related in the chapter took place. There are moments when the narrator addresses his listener directly ("As true as I'm drinking this porter . . ." or: ". . . true as you're there."). This is plain sailing but there are similar passages where the changing time perspective has misled some translators. In one such passage (298. 27-29)[1] the narrator takes a

1. Page and line numbers refer to James Joyce, *Ulysses*, New Random House edition, New York, 1961.

swig from a pint before him while reliving the gratifying experience of Joe Hynes offering him his first drink after opening time:

> Ah! Ow! Don't be talking! I was blue mouldy for the want of that pint. Declare to God I could hear it hit the pit of my stomach with a click.

As I see it, the speaker expresses the satisfaction he finds in the actual drink in his hands ("Ah! Ow! Don't be talking!") while impressing on his listener an identical satisfaction he derived from his first drink of the afternoon a few hours before.

In the modern German translation of *Ulysses*[2] this phenomenon of double vision, suggesting two parallel activities, one of which should be seen in retrospect, has been disregarded. The translator has transposed the entire paragraph into present tense, conveying the impression that the narrator is solely talking about the drink in his hand, the drink he has just been offered by the listener:

> Ah! Oh! Nicht lange gefackelt! Ich bin schon richtig verdorrt und ausgetrocknet, so nötig hab ich die Pinte. Also ernstlich, ich erklärs bei Gott, wie das Zeug mir in den Magen runtergeht, da hör ichs direkt zischen.

This translation – which is, in fact, an interpretation – does not make sense, if only because the narrator at this late hour could hardly have had to swallow his drink on an empty stomach.

The close-knit way translation and interpretation are interrelated may be demonstrated more fully by referring to the story of Bob Doran, who plays a minor role in this chapter. In Joyce's *Dubliners* he figures as the protagonist of the story "The Boarding House", a young man whose instinct urges him to remain free but who is trapped into marriage, having been seduced by his landlady's daughter, Polly Mooney. Giving in to the pressure brought to bear upon him by his environment, he conforms to the basic pattern underlying most stories in *Dubliners*. His shotgun marriage must have been common knowledge in Dublin. The narrator seems to know all about him anyway, introducing him as "sitting up there in the corner . . . snoring drunk, blind to the world . . ." (298.37-38). This, however, is not the first time Bob Doran is referred to in the novel. Sometime between 10 and 11

2. James Joyce, *Ulysses*, trans. Hans Wollschläger, Frankfurt a.M., 1975, 2 vols, consecutively numbered.

a.m. that day, Bloom learns from M'Coy, by whom he is buttonholed in the street, that Doran is on his yearly drinking spree (74.1-3):

> – I was with Bob Doran, he's on one of his periodical bends, and what do you call him Bantam Lyons. Just down there in Conway's we were.

Bloom's mind is elsewhere at the moment but somehow the words must have registered, for later in the day he remembers what M'Coy told him. The scene is Grafton Street. Thinking of sunspots and eclipses, Bloom now remembers Mrs Breen, whom he had met in Westmoreland Street, saying that there must be a new moon out, because then her husband's condition always gets worse. Bloom checks this by reckoning back to the night of the full moon a fortnight before, evidently a significant landmark in his emotional life, the night Molly must have started her affair with Boylan. Greatly perturbed by these memories he tries to calm down by concentrating on his immediate surroundings and that is when he spots Bob Doran (167.19 ff.):

> Wait. The full moon was the night we were Sunday fortnight exactly there is a new moon. Walking down by the Tolka. Not bad for a Fairview moon. She was humming: The young May moon she's beaming, love. He other side of her. Elbow, arm. He. Glowworm's la-amp is gleaming, love. Touch. Fingers. Asking. Answer. Yes.
>
> Stop. Stop. If it was it was. Must.
>
> Mr Bloom, quick breathing, slowlier walking, passed Adam Court.
>
> With a keep quiet relief, his eyes took note: this is street here middle of the day Bob Doran's bottle shoulders. On his annual bend, M'Coy said. They drink in order to say or do something or *cherchez la femme.* Up in the Coombe with chummies and streetwalkers and then the rest of the year as sober as a judge.
>
> Yes. Thought so. Sloping into the Empire. Gone. Plain soda would do him good.

When Bob Doran is seen next, the time is somewhere between 3 and 4 p.m. and the place Grafton Street in front of *Maison Claire* the dressmaker's. As this is in the immediate vicinity of the Empire Buffet (Adam Court, off Grafton Street), Doran must have spent quite a few hours there. The scene is one of the interpolations that occur in many sections of the Wandering Rocks chapter, brief interruptions of the narrative proper where the reader finds himself stumbling over some fragment dislodged from some other section; they differ significantly from the interpolations in the Cyclops chapter in that there is no break in the chapter's narrative style. So in section fifteen, the scene of which is Parliament Street, not quite half a mile to the north-west of the Empire Buffet, we come upon the following lines (246.33-35):

> Outside *la Maison Claire* Blazes Boylan waylaid Jack Mooney's brother-in-law, humpy, tight, making for the liberties.

Apparently, readers are supposed to know that Jack Mooney's brother-in-law, the man who has married Jack's sister, is none else but Bob Doran. If they do not they will have to wait till the Cyclops chapter, in which more information about the Mooney family will be forthcoming. Meanwhile, one might ask whether any motive could be adduced for this fragment to be inserted just here. I think there could. A few lines higher up in this section Nolan, Cunningham, and Power have been discussing Bloom's generous contribution to the fund that is being raised in aid of Dignam's widow, Nolan winding up by quoting, "I'll say there is much kindness in the jew" (246.27). Thereupon the interpolation draws attention once more to *la Maison Claire*, focussing on the spot where Bloom, kind Jew, was passing by a few hours earlier (167.18), where he was troubled by thoughts of Boylan, and where he happened to see Bob Doran. All these elements are bundled together in this one interpolation.

Now the scene itself, Boylan meeting Doran, which figures as an intrusion in section fifteen, has still to fall into its proper slot as an organic passage in its own right. This happens in section eighteen, but there the scene is observed through the eyes of a boy, Pat Dignam, and so the wording is quite different. Young Dignam has been sent to the butcher's to buy porksteaks and is dawdling along Grafton Street. Nearing the corner of Nassau Street he sees two men engaged in a rather one-sided conversation, without, apparently, realizing who they are. The reader, however, will easily recognize Boylan by the carnation he has picked up in Thornton's and by his nice shoes (*cf.* "Blazes Boylan's smart tan shoes creaked on the barfloor . . ." – 264.36), which become "a swell pair of kicks" in Pat's school boy's slang (251.15-17):

> In Grafton Street Master Dignam saw a red flower in a toff's mouth and a swell pair of kicks on him and he listening to what the drunk was telling him and grinning all the time.

So now we have come back full circle to the Cyclops chapter and, as we have seen from a brief glimpse above, here we find Bob Doran in Barney Kiernan's pub in Little Britain Street – quite a distance for him to have walked there all the way from Grafton Street where he was seen last, especially in the state he must have been in. The narrator spots him the moment Alf Bergan comes in (298.35-38):

> Little Alf Bergan popped in round the door and hid behind Barney's snug, squeezed up with the laughing, and who was sitting up there in the corner that I hadn't seen snoring drunk, blind to the world, only Bob Doran.

What with Alf's laughing (at Breen, a notorious idiot, who is passing outside) and the Citizen's dog's growling, Bob wakes up. He recognizes Alf's voice and, bad-tempered, keeps asking what it is all about, without getting any response. Meanwhile the Citizen has spied Bloom walking up and down in front of the pub. In answer to the narrator's inquiry after one Willy Murray, Alf Bergan mentions to those present that he "saw him just now in Capel street with Paddy Dignam" (300.28). Understandably, this statement causes some consternation, as all are aware that Paddy Dignam was buried that very morning. Told about this, Bergan keeps muttering, "Good Christ!" over and over, as he was really under the impression of having seen Dignam alive and well not five minutes before. As the narrator comments, "he was what you might call flabbergasted" (301.12). This is followed by an interpolation of some length, parodying the account of a spiritualist séance (in keeping with Joe Hynes's remark to Bergan that he must have seen Dignam's ghost), in the course of which Dignam's spirit is called up from beyond the grave. The action goes on, the Citizen pointing out that Bloom is still to be seen outside. Alf Bergan is still stunned as he could have sworn it was Dignam he saw. Bob Doran, disgruntled as before, chimes in with a piece of blasphemy. This scene runs as follows (302.18 ff.):

> – There he is again, says the citizen, staring out.

– Who? says I.

– Bloom, says he. He's on point duty up and down there for the last ten minutes.

And, begob, I saw his physog do a peep in and then slidder off again.

Little Alf was knocked bawways. Faith, he was.

– Good Christ! says he. I could have sworn it was him.

And says Bob Doran, with the hat on the back of his poll, lowest blackguard in Dublin when he's under the influence:

– Who said Christ is good?

Having been warned off by the barman, Bob Doran stops blaming Christ and starts weeping instead, drunkenly lamenting Dignam's death. His behaviour gives rise to a sneering commentary by the narrator (303.1-7):

> The tear is bloody near your eye. Talking through his bloody hat. Fitter for him to go home to the little sleepwalking bitch he married, Mooney, the bumbailiff's daughter. Mother kept a kip in Hardwicke street that used to be stravaging about the landings Bantam Lyons told me that was stopping there at two in the morning without a stitch on her, exposing her person, open to all comers, fair field and no favour.

In various respects this passage has proved a stumbling-block to translators. As said before, translation depends largely on interpretation, and interpretation in its turn will often have to rely on background information. In this instance such information is available in the *Dubliners* story mentioned above. As Halper[3] says, we should be careful about applying what was written at another time and in another book, but *Ulysses* after all is a book about Dubliners too, and whereas readers may or may not care to profit from the inside information contained in Joyce's earlier stories, translators, I believe, cannot afford to miss any relevant detail these stories may add to our store of knowledge about characters and situations in *Ulysses.* Halper is right, I think, when he concludes that what we are told in *Ulysses* about Bob Doran's case history, has been implied already in the story, "The Boarding House". Looking back we understand that the frustration the

3. Nathan Halper, "The Boarding House", in Clive Hart, ed., *James Joyce's Dubliners: Critical Essays*, London, 1967, pp. 72-83.

STER ZUSTER SCHWES
N JACK MOONEY'S SOE
'HE OLD PROSTITUTE
QUERELLE DE MÈRE
RE VON MUTTER VER
OMS TO STRASSENPÄR
MAARLUI VAN DE STE
AMBRE À L'HEURE E
CHTE JACK MADE HI
RES MARCHER DROIT
E LINE TOLD HIM W
RÉPARAIT PAS PAT
E POT endlich DIE F
EHT JEZUS JEZUS J
N ZOU HIJ HEM STRO
CK THE SHIT OUT SCH
S ARSCH VRETEN LA
I DÉFONCER LE TABI

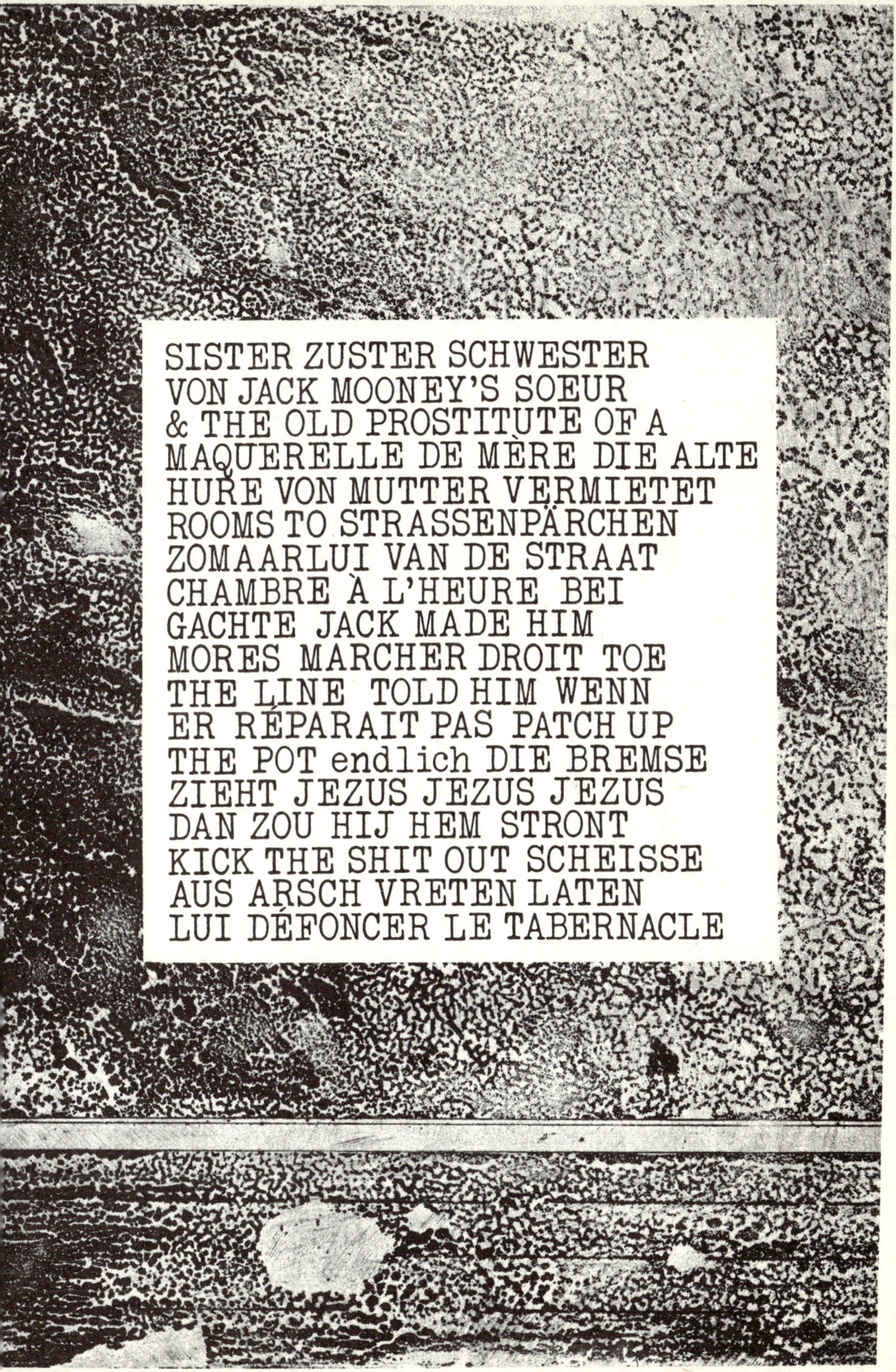

SISTER ZUSTER SCHWESTER
VON JACK MOONEY'S SOEUR
& THE OLD PROSTITUTE OF A
MAQUERELLE DE MÈRE DIE ALTE
HURE VON MUTTER VERMIETET
ROOMS TO STRASSENPÄRCHEN
ZOMAARLUI VAN DE STRAAT
CHAMBRE À L'HEURE BEI
GACHTE JACK MADE HIM
MORES MARCHER DROIT TOE
THE LINE TOLD HIM WENN
ER RÉPARAIT PAS PATCH UP
THE POT endlich DIE BREMSE
ZIEHT JEZUS JEZUS JEZUS
DAN ZOU HIJ HEM STRONT
KICK THE SHIT OUT SCHEISSE
AUS ARSCH VRETEN LATEN
LUI DÉFONCER LE TABERNACLE

young man in the story falls a victim to, may over the years have turned him into what he is now, a chronic alcoholic. As to some details revealed by the narrator, we should do well to realize that exaggeration comes natural to him. According to Halper, in *Ulysses* we have an account of Polly naked on the landings. That is true, but this account is based on hearsay and may have been embellished by the narrator. Maybe it is not so much exaggeration, strictly speaking, not hyperbole as a figure of speech, but rather a bitter and sneering way of speaking the narrator affects, as when he refers to Bloom's wife as "The fat heap he married" (305. 38).

Now let us take three translations of *Ulysses* and see how the translators have coped with the text in this case.

> Autant dire qu'il pisse de l'oeil. Il dévide il dévide son sacré rouleau. Il ferait mieux d'aller retrouver la petite fleur de macadam qu'il s'est embellemerdé avec, la Mooney, la fille à l'huissier. La mère tenait un garno dans Hardwicke Street et qu'elle se baladait sur le palier, c'est Bantam Lyons qui y a été un temps qui me l'a dit, à des deux heures du matin avec pas un fil sur elle et montrant son anatomie à qui voulait, entrée libre et pas de tour de faveur.[4]

> De tranen staan hem verrekt na. Al die verrekte onzin die hij uitkraamt. Kon maar beter naar huis gaan naar die slaapwandelende temeie met wie hij getrouwd is, de dochter van Mooney, de deurwaarder. Haar moeder hield er een hoerenkast op na in Hardwicke Street en altijd kon je haar op de overlopen zien zwalken heeft Bantam Lyons me verteld die daar een keer om twee uur 's nachts geweest is en geen barst aan, haar hele persoon tentoongespreid, voor wie maar wilde, vrij entree en geen voorkeur.[5]

> Und da fängt man verdammt bald selber das Heulen an. So ein verdammter Quatschkopf. Sollte lieber machen, dass er nach Hause kommt, zu der kleinen mondsüchtigen Nutte, die er

4. James Joyce, *Ulysse*, trans. Auguste Morel, Paris 1929, p. 296.
5. James Joyce, *Ulysses*, trans. John Vandenbergh, Amsterdam, 1969, p. 351.

> geheiratet hat, Mooney, die Büttelstochter. Die Mutter hatte nen Puff in der Hardwicke Street, lungerte dauernd auf den Treppenabsätzen rum, hat mir Bantam Lyons erzählt, früh um zwo stand sie da, ohne ein Fitzchen an, und liess sich begaffen, egal wer kam, immer hereinspaziert, gleiche Chancen für alle.[6]

Note that I am not concerned here with the literary qualities of the translations as such. To evaluate them, no mean task certainly, would require a study in itself. The point I am trying to make here is that no translator may hope to achieve an adequate translation of *Ulysses* without taking full advantage of all the information he can get from Joyce's earlier works. *Dubliners* above all is important, among other things because, as Burgess remarks, "it provides *Ulysses* with a ready-made cast of extras".[7]

Turning again to the passage in which the narrator shows his contempt of one of these extras, the protagonist of the story, "The Boarding House", now in his decline, we find that the very first sentence entails a problem of interpretation. As to tone, the translations do differ substantially but Morel's and Vandenbergh's are similar in that they substitute third-person pronouns for the second-person pronoun of the original. This implies that they attribute the state of near-crying to Bob Doran, which is very unlikely as the latter is actually crying already. I think, therefore, that Wollschläger is right in taking the sentence to be an aside addressed to the listener, inviting his sympathy, leading up to the comment proper the narrator has in mind, and conveying something like: "Would you believe it? Listening to that snivelling drunk, a person would almost start crying himself, but let me tell you a few things about this sensitive Mr Doran and his precious home life you may be surprised to hear." The next sentence does not offer any difficulty but interpreting the rest of the paragraph in a way that makes sense, requires the reader to possess information only to be obtained from the *Dubliners* story, which tells us in a few economical lines all about Mr Mooney's unlucky career. He has come down in life from running his own butcher's shop to being a sheriff's man, a so-called bumbailiff, who has to sit all day long "in the bailiff's room, waiting to be put on a job". In *Ulysses*

6. Trans. Wollschläger (see note 2), p. 419.
7. In Morris Beja, ed., *James Joyce, Dubliners and A Portrait of the Artist as a Young Man, a Casebook*, London, 1973, p. 239.

we have already heard Bob Doran referred to as "Jack Mooney's brother-in-law", so he must have married a girl whose maiden name was Mooney. Therefore, "Mooney, the bumbailiff's daughter" should be understood as meaning "the daughter of Mooney, the bumbailiff", although we might have preferred a different punctuation so as to avoid ambiguity. Anyway, a look at the translations shows that Vandenbergh has the only non-ambiguous reading. Both Morel (speaking of "la Mooney", as Greta Garbo might be called "la Garbo" in French) and Wollschläger seem to believe that the narrator calls the young woman by her family name. This is rather improbable, I think, but hard to disprove. The following sentence contains some puzzling details. On the surface, it seems to state that Mrs Mooney, who kept a boarding house in Hardwicke Street (where Bob Doran was one of the lodgers), used to walk around the house at night "without a stitch on her", and the translations, all three of them, apparently conform to this view. I am inclined to doubt this, however, for several reasons. For one thing, I find it hard to believe that such a person could be identical with the woman of whom we are told in *Dubliners*: "She governed her house cunningly and firmly, knew when to give credit, when to be stern and when to let things pass. All the resident young men spoke of her as *The Madam.*" Furthermore, why would the narrator call Bob Doran's wife a little *sleepwalking* bitch (a detail left out by Morel), unless it was she, not her mother, who used to roam about in the small hours in her nightdress? I think we may safely discredit Lyons' account of Polly parading in the nude as a typical exaggeration of the version he may have heard from Bob Doran himself, the story as we find it in *Dubliners*, Polly tapping at Bob's door late one night, fragrant from having had her bath and wearing "a loose open combing-jacket of printed flannel", wanting to relight her candle that had been blown out, as she said. Finally, the reader should constantly bear in mind the essentially oral nature of the account, the narrator improvising as he goes along, filling the listener in on details the speaker expects him to be interested in. As I see it, the statement about the mother is just an aside and so is the information that the narrator's informant, Bantam Lyons, was stopping there once, which means, of course, that Lyons was a lodger in the same house as Bob Doran at one time, a detail confirmed by the story in *Dubliners*. Wollschläger leaves out the "was stopping" part altogether, Morel has got it right on this point (apart from skipping the "sleepwalking" bit, as said before: could he – his phrase, "petite fleur de macadam" does suggest it – have been thinking of "streetwalking"?), but Vandenbergh is clearly wrong in presenting the scene as if Lyons was just passing by there once at 2 a.m. ("die daar een keer om twee uur 's nachts geweest is"), a highly improbable event, to say the least. Thus the way I interpret the passage from the third sentence on, it might be rewritten as follows:

> Fitter for him to go home to the little sleepwalking bitch he married (the daughter of Mooney, the bumbailiff, you know) . . . (*aside*: Her mother kept a boarding house in Hardwicke Street) . . (that little bitch, you know) that used to be stravaging about the landings . . (*aside*: I have this from Bantam Lyons, who was lodging there in those days) . . at two in the morning . . etc.

What it boils down to is that we have to think of some of the narrator's remarks as a kind of asides-within-asides.

Returning to the pub scene we find that meanwhile Bloom's entrance has created a diversion. Bob Doran, having understood that Bloom is waiting for Martin Cunningham to accompany him to the deceased's house in order to attend to the widow's insurance problems, starts shaking Bloom's hand, and begs of him to be sure and tell Mrs Dignam how very sorry he is and all that, after which he leaves, "trying to walk straight", as the narrator comments. Reminiscing about Doran's not too sure-footed exit ("boosed at five o'clock") he treats his listener to another of his spiteful, derogatory comments on Doran, his wife, and his in-laws (314.9-28). Again, translators have encountered difficulties inherent in the narrator's allusions to what must have happened to Bob Doran prior to his marriage. It will suffice to quote only the latter half of the passage, the lines 314.22-28, followed by translations of the last few sentences.

> Then see him of a Sunday with his little concubine of a wife, and she wagging her tail up the aisle of the chapel, with her patent boots on her, no less, and her violets, nice as pie, doing the little lady. Jack Mooney's sister. And the old prostitute of a mother procuring rooms to street couples. Gob, Jack made

> him toe the line. Told him if he didn't patch up the pot, Jesus, he'd kick the shite out of him.

> La soeur de Jack Mooney. Et la vieille maquerelle de mère qui loue des chambres à l'heure. Gachte, Jack l'a obligé à marcher droit. Lui a dit que si il réparait pas, bondieu, il lui défoncerait le tabernacle. (p.308)

> De zuster van Jack Mooney. En die oude prostituée van een moeder die kamers verhuurt aan zo maar lui van de straat. Gossie, Jack heeft hem wel mores geleerd. Zei hem dat als hij zijn leven niet beterde hij hem zijn eigen stront zou laten vreten. (p. 365)

> Jack Mooneys Schwester. Und die alte Hure von Mutter vermietet Zimmer an Strassenpärchen. Bei Gott, Jack hat ihn sich aber vorgeknöpft. Hat ihm gesagt, wenn er nicht endlich die Bremse zieht, Jesus, dann tritt er ihm die Scheisse ausm Arsch. (p.436)

We know already that the narrator does not have any very high opinion of Mrs Mooney but, once more, we should not accept without qualifications what he says about her being a prostitute herself. As to the statement about her procuring rooms to street couples, Halper remarks, "Since the speaker is scurrilous, this may or may not be true, but at any rate, it is not mentioned in 'The Boarding House' ". He is right in so far as such things are not mentioned explicitly in the story. Still, the narrator's comment sheds some light on what is at least hinted at in *Dubliners*, when Bob Doran sits pondering helplessly on the way fate has forced his hand, making marriage with Polly Mooney seem unavoidable:

> He had money enough to settle down on; it was not that. But the family would look down on her. First of all there was her disreputable father and then her mother's boarding house was beginning to get a certain fame. He had a notion that he was being had.

Now what has been Jack Mooney's role in Bob Doran's life? The narrator is quite outspoken on this point. According to him, Jack made Bob do as he was told, made him marry Polly, threatening to give him a terrific beating if he did not "patch up the pot", that is, if he refused to marry the girl he had made pregnant. In the *Dubliners* story, as might be expected, this is all much more vague and subtle. When Bob is going down the stairs to the impending interviews with Mrs Mooney he meets Jack coming up from the pantry with a few bottles of beer. He has a fleeting impression of "a thick bulldog face and a pair of thick short arms". Having reached the foot of the staircase he glances up and sees Jack looking down on him. In that instant this threatening figure at the head of the stairs reminds him of something that had happened some time ago and that must have scared him even then:

> Suddenly he remembered the night when one of the music-hall *artistes*, a little blond Londoner, had made a rather free allusion to Polly. The reunion had been almost broken up on account of Jack's violence. Everyone tried to quiet him. The music-hall *artiste*, a little paler than usual, kept smiling and saying that there was no harm meant: but Jack kept shouting at him that if any fellow tried that sort of a game on with *his* sister he'd bloody well put his teeth down his throat, so he would.

Of the interview with Mrs Mooney itself we are not told anything, but we may assume that the memory of the scene quoted above must have clinched the matter for Bob.

To wind up Bob Doran's story let us have a brief look at what the translators have made of the narrator's remarks about Jack Mooney. Curiously enough, two of them, Vandenbergh and Wollschläger, apparently fail to see the connection between Jack's threats and Bob's marriage. Morel, on the other hand, uses the same term we find in *Dubliners*, "reparation". Mrs Mooney, turning over the matter in her mind before the interview with Doran she has planned, asks herself, "What reparation would he make?" – for she knows quite well: "There must be reparation made in such cases." In my opinion this proves that Morel is on the right track. Vandenbergh and Wollschläger both seem to suppose that Jack told Bob simply to mend his ways in general, maybe urged him to stop drinking. Vandenbergh is even quite explicit: "Jack heeft hem wel mores geleerd" (Jack punished him for behaving badly) and: "dat als hij zijn leven niet beterde" (that if he did not mend his ways). Wollschläger uses metaphor: "wenn er nicht endlich die Bremse zieht" (if he does not put on the brake at last), but by smuggling in an extra adverb ("endlich") and above all by using present tense throughout, Wollschläger makes it abundantly clear that in his view Jack's threats refer to Bob's present condition. Now the narraror, fully aware of the hopelessness of that condition as we know he is (from previous comments), would not dream of presenting a state of affairs in which there might be a ray of hope left, however feeble, for Bob Doran. Moreover, the past tense he uses, shows that the whole thing is over and done with: Jack *made* Bob toe the line, Bob obeyed orders, he "patched up the pot", he married Polly. Whatever might befall Bob and Polly after that, ought not to be any concern of Jack's. If Bob is now slowly going downhill, that is just his bad luck, his and Polly's. Mrs Mooney must have reasoned along the same lines. Her aim in life has been to get her daughter off her hands and this she has achieved. She may look at her own face in the mirror with satisfaction, indeed, that Sunday morning just before she is going to have her talk with Mr Doran: "The decisive expression of her great florid face satisfied her and she thought of some mothers she knew who could not get their daughters off their hands." It may not be a face apt to launch a thousand ships, it certainly is a face that will leave Bob Doran in no doubt as to what is expected of him.

Thus Bob Doran's trivial story while illustrating the links between translation and interpretation, may at the same time have shed some light on the importance of acknowledging the workings of what might be called factual intertextuality, especially where *Dubliners* and *Ulysses* are concerned.

Groningen Paul P.J. van Caspel

"THE FAMOUS CLERK ERASMUS"

Many Dutch influences in sixteenth-century England were the result of the collective activities of immigrants or visiting tradesmen and artisans who have remained anonymous, but to some influences we can attach the names of individuals, as, for example in the case of several generations of Dutch painters and engravers in Tudor England. Occasionally, even the humbler arts can be associated with individual people.[1] But on the whole the names that continued to be remembered throughout the century were "great names": scholars and statesmen whose words and works remained famous even after their author's death. One is often inclined to assume that if their names continued to be mentioned, their influence, too, must have continued. But does Fame equal Influence?

Erasmus' reputation in Elizabethan England (and in the Low Countries) is a subject that needs to be studied precisely in these terms — fame or influence? — as the following example will show. In December 1585 John Stow saw a statue of "the famus clearke Erasmus in a pulpet" on the Rotterdam market place, a statue which probably represented the Dutchman in a scholar's gown, holding an open book in his right hand and addressing an audience, while pointing to an inscription that gave the dates and places of his birth and death.[2] One of a long series of Rotterdam-produced

1. For instance "Mistress Dinghen van den Plasse" who in 1564 first introduced the art of starching ladies' ruffs — who can think of the Elizabethan Age without actually seeing them? But once she had taught the London housewives how to do it, her name would have vanished from people's memory if John Stow had not recorded it in his *Annals* (1615).

2. See the drawing (above, p. 295) by van Buchell, also reproduced in N. van der Blom, *Erasmus en Rotterdam*, Rotterdam/The Hague, 1969, where the involved history of the statues of Erasmus is discussed — including the famous case of the Erasmus figurehead of the ship *De Liefde*, wrecked on the Japanese coast in 1598, which until 1926 adorned

images of Erasmus, this particular statue may have been commissioned for a great Anglo-Dutch occasion: the official entry into Rotterdam (en route to The Hague) of Robert Dudley, Earl of Leicester, shortly before he became Governor-General of the Northern Provinces.[3] One thing is certain: the Earl and his distinguished attendants were escorted to "the middle of the market place" where Erasmus stood, "very memorably". When in 1964 Roy Strong and I commented upon this scene, we perhaps made a characteristic mistake when we wrote: "Whether Leicester grasped the message of liberal reform and religious tolerance which the statue embodied, it is difficult to say."[4] Evidently, we assumed that Erasmus was a living influence in 1585. Yet it is perfectly plausible that the only reason why a rather insignificant town such as Rotterdam persistently erected Erasmus statues was that Erasmus was indeed famous (as John Stow, too, observed) and that his name and memory were used on every occasion simply because this was the town's only claim to fame.

Our mistake, if it was one, seems typical. The name of Erasmus produced instant associations which we then tried to apply to the time and circumstances with which we were concerned. I am not sure now whether Leicester could have "grasped the message". The meaning of the name Erasmus has changed, especially since the introduction of the adjective "Erasmian" and its decapitalized variant "erasmian"; and it seems safe to say that nowadays both the name and its derivatives have acquired benevolent overtones which they did not have before. According to the *O.E.D.* neither the noun nor the adjective "Erasmian" appear to have existed in English before the late-nineteenth century. Their meaning was strictly factual: "pertaining to ... Erasmus", "a follower of Erasmus", "one who follows the system of Greek pronunciation advocated by Erasmus". More recently, however, specialist and non-specialist speakers and writers have adopted the word as a learned synonym for "tolerant", and many historians of the

a Japanese temple as the image of "A Dutch Barbarian". (It is a pity that the author of the best-selling novel *Shōgun*, which treats the adventures of one of the crew of *De Liefde*, appears to have been ignorant of this significant detail.)

3. See R.C. Strong and J.A. van Dorsten, *Leicester's Triumph*, Leiden/London, 1964.

4. *Ibid.*, p. 39.

sixteenth century have joined the trend. Thus, to take three random examples, Charles Wilson in 1970 observed that William the Silent "wanted no monopoly for Calvinism, no theocracy,... he was an Erasmian, in some sense a *politique*";[5] in 1975 Frances Yates remarked that Catherine de Medici's "policy had always been Erasmian and tolerant";[6] and even Elizabeth Eisenstein, who in *The Printing Press as an Agent of Change* (1979) consistently used "Erasmian" to define a particular form of philological scholarship, on one occasion wrote: "... an international peace movement was being quietly shaped. 'Erasmian' trends were persistently propelled throughout the entire century-and-a-half of religious warfare."[7] Mrs Eisenstein's quotation marks seem to emphasize my point.

This essay does not intend to trace the curious history of an adjective, nor does it propose to analyze how scholars like Huizinga and Bataillon, and an increased interest (because of two world wars and what came after) in the roots of pacifism, may have caused it to change its meaning. The point is simply that more and more people use it, as Strong and I used it, to mean "liberal, tolerant, and pacifist" (in the modern sense of these words). Unlike the original Latin form "Erasmianus" which Reformers and Jesuits alike adopted in their controversial writings — sometimes claiming Erasmus as one of them, and sometimes, if the occasion demanded, rejecting him because he was not — "Erasmian" has become a term of approval, applicable to persons and things which are agreeably uncontroversial.

Three conclusions may be drawn. Our age appears to have created an image of Erasmus which is probably closer to the ideals of twentieth-century liberal humanism than to the Prince of Humanists himself; and it has naturally been inclined to project that image upon its interpretation of earlier events. As a result, modern scholarship has cultivated a poorly defined term, "Erasmian", to denote certain elusive (but attractive and probably very important) trends in the second half of the sixteenth century in which we see, or wish to see, conciliatory movements in matters of

5. *Queen Elizabeth and the Revolt of the Netherlands*, London, 1970, p. 51.
6. *Astraea*, London, 1975, p. 133.
7. Cambridge U.P., 1979, p. 449.

church and state. Lastly, Erasmus' continuing fame has encouraged twentieth-century scholars to believe that his influence, whatever it was, must have been significant in his own century — including the later decades of the sixteenth century, therefore, which were crucial years of religious and political settlement both in England and in the United Provinces. But how significant was it? How can we be sure that the learned clerk continued to exercise an influence? Indeed, was he read at all?

In order to be influential, an author needs to be read. In the post-Gutenberg era this means an adequate supply of printed copies of his works. Erasmus himself was much aware of the importance of the new medium and used it to great advantage. His fame as a scholar was acquired in the modern way: instant publication of his writings, wide circulation as printed books. The demand for copies of his works, which is reflected in the production of new editions, can therefore indicate how widely he was read in later years. Oddly enough, many studies of Erasmus have ignored such simple data. But how can we discuss a scholar's continuing influence without considering the popularity and availability of his books?

Let us first consider his native country, at a time when "Erasmian" books might seem (to us at least) to have had a very special relevance: the period of the Dutch Revolt (1568 ff.). How "available" were these books? In his inaugural lecture *Erasmus, the Anabaptists and the Problem of Religious Unity* the Amsterdam church-historian Irvin B. Horst emphasized the importance of the *Liber de Sarcienda Ecclesiae Concordia* as a very personal document "which Erasmus came to write towards the close of his life as a final plea for religious unity and much else dear to him". In the Netherlands, Horst added, "it went into more editions during the sixteenth and the seventeenth century than in any other land".[8] This is true enough; but Horst overstates his case because in the Netherlands the *Liber* was printed only six times which is rather less than many other works by Erasmus. Moreover, the last edition to appear in the Southern Netherlands came out in 1567. Even more revealing, no edition appeared in the Northern Netherlands before 1611. In other words, there is no evidence that there was any great demand for this *Liber* in the Dutch Republic until after

8. I.B. Horst, *Erasmus, the Anabaptists and the Problem of Religious Unity*, Amsterdam, 1967, p. 7.

the Twelve Years' Truce had been concluded (1609).

The printing history of Erasmus' "final plea for religious unity", both in its distribution and the curious gap of forty-odd years, is fairly typical. In the middle of the sixteenth century the popularity of his works in the Southern Netherlands is evident from numerous editions, even after he had been given a prominent place on the *Index* of Pope Paul IV in 1559. But as soon as hostilities broke out in Flanders in the late 1560s, most of his works ceased to be printed. Perhaps this is not surprising; but it is curious to see that the North did not take over even some of his most popular works. The famous *Adagia*, for example, did not appear there until 1649 (exactly one year after the end of the Eighty Years' War) and ceased to be published in the South after 1566[9] — nor were they ever translated into Dutch.[10] Similarly, the very popular *Colloquia*, to which the various *Indices* objected so strongly and which disappeared from the Southern presses in 1567 (except for one Antwerp edition in 1604), were pretty well ignored by the translators and only began to be printed in the North as late as 1610. Such is the pattern; and the only book to really break it is the best-selling *Praise of Folly*, the *Moriae Encomium* which continued to be printed and translated in both parts of the Netherlands throughout the period.

Naturally, there are some exceptions and borderline cases. An obvious one is the translation and publication (Amsterdam, 1594) of the *Paraphrases* by Ellert de Veer, once the eloquent supporter of the Earl of Leicester to whom he owed his appointment in 1586 as notary public in Amsterdam. (His son Albert rose to even greater prominence and was knighted in 1610 by King James.) All such exceptions would require individual comment and explanation, for which there is no place in an essay like this. The story of Erasmus' popularity in the late sixteenth-century Netherlands is a complex one. Coornhert, for instance, whose 1561 translation of Cicero's *De Officiis* had included passages from two Erasmus letters, towards the end of his life (d. 1590) also attempted a translation of the *Paraphrases*, which is no longer extant; yet he

9. For these and other details, see F. Van der Haeghen, *Bibliotheca Erasmiana*, Ghent, 1897-1907.

10. On the translations into Dutch, see S.W. Bijl, *Erasmus in het Nederlands tot 1617*, Leiden, 1978.

was not, according to his recent biographer, "an erasmian".[11] The Protestant scholar-poet Charles Utenhove of Ghent, to take another example, grew up in a highly Erasmian milieu. In his student days he was even sent to mid-century Basel where in former years his grandfather and his father (the "Carolus" of Erasmus' Colloquium on "Talorum lusus", the game of dice) used to converse with the author of the *Colloquia*; but I do not remember having come across Erasmus' name in the published writings of Carolus Utenhovius the Younger.[12] There are numerous other instances where, for varying reasons, the name of Erasmus crops up in the biographies of sixteenth-century Dutch scholars. In a proper survey (which does not exist) each case would have to be considered and evaluated in the light of this very basic question: how widely read and how influential was the famous humanist in these years? But for the purpose of this discussion it is enough to note the remarkable fact that, by and large, the Dutch presses showed a reduced interest in Erasmus' writings between the early years of the Revolt and the first few decades of the seventeenth century.

Perhaps, then, his influence remained strong in England? Erasmus himself was deeply attached to England and to his friends there, and his biographers agree that he was much indebted to the country in which he spent almost six years of his life. His first visit took place in 1499 (when he wrote the often quoted letter about the agreeable kissing habits of English girls); the last visit was in 1517 when he was officially released at last from his monastic obligations. During his longest stay (1509-1514, except for a few months' absence in 1511) he wrote the *Moriae Encomium*, in Thomas More's house, revised the *Adagia*, and worked hard on two other major publications, Jerome and the Greek New Testament. Erasmus liked England, even though he disapproved of the weather in Cambridge. And England responded enthusiastically to his writings. His books became immensely popular. More translations of them appeared in England than in any other country, the Netherlands included: Devereux has listed eighty-eight different English

11. H. Bonger, *Leven en Werk van D.V. Coornhert*, Amsterdam, 1978, p. 261.

12. Cf. my *Radical Arts*, 2nd ed. Leiden/London, 1973, App. ii.

translations, many of which were reprinted frequently.[13] Thanks to the happy interaction between the Dutchman and the English humanists, his name became for ever associated with the England of More and Colet. In fact, Erasmus grew more English than he ever was "Roterodamus".

Yet in the course of the sixteenth century his popularity waned, as it did in the Netherlands and elsewhere.[14] During the reign of Queen Elizabeth "his name continued to be prominent, even authoritative, in exegesis",[15] but fewer and fewer editions of his books came out. Except for two 1576 re-issues of William Tyndale's translation (c. 1522) of the *Enchiridion Militis Christiani* and two editions (c. 1560, 1577) of Sir Thomas Chaloner's rendering of the *Moriae Encomium*, first published in 1549, English translations of his works which used to be so popular almost disappeared in the Elizabethan period. At the 1969 Erasmus Conference at Rotterdam these facts were noted. It was suggested that foreign (Latin) editions had begun to dominate the market;[16] but the evidence is far from conclusive, and there is no reason why English printers should not have continued to produce Erasmus editions if the demand had been there.

The demand, clearly, was there no longer. In some fields his reputation remained high, most notably in education where many of his ideas had become standard thanks to the efforts of Sir Thomas Elyot and Roger Ascham, Queen Elizabeth's tutor, both of whom had continued to emulate the example of the More-Erasmus circle. Similarly, his name continued to occur in Anglican defences, for Foxe's *Acts and Monuments* and Jewel's *Apology* remained popular. But Erasmus himself does not appear to have been read extensively by the Elizabethans. The *Paraphrases*, which are often mentioned as an example of his lasting influence in Elizabethan England,[17] are an interesting case in point. In 1547 royal injunctions had ordered the clergy to have one copy of the

13. E.J. Devereux, *A Checklist of English Translations of Erasmus to 1700*, Oxford Bibl. Soc. Occasional Publication no. 3, Oxford; 1968.

14. Cf. Bijl, *Erasmus*, ch. xxix.

15. Craig R. Thompson, "Erasmus and Tudor England", *Actes du Congres Erasme Rotterdam 1969*, Amsterdam, 1971, p. 57. This important article is the best survey available.

16. *Ibid.*

17. For instance, see n. 4.

Bible plus one copy of the *Paraphrases* in English "set up in some convenient place within the ... church that they have cure of, whereas their parishioners may most commodiously resort unto the same, and read the same."[18] Although the clergy may not have unanimously observed these costly injunctions, quite a number of copies must have been around. The volumes, therefore, will have been familiar enough — but how many parishioners actually resorted unto the same to read them? Quite soon afterwards, during the reign of Mary Tudor, the *Paraphrases* came under heavy attack; a little later they appeared on the *Index* along with Erasmus' other translations and exegetic writings; and after Elizabeth had ended the Catholic *interregnum*, no English edition of the *Paraphrases* ever appeared again. Thus, even if they continued to be on show in the parish churches, the volumes of the *Paraphrase of Erasmus upon the Newe Testament* had become *livres d'ameublement*.

The more one looks at the evidence, the more one suspects that in the late-sixteenth century most of Erasmus' works were actually read only by a small number of people, Anglican apologists mainly, and educationalists. Erasmus probably continued to be appreciated also by some philologists who admired and copied the humanistic life style of an earlier age: Ascham's patron, for instance, the arch-conservative William Cecil and his learned wife Mildred Cooke, a Greek expert.[19] Otherwise, Erasmus appears to have become a famous name. In this he seems to have suffered the fate of many other great men from the past — one could think of some modern parallels — to whom one can occasionally refer without ever having read the books.

Perhaps, therefore, the name of Erasmus should be used more cautiously when we discuss the elusive conciliatory trends of the late-sixteenth century, whether in England or in the Netherlands. Some scholars even argue that the Erasmian *Philosophia Christi* had in fact been superseded quite early in the century by confessional approaches, so that from then on any attempt to reconcile

18. As quoted by Thompson, "Erasmus and Tudor England", p.53.

19. Cf. my article "Mr. Secretary Cecil, Patron of Letters", *English Studies*, L (1969), 1-9; and "Literary Patronage in Elizabethan England: the Early Phase", in *Patronage in the Renaissance*, ed. S. Orgel, Princeton U.P.

the warring parties of Christendom was based on "the doctrinal ground established by Luther, Bucer and Melanchthon, not Erasmus".[20] Such a strict reading of sixteenth-century church-history appears to ignore the highly unorthodox "solutions" that abounded in mid-century Europe and which had their repercussions in England and the Netherlands "during that brief, chaotic moment when positive efforts towards a reconciling of the Churches were still not entirely unrealistic";[21] or the various "tolerant" trends in the later sixteenth century in which a deep distrust of theological solutions is manifest.[22] But clearly, here the term "Erasmian" cannot apply either. Many of such trends were Anabaptist in origin — and we all know how Erasmus felt about the Anabaptists. For a while at least, the famous clerk recedes into the background.

This is not surprising. Some of the things he stood for had long become accepted, for instance in education; and much else had become irrelevant. In religion, "battles had been won, questions settled: monks and monasteries had disappeared".[23] In the Protestant parts of Post-Tridentine Europe — a Europe which Erasmus could not have foreseen — new issues now called for new solutions, none of which were to be found in his writings. Erasmus had not left behind a useful "method" to solve such problems. Even in the history of religious toleration in this period, "the chief hero is not Erasmus of Rotterdam".[24] Both in England and in the Low Countries the political situation demanded the formulation of entirely new concepts. How could a scholar who always disliked *novitas* be their guide? Indeed, for many years the voice of Erasmus — ambiguous, discursive, contradictory — seemed to have little relevance. His fame, of course, remained.

The real Erasmus revival came later. In the seventeenth century

20. Dermot Fenlon, "*Encore Une Question*: Lucien Febvre, The Reformation and the School of *Annales*", *Historical Studies* IX, Belfast, 1974, 73.

21. *Radical Arts*, p. 13.

22. I have tried to indicate some of these trends in "Temporis Filia Veritas: Wetenschap en Religievrede", *Tijdschrift voor Geschiedenis*, 89 (1976), 413-19.

23. See n. 15.

24. A.G. Dickens, *The English Reformation*, London, 1964, p. 323.

numerous important editions of his works appeared. Erasmus was once again read and studied extensively on both sides of the North Sea, and his writings resumed their role in the history of Anglo-Dutch relations. But that is a different story.[25]

Leiden

Jan van Dorsten

25. This article is based upon a paper read for the Renaissance Society, London, in November 1976. I have not succeeded in finding a copy of Bruce Mansfield, *Phoenix of his Age*, Univ. of Toronto Press, scheduled for publication in 1980, which according to the publisher's announcement deals with "the decline, fall, and recovery" of Erasmus' reputation.

A RAINDROP ON A THORN: AN INTERVIEW WITH SEAMUS HEANEY*

The very first question I want to ask you is, what, exactly, does being a poet mean to you?

Well, that's a very difficult question. I think that part of the activity is the pursuit of the answer to that question. You keep writing and you keep going on – at least, I have done – in the search for the answer. I think the word "poet" is quite a large word. It means a "maker", so I think being a poet means the satisfaction that comes from making things. But somehow, since the Romantic movement anyway, we have invested the word with an extra dimension. And since the outbreak of the troubles in Ireland, since the forcing of some kind of public role, willy nilly, on the writers there, my investigation of what the word "poet" means concerns his function within a community, within a society. That question has been uppermost in my mind; and I've gone different ways, I suppose, in pursuit of an answer to it. I suppose *North* was an attempt to answer those questions, although not directly. At the end of *North*, there are these poems which in a sense *anybody* could write, if they could make. They're just telling – one kind of telling. But then there are other poems which are more symbols, more oblique. They are a kind of pleasuring in the language; and that's more following the material of the language itself, seeking for its mysteries, you know. I think that's part of being a poet also.

Do you see poetry as something you dedicate yourself to? In a bardic sense, I mean?

*Seamus Heaney visited the Netherlands in March 1978, giving readings at the universities of Groningen, Amsterdam, Leiden, and Utrecht. Robert Druce talked to him on March 2, and the following records part of their conversation. The references to the *Sweeney* poems on p. 34 is to a Middle-Irish romance, *The Madness of Suibhne*, which Heaney calls in the translation he is working on, *Sweeney Astray*.

I think so, yes, I don't know of any writer in the poetry line who didn't have that sense of dedication. I think it operates differently at different times. Pope was clearly a dedicated poet, and he had a sense of an historical perspective in which he was working. He had a sense of his forbears and a sense of the classics, and a sense of himself as a guardian of certain standards both linguistic and moral, if you like. We make a lot of play on the moral side of Pope. But he was naturally outraged at certain things, and it was as much a stylistic outrage as it was anything else. It all changes when you come to Wordsworth. And if you're living in Ireland, you have Yeats and Joyce as the two giant dedicated geniuses at the beginning of the century. Somehow, when you begin to ponder – which is a dangerous thing to do – when you begin to wonder about what it means to be a poet, all those exemplars are there.

I'd like to return to Yeats and Joyce in a moment. Meanwhile, I'd like to ask how you see yourself as a poet writing within the tradition.

Well, I don't know; I don't think I can do that.

Not yet.

No. I mean, I began writing with a stronger sense of contemporary English and Scottish verse, really. And Irish verse in the shape of Patrick Kavanagh. When you begin to write, you're just desperately hoping that you *can* write, and so you follow the examples that you think would help you. And I read Patrick Kavanagh, I read Ted Hughes, I read R.S. Thomas, I read some of the younger Irish poets, like John Montague and Richard Murphy, I read Norman MacCaig. And all of their subject matters, the elements of the poetry, were the natural world: were somehow eccentric experiences, not urban, not metropolitan. And that gave me confidence in the elements of my own experience. The poet who had most affected me early on was Hopkins, and I wanted to make noises like that, over my own ground; and that's how the poems came to be written. I'd no sense, really, of tradition; I mean, you're scrambling for your own voice. I suppose one then becomes more conscious, more *self*-conscious even.

There are all kinds of ways in which you can, I suppose, opt for a sense of belonging. It's a kind of political thing, almost, you know? It's a difficult question. But I think that I am tending to see myself more in terms of an Irish tradition. . . But then, the minute you say that, you know that's lies, because everything written affects you. The *Penguin Modern European Poets* even more than the *Penguin Book of Irish verse.*

Do you see yourself as a nature poet, primarily?

No, I don't think of myself as a nature poet. It just so happens that language, for me, has always come alive and become more excited when it is hovering over natural things. And when it is paid into by memory.

Yes. How do you see yourself in relation to the ironist vein in poetry: the Larkin tradition, as it were?

Well, it's not my noise, if you like, or posture. I read them, with pleasure, but I don't think I have that kind of gift, the gift for trusting first of all in discourse. Larkin has the ability to turn discourse of some kind into music, almost; he's not altogether in pursuit of an image. As Yeats said, I seek an image, not an idea. I think I have to, in some ways, be rolling an image under my feet. There has to be an original growth point, a nub of some kind which has a field of force around it that draws all our thinking into it. And the poems proceed not so much by force of argument and intellection and intention, as by some sort of intuitive gathering up or spreading out.

Again, it's a matter of tone. If I try to use a tone that is ironical, I can't. Because the tradition of my speech – I mean, the very basis of my ear – was in a rural community where that kind of social tone did not exist. The Larkin tone implies a certain social, almost class milieu. He has, of course, the unique break in his own voice, in his own melancholy; his own personality is in the thing. But his common language is entirely different from my common language, and I think that a writer has to obey the primary noise that is in him.

How do you face up to Yeats?

I don't face up to him: I turn my back and run!

Ah well, when I was going through this little crisis – I overstate it when I say it's a crisis: I resigned from teaching in 1972 and I was a free-lance writer in Wicklow; having moved from Belfast, having taken my family into the wilderness, if you like – I was wondering then about your first question all the time: what did it mean to be a poet? Perhaps wondering too much about it. And I learned a lot, I think, for my own satisfaction, from Yeats' prose. Yeats had a notion of the relation of the artist to his community which was very strong. He had a belief in the efficacy of art as a binding force for a community. He had a belief in images; you know, if you get the right image, you bind the group together with it. And that kind of thing was important to me because I thought to myself – I'm always thinking to myself – "when people are killing one another, what are *you* doing?" And I can say to myself, well, this bog is deeper than those bullets, in some way. And I came to this notion that, in a time of politics or violence, it wasn't the artist's function just to be liberal and deplore it, but if you believed in one set of values over the other, to maintain those values in some way. You needn't necessarily maintain that belief by writing political poetry or writing deploring the army, or anything like that. I think that's crisis poetry, if you like: once its occasion is over, the energy of the poetry is over. But I think you can write about, or write out of, a sensibility or a set of images which imply a set of values. And that, roughly, would have been the conclusion I finally came to. I think Yeats helped me towards that, to realise that by choosing certain material, almost, you were maintaining certain values.

I wanted to ask you about your resettling yourself in Southern Ireland. What effect did this have, do you think, on your writing? Did you, in moving from Ulster and settling yourself in the South, in Wicklow, did you feel it allowed you to define or redefine your own Irish loyalties?

Yes, I certainly felt that it allowed me to define or redefine: to get freedom or space for myself. But the way we have been talking, the Irishness of the business has been creeping into our conversation in a definitive way, which wasn't there at the time. I would certainly have moved from Belfast anyway. At the time when I was changing from teaching to writing, I didn't want to be in the same rhythms and among the same company: I couldn't have worked in a new way; I'd just have kept the same patterns. I hadn't in my mind that I'd move south. We were, you know, somnambulist towards a change. We were half thinking of going to County Tyrone, going outside Belfast. It's still in the North. But we got the cottage offered to us in Wicklow, and we went to see it, and we were entranced with it. Of course I realised that there would be an emblematic significance in moving south of the Border. But what happened then was that it *was* mythologised actually, immediately, because it was in the newspapers. "Heaney moves South." There was an editorial in *The Irish Times*. And of course that affected my sense of what I was doing, too. I suppose that's what drove me into thinking about the relationship between public and private life. But I don't think that the move south meant that I became more "Irish" in any way. I think I tried to explore what I really felt.

Didn't you feel that it gave you a greater sense of freedom, as it were, being away from conflict, being away from people like Paisley mentioning your name in the papers?

Exactly. I felt for a while in Belfast that I was creeping into the position of being a representative of the Catholic community. Speaking liberally and with well-behaved tongue. And you had to do that for reasons of manners, civility, politics and – finally – civilisation, you know? But in oneself there was this other deposit of tribalism, of scepticism; one half of yourself was mocking the other half all the time. So the move took me out of that useless focus, where I seemed to be speaking as a spokesman.

It took away the political colouring from your utterances?

Exactly. Yes. Yes.

How important is Catholicism to you? There are two questions there, really. How much is it important to you; how far is it your own ground-bass, as it were? And how important is it, do you think, to your poetry? Or is it not?

I don't know about that. I mean, I'm not conscious of that. I have been thinking recently, though, about the whole Catholic/pagan/ Gaelic ethos, which was in the rhythm of the year, and in the rhythm of the seasons. I think that was and is important. In February on St Brighid's Day, we made the Brighid's crosses in honour of St Brighid. I remember this old woman Annie Devlin sitting in the middle of the floor with the green rushes all around her, making those crosses. Then they were hung up everywhere throughout the year. In May you pulled the flowers for the May altar for the Virgin; at Hallowe'en you had the turnip man. In some way, I'm sure, all that binds you to the world around you: in

The Tollund man who died 2000 years ago: "His last gruel of winter seeds/Caked in his stomach,/Naked except for/The cap, noose and girdle . . .".

a way that a kid, say, growing up in Camden or Kilburn wouldn't possess his ground.

I think Catholicism meant *everything* to me, in some ways; because it was my whole life. I was at a Catholic boarding school, and the community that I lived in moved on the poles of the Church and the Gaelic football team. Those were the two central congregating areas, and they both overlapped. And in the countryside, in the rural outback, the only place for the people to come together *is* the Church or the village hall. In the North of Ireland, of course, that village hall was not a mixed area: Catholics went to their village hall, and Protestants to theirs. So, in a way, everything for me was dominated by that.

And then, of course, I met the secular, humanist world of the university and Modern Letters. But I think I didn't feel any need to reject anything: they just lay together in a sceptical relationship. That whole trauma of rejection and anti-Clericalism and disbelief has been gone through. I mean, from a literary point of view, there's not much point in writing *A Portrait of the Artist as a Young Man* all over again.

I think we have become more aware, maybe, through the popularising of the insights of anthropologists and mythologists, of the deep value of some kind of belief, of some kind of ritual. Of their value as fictions, if you like, or as structures. And I suppose I am grateful for the whole burden of Catholicism in that way.

It's obviously one of the strands that pulls a book like North *together, together with the other strand of your own myth. How conscious were you of seeking a myth? Did you recognise that you were looking for a myth, at the point at which you found it?*

No, I didn't. No. But I realised that there was something there.

Was it chance that led you to Glob?

It was chance in so far as I noticed the book, though I'm sure I'd have seen it sooner or later. But the minute I saw the photograph and the reviews I sent for it . . . The "Bogland" poem was the first poem of mine that I felt had the status of symbol in some way; it wasn't trapped in its own anecdote, or its own closing-off: it seemed to have some kind of wind blowing through it that could carry on. And so I sent for this book, and the "Tollund Man" came out of it then. And in fact, Ted Hughes said to me, "You should write a lot more of those, you know: this is your ground." And I knew it myself in a way.

So you went to Denmark.

I hadn't been in Denmark when I wrote the "Tollund Man". But I went twice, and after the second time, I wrote the "Grauballe Man". But I had to beware of writing too many of these poems, also. You know? There seem to be a lot of them, but in fact if you count them there are only about seven or eight. But one is pleased because they seem to have a kind of resonance, and because the material itself is so strange.

It gives you a shape, for looking at Ireland and the successive invasions, of course.

That's right. Through reading around that, I got involved in archeology. And at the same time in the early seventies in Dublin, Brendan O'Riordan was doing a lot of excavation. In the school history books, the Danes had been known as the villains – you know, "the Danes came and destroyed the early monasteries" and all that. But now they were being rehabilitated; and they were seen as being the founders of Dublin, an early domestic settlement. So, at the time, on the ground in Dublin, this connection – the Viking connection, if you like – was being explored. And I was quite interested in that kind of thing, in an amateurish way. I became interested in archeology, and began to see a perspective other than the recent perspective on events. And so the poems in *North* arose out of that. Some people objected to the book, because they said it sounded more like an archeological book than a book of poetry; and I can see what they meant. Some of the vocabulary *is* technical in that way. But again, to go back to what we were saying earlier, it's those elements around which the language can come alive – *that's* the most important thing for poetry. And whether it sounds like archeology or not doesn't matter to me. There was an excitement and a vitality there, and the language moved. And that is what, I suppose, you're always in pursuit of.

Obviously, Joyce has been an enormous influence on you.

Again, unconsciously, I suppose; yes. I suppose it's the fondling of words, for a start. But I don't know if I'm consciously influenced

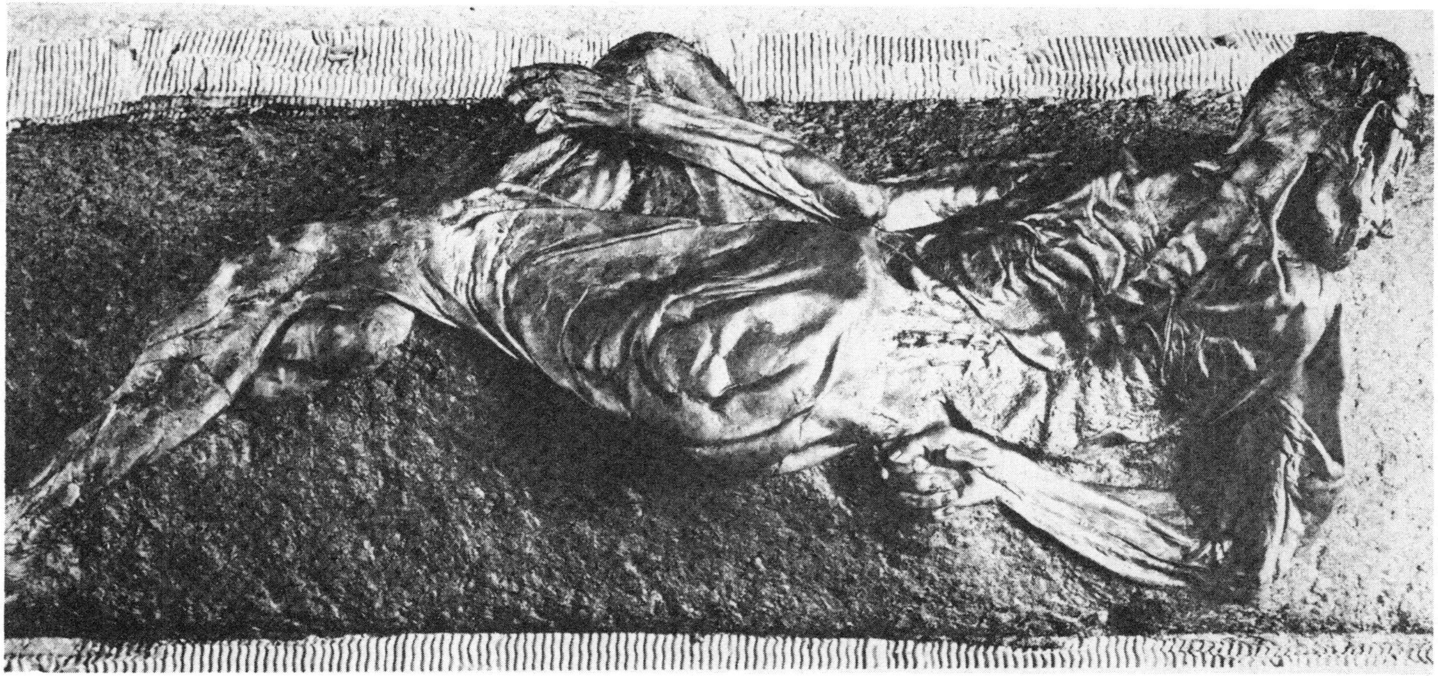

The Grauballe man after excavation: "As if he had been poured/in Tar, he lies/on a pillow of turf/and seems to weep/the black river of himself."

by him. When you say that, what would you be thinking of?

I was thinking of the care with words; but also Joyce as myth-maker. As, as it were, centralising himself constantly in Ireland; and exiling himself in order to do so.

I suppose, yes, Joyce is an influence upon every Irish writer in some way. Just the structuring of your thought about writing involves dedication, language – love-making to language, almost. And some kind of handling of the Irish material, yes. I think Joyce is more exemplary than Yeats, in a way, where it comes to that, because Joyce handles the Ireland that is there. And Yeats imagines – he says so himself – an Ireland that isn't there. To a certain extent, Joyce knows all about the majority of people in Ireland, the Catholics. Yeats has them as ideal fishermen on the West Coast, but Joyce has the East Coast himself. There's a friend of mine, Tom Flanagan, who has written on the Irish novel: he takes the two towers as emblematic of the two writers. Joyce's tower in Dublin Bay, modern, built about 1800, watching the shipping, and surrounded by suburbs. And Yeats' tower, Norman, surrounded by this heathery countryside where Raftery the blind poet had praised Mary Hynes, surrounded by the peasant Gaelic deposit on the one side, and on the other by Coole Park and Lady Gregory's house over there. The democratic versus the aristocratic and so on and so forth: you can make up a good myth out of that.

Yes. But to come back again to this political question: can a writer avoid writing political poetry today?

Oh yes, I think so. He can write love poetry. I mean, did Sylvia Plath write political poetry in any sense? But then you can go the whole hog and say everything's political.

But, in a sense, is a failure to write political poetry in an Ulsterman a –

– a failure of nerve? or of imagination?

Well, yes. Or is it a deliberate declaration that you are not prepared to make a political statement?

It would depend, I think, upon which tribe you came from. I think that a Protestant or Unionist poet doesn't really have to, if he doesn't want to. Because the status quo is what he wishes for, politically. He sees the Provisional IRA as "irritants", "terrorists", "disturbers"; and when they're over and done, everything will continue exactly as before. So he can continue to write – if he wants to, I suppose – love poetry, without disturbing or being unfaithful to the blueprints of his sensibility. But I think for somebody from the Catholic community with a sense of being an Irish nationalist, with some sense of the tension between being and thinking of yourself as Irish, and living in a province which calls itself British – I'm not saying that people are torn apart by this by any means, they are not – but usually, I think, if he wants to explore himself, he'll have to explore this aspect of things. There are Catholic and Protestant sensibilities, Catholic and Protestant being mirror images in some ways of each other . . . But to go back to the question, is it inevitable that you would write political poetry – I think it was probably inevitable that I would write political poetry, in some way.

But "political", you see, is a strong word again. Some people would ask for Marxist solutions: I don't think you can write poetry like that. You can't bring in a programme and impose it. You can if you're a political speaker; but I think you have to be true to the grain of the emotions and personality generally of the community and the society. And that is rarely consonant with any kind of large doctrine.

Can we turn to the Sweeney poems at this point? What sort of problems have they given you? problems of translation, and so on; problems of organisation? Do you see any interference from Eliot's "apeneck Sweeney"? Is he a kind of irritant standing between you and Suibhne?

Ah, I don't think so, no. *Sweeney* is a long story. Literally. It's about one hundred and twenty pages of manuscript, in prose and verse. I began it when I moved in 1972 to Wicklow, because I wanted to have this task that I could occupy myself with, day after day. It was a discipline, if you like. But as I thought about Sweeney at that time, I found that he was a very useful mask – or a very useful objective correlative: whatever term you want to use – in so far as I began to think of him as being like myself. You have to do that, I suppose, when you're working.

It was after the battle of Moira that Sweeney had been turned into a bird, a roamer of the countryside; after the noise of battle. So I had this notion of how, out of the clash of arms in the North,

I was living among the hedges myself, here in Wicklow. And then there were these tinkers called Sweeney whom I had known as a child, and used to see camped in the hedges. So that Sweeney became a medium through which I could bring back that childhood intimacy with hedges and tinkers. And I began to think of him also as a kind of figure like Poor Tom in *King Lear*: a civilised man in disguise, tasting the primitive facts, and so on.

And apart from all that – which is all on the circumference of the Sweeney myth – at the heart of it, in the centre, in the poems themselves, there is this beautiful, specific entangling of the imagination with the landscape itself. And there are opportunities, I think, to write and discover beautifully rich, specific, simple poems. I was obsessed with it. I did it through once; and then I left it.

My unease was that I hadn't dealt with the Irish – I worked from a parallel text, Irish on one side, English on the other – and in order to hurry and not lose my excitement, I kept moving at a great pace. I did a lot each day, and that gave it a kind of excitement. But it meant that I was paying more attention, really, to the English crib, than to the Irish itself, and that I was reshaping the thing in terms of the sense that I got from the English. At first I wrote a lot of free verse for the speed of it. I was possessed by it then: I was well into the material, and the material was well into me. I'd just published *Wintering Out*, and there was a kind of movement, a softish, drifting, free-versy movement in some of the short poems in that book that I felt worked with *Sweeney*.

Then as I came towards the end of the manuscript, I became more interested in the Irish, in the formal aspects of the language. I began to grow more metrical and rhymed. I began to get great pleasure out of just the sheer technical challenge and, I hope, achievement. Occasionally doing, say, forty or fifty quatrains, and making them not too boringly repetitive. But as I came towards the end of the work, the tang of the thing was beginning to change. The speed slowed down. And I think that the work I was doing at the end was richer in some ways than the work I was doing at the beginning. So I felt that I would have to go back and repeat it. But I have hesitated on that brink for some time.

Did you find that the Irish language was feeding your own English speech, your own English rhythms? Or not?

Not really. And maybe that's part of my hesitation.

I had one thing I was determined not to do; and that was to write translatorese. And Irish translatorese has a particularly – well, you know, Douglas Hyde quality: there's a Synge-song element, and Anglo-Irish element. And I didn't want to do that; I wanted it to be English. I didn't want it coloured with the picturesqueness of Irish idiom. At the same time, I wanted it to have an Irish tang.

I think the genius of the English language, certainly since the Norman invasion, has changed. The temperature of the language changed, and became warmer. The temperature of English poetry, on the whole, is a little bit warmer than the temperature of actual English weather – except for Thomas Hardy, maybe, and a few places in Wordsworth. But the temperature of the Irish language, and the emotional weather in that early Irish verse, is colder. It's purer. I always think of a raindrop on a thorn. If the sunlight is winking through that, it isn't a balmy, "Ode to Autumn" sunlight. So the challenge is to find an idiom in English that renders that. There's one tuning-fork for that music, I think, in Shakespeare: "Still through the hawthorn blows the cold wind." You know that line?

Now, I was slightly dissatisfied with what I had because it had more the temperature of English verse; it was more kindlier, more benign. It's not thorny and raindroppy enough.

Or like "the bleb of the icicle".

Or the bleb of the icicle: the very thing, yes.

It's interesting that you keep coming back to this image of a hedge. I mean, one sees a hedge as a divider of fields, and as a sort of interface between one piece of territory and another, but then, again, it remains its own territory.

Yes, I'd never thought of that myself.

For me, one of the happiest things I ever do, is just going and sitting under a hedge.

Well, I suppose I began to think of Glanmore as my hedge-school, in fact. I did a little series of so-called prose poems, which I was thinking of calling "Hedge-School".

What are the other problems that you're wrestling with now?

Does Sweeney represent in any way part of the edge of a new myth?

He could be. Sweeney could be actually used, yes.

We were talking yesterday about the danger that can come when a poet knows he has the skill to turn a poem by craft rather than by truth. I wonder if you're sensitive to the same problem with myth? That once, as it were, you've seen the enormous importance of a myth, you might then begin to think, "I could turn that myth."

Well, I think a myth has to come up in you unconsciously, and be discovered in you. And I've discovered something of Sweeney in me. And the question is, in a sense, whether one is content to take Sweeney as he appears in the manuscript, and to invest that version of the manuscript with things from within myself. Or whether to take Sweeney out of the old fable, and make him *Sweeney Redivivus*, and make him bear other experiences.

To make him a twentieth-century Sweeney.

Yes, exactly. But those questions, I think, should be left unanswered for a moment. I've been writing some elegies recently, and love poems, much more casual occurrences. . . but I think it was Eliot who said, every ten years you have something to say. Or that your experience re-orders itself. I think that's probably true.

Robert Druce

Acknowledgements: the photograph of Seamus Heaney on p. 1 is by Fay Godwin. The pictures of Tollund man and Grauballe man on pp. 29 & 31 are taken from P.V. Glob, *The Bog People*, first published by Faber & Faber in 1969, reissued as a Paladin paperback in 1971. The quotations in the captions are respectively from *Wintering Out*, p. 47 and *North*, p. 35.

LITERATURE AND LINGUISTICS: 1950-1970

1. Backgrounds to the Linguistic Study of Literature

When I read English at the University of London in the fifties, I had to make a choice between "the literature syllabus" and "the language syllabus". The former entailed concentration on post-Renaissance literature; the latter reduced the literary corpus, doubled the Old and Middle English, and allowed students to study such allegedly "linguistic" subjects as Anglo-Saxon Art and Archaeology, Old Icelandic, and Philology. This choice of alternative emphases reflected a traditional division in the field of English studies. At London, Oxford, and the majority of the civic universities, English departments were staffed by people with two different kinds of training and interests. The "language staff" were the descendants of generations of Anglo-Saxonists in a tradition of scholarship dating back to the seventeenth century. In the nineteenth, the antiquarianism of the early Anglo-Saxonists blended with the "scientific" spirit of the new comparative and historical philology. By the close of the century there was in existence an army of scholars with advanced professional interests in the structure and early history of English and the other Germanic languages. When English was established as a university subject – effectively displacing classics as the central arts subject – philological medievalism found a prominent place in the syllabus. Regrettably, this presence has been a source of continuous strife with staff on the other side of English departments: staff with predominantly "literary" interests. In this context "literary" came to mean "post-medieval", and so a rather awkward division of labour was institutionalized. Literature written before about 1500 was taught by philologists; their responsibilities also included phonetics, history of the English language, etc.: they were not expected (and in some cases, not allowed) to teach post-medieval literature, except perhaps for the occasional foray into Shakespearean or Miltonic syntax or Spenserean diction. As literary studies gained the ascendancy, "language" was presented as an archaic irrelevance at best and an inimical source of potential contamination at worst. The position of the philologists and medievalists became an entrenched defence under constant attack. Undergraduates resented having to learn Anglo-Saxon, faculty resented staff places being taken up by Anglo-Saxonists. By the time I came into university teaching, there was a regular Berlin Wall down the middle of English studies.

One of the allegations made against philology and medieval studies was that they are irrelevant to the study of modern literature; another, that Anglo-Saxon is, through distance, culturally irrelevant; a third, that "language" studies maintain a pursuit which is impertinently "scientific". Philology deals in "facts" (so does editing, a necessary preoccupation of medievalists), possesses analytic "techniques", employs "jargon". The study of literature entails consideration of "values", and values are felt to be the antithesis of facts and thus unamenable to scientific study.

Because of these difficulties of communication between linguists and critics, the applicability of linguistic method and ideas has still, apparently, to be justified; this is in spite of a good deal of practical work and theoretical argument by linguists during the last twenty years. I would date the beginnings of modern interest in "linguistic criticism" from this statement by Harold Whitehall in 1951: "as no science can go beyond mathematics, no criticism can go beyond its linguistics." This is certainly an extravagant claim; I do not think any contemporary linguist would commit himself to such a sweeping assertion. Yet some critics evidently believe that this is the claim which linguists generally are making: the claim that criticism should be based on linguistics, and that criticism can only be as good as the linguistics which informs it. To understand why anyone should have made such an audacious statement, and why no-one would maintain such a position today, it is necessary to understand that linguistics had been completely revolutionized since the early fifties: the claim arises from a style of linguistics which is almost universally condemned today. It is now necessary to moderate the excesses of the early claims, and restate as clearly as possible what critical functions it is proper for the contemporary linguist to perform.

The confidence of Whitehall's proposal stems from the mood of American linguistics at the time. In 1951 two extremely influential books were published: Z.S. Harris' *Methods in Structural Lin-*

guistics, and *Outline of English Structure* by G.L. Trager and H.L. Smith. With the publication of these books it seemed that American structuralism, the foundations of which had been laid in the twenties and thirties, had attained methodological perfection. Harris' book, and a body of articles by authors in the same school, laid out a set of efficient techniques for discovering the structure of languages; Trager and Smith's monograph provided an example of a description in which the essentials of the structure of a natural language were set out symmetrically and economically. A historian of modern linguistics, John T. Waterman, nicely (but without irony) captures the spirit of that time: "With the publication of *Methods in Structural Linguistics* American structuralism clearly reached its majority, and could take its place in the world of scholarship as a mature discipline uncompromisingly dedicated to the scientific study of language."

Descriptive linguistics was regarded as a strictly empirical science. Its data consisted of samples of speech ("texts", "utterances"), ideally collected in accordance with set field-work procedures. The language corpora so built up were then subjected to a succession of analytic techniques: they were first recorded in phonetic notation, that is, transcribed as sequences of sounds. Distributional techniques could then be employed to reveal which classes of sounds ("phonemes") were used in that language to effect differentiations of meaning. Next came the discovery of syntactic units: morphemes, words, phrases, clauses, sentences, etc. These units, or classes of units, were observed to have regular privileges of occurrence relative to each other – for example, the class of articles regularly precedes the class of nouns, with adjectives optionally occurring in between. Thus the structure of sentences, texts, or languages (seen as collections of texts) could be presented in terms of the distributional privileges of units relative to each other. Structure was a generalization, or abstraction, extracted from texts by the application of techniques of *segmentation* – chopping the texts into linearly juxtaposed units – and *classification* – sorting the resulting segments into different categories according to the similarities and differences of their distributional behaviour. And it was believed that this structural analysis could be carried out in a mechanical fashion: that linguistic technicians could be trained in the methods so effectively that two separate analyses of the same data would yield the same results (the empiricist criterion of "reproducibility of experiments"). What is more, the structuralists argued the practicality (and necessity) of conducting analysis without recourse to the *meanings* of the utterances under investigation. In theory, this condition meant no more than that syntactic and phonemic tests were best conducted without appeal to semantic criteria; it did not necessarily mean that no statements were to be made about the semantic dimension of language, although it was acknowledged that such statements were very difficult to make. In practice, linguists had to make constant surreptitious references to meaning in order to establish their phonemic and syntactic units, while at the same time the frontal description of meaning was almost totally neglected.

The general characteristics of American structural linguistics that I want to emphasize are these: the belief current among that generation of linguists that their discipline was defined by a set of analytic methods with the status of *discovery procedures;* and, relatedly, that linguistic description consisted of the induction of structure, of patterns of abstract units which were inherent in the linguistic materials under consideration. In passing, we might note that these assumptions are very close to certain governing principles of New Critical theory: the view of the poem as an enclosed, autonomous object to which the critic gains access by his analytic techniques; and the insistence on the primacy of abstract structure as against cognitive meaning.

The next stage in the recent history of linguistics is all too familiar to a whole generation of American schoolteachers. The structuralism of the fifties was aggressively innovatory, claiming overwhelming advantages over "traditional" or "school" grammar. Many English teachers were persuaded to introduce the new methods into their teaching. But no sooner had they learnt the new jargon, the new styles of diagramming sentences, than they were told that they had to learn linguistics all over again. In 1957 Noam Chomsky, who had been a pupil of Z.S. Harris, published a little book called *Syntactic Structures* which heralded a new style of linguistics, *transformational-generative grammar.* The repercussions of this study have literally revolutionized linguistic theory. Although the details of the approach have been hotly controversial, there is no doubt that it has completely changed our way of thinking about langugage. The analytic-technical proposals of Chomsky and their philosophical and psychological implications, have been so fully documented and debated in recent years that it is unnecessary for me to offer a detailed exposition here.[1] I will simply point to an important modification in the general conception of linguistic analysis which has noteworthy repercussions for the verbal analysis of literature.

It might seem that Chomsky merely suggested some mechanical improvements in the technique of syntactic analysis. In fact, the consequences of his approach are much more far-reaching: the whole conception of linguistics has changed. We now no longer regard linguistics as an "analytic" discipline in the sense proposed by the structuralists. That generation of linguists regarded the goal of linguistics as discovering structures in sentences, and listing and classifying those structures and the units which entered into them: the resulting catalogue was claimed to be the grammar of the language. Clearly, structure was felt to be somehow inherent in sentences, and this inherent structure was the subject-matter of linguistic description. This view is not obviously well-founded. It is arguable that the subject-matter of linguistics is not sentence-structure, but rather the linguistic faculties of speakers. It follows that sentences are not *subject-matter,* but *data,* interesting only insofar as they provide access to the vital, human dimension of language: what speakers know which enables them to produce and understand sentences.

I will explain this in a little more detail. A language (*L*) may be defined as a(n infinite) set of sentences. A language is described by a grammar. A grammar is a device which *generates* or *enumerates* the set of sentences which constitutes *L*. It does this by assigning structural descriptions to all the utterances which are grammatical sentences of *L* and to none of the ungrammatical ones. For instance, the structural description of the sentence. *The dogs were chasing a*

1. See N. Chomsky, *Syntactic Structures,* The Hague, 1957, and *Aspects of the Theory of Syntax*, Cambridge, Mass., 1965; J.J. Katz and P.M. Postal, *An Integrated Theory of Linguistic Descriptions*, Cambridge, Mass., 1964; J.A. Fodor and J.J. Katz, eds, *The Structure of Language*, Englewood Cliffs, N.J., 1964; D.A. Reibel and S.A. Schane, eds, *Modern Studies in English*, Englewood Cliffs, N.J., 1969; R.A. Jacobs and P.S. Rosenbaum, *English Transformational Grammar*, Waltham, Mass., 1968; J. Lyons, *Introduction to Theoretical Linguistics*, London, 1968; and *Chomsky*, London, 1970; M. Lester, ed., *Readings in Applied Transformational Grammar*, New York, 1970.

cat includes the information that the sentence contains two Noun Phrases, each of which is a sequence Determiner plus Noun. The grammar contains a rule *NP* → *Det* + *N*. What is the status of that rule? Does it simply acknowledge the presence of sequences *Det* + *N* in many English sentences? It can be argued that such a rule does something more than notice one regularity in English sentences. Contemporary linguists would assert that a linguistic rule has roughly the following significance. Speakers of English are observed to produce sentences which include the pattern represented by *the dogs, a cat, an apple, the books, some cheese* etc. This patterning reflects a certain knowledge speakers of English possess which is part of "knowing English". The rule *NP* → *Det* + *N* is an abstract representation of part of what a fluent, mature, speaker of English knows which allows him to produce and understand English sentences which contain that structure. Sentences (and therefore, texts also) are not regarded as interesting in themselves; when we analyse them, we are asking, not What is their structure? but What does a speaker know which enables him to produce and understand sentences with these observed characteristics? A grammar is said to be a hypothesis about *linguistic competence*: about the knowledge speakers possess which makes *linguistic performance* possible. A linguist is interested in texts as samples of performance, as concrete reflections of competence.

2. The Position of the "Linguistic Critic"

In a sense there have always been "linguistic critics", if by that is meant students of literature who pay particular attention to the language dimension of literary texts. As far back as we have written records, there have been scholars whose linguistic and critical studies have amalgamated in their work on sacred texts, or texts which have been revered for other reasons, for instance their antiquity. Textual exegesis, and efforts to conserve ancient and honoured forms of language, have traditionally nurtured a linguistic science in intimate contact with the value and meaning of texts. The oldest, best-known and most influential example would be the work of the Sanskrit Indian grammarians in the preservation of the language of the Vedic religious texts, several centuries before Christ. Much nineteenth century philological scholarship, directly influenced by the rediscovery of the Sanskrit grammarians, carried on this spirit of enquiry: linguistics remained closely attached to textual discussion. It is only in this century that linguistics and literary studies have lost their interdependence. So, as we have seen, recent proposals to "apply linguistics to literature" have appeared awkward and even shocking, despite the existence of a long heritage in this kind of study.

But once the proposal had been made, a steady flow of linguistic-literary analyses appeared on both sides of the Atlantic. Whitehall's recommendation that the Trager-Smith phonemic analysis should be applied to poetry bore fruit, especially in the field of metrics. His review was published, in an extended form, in the 1956 *Kenyon Review*, followed by a symposium on verse structure in which Seymour Chatman made his first important contribution to metrics; in 1959 we had Epstein and Hawkes' *Linguistics and English Prosody*; in 1961, John Thompson's *The Founding of English Metre*; in 1965, Chatman's book *A theory of Meter.*[2] Samuel R. Levin in 1962 published his monograph *Linguistic Structures in Poetry*; in the same year, papers by Levin and M.A.K. Halliday at the Ninth International Congress of Linguists attracted much discussion.[3] Already a large (and inconclusive) interdisciplinary conference on style had been held at Indiana University in 1958; the proceedings were edited by Thomas A. Sebeok as *Style in Language* (1960), a volume which, by providing a range of theoretical discussions and models of analysis, did a great deal to promote interest in this subject. A statement of method by British linguists is Spencer and Gregory's *Linguistics and Style* (1964); and in 1965 the journal *A Review of English Literature* devoted one issue to "New Attitudes to Style", in which more writings by British "stylisticians" appeared. One of the contributors, Geoffrey N. Leech, has provided an elementary textbook: *A Linguistic Guide to English Poetry* (1969). And throughout this period there have appeared scores of specialized, popularizing or polemic articles: many of the most important are collected in anthologies.[4] It now

2. For full bibliographical details of these and other writings on metrics, and critical discussion, see my "Structural Metrics", *Linguistics*, 27 (November, 1966), 49-64, and "What is Metrical Analysis?" *Anglia*, 86 (1968), 280-320.

3. *Proceedings of the Ninth International Congress of Linguists*, ed. H.G. Lunt, The Hague, 1964.

4. Seymour B. Chatman and Samuel R. Levin, eds, *Essays on The Language*

seems that we have a fertile discipline of "linguistic criticism", however controversial the productions of that discipline might be. Reading materials – both scholarly and pedagogic – abound.

Before proceeding further, we should evaluate the claims that have been made for linguistics in literary studies. We may do so by asking three questions:

Is criticism in any way dependent on linguistics?

Can linguistic analysis serve as a mode of criticism?

What specific contributions (other than under the two general heads above) can linguistics make to literary studies?

The first two questions imply very strong claims for linguistics; claims which are almost certainly too strong and in any case stronger than most of the proponents of "linguistic criticism" would put forward. But Harold Whitehall's statement may be construed as an emphatically affirmative answer to the first question: "no criticism can go beyond its linguistics." If this assertion means that a theory and practice of criticism must have an explicit linguistic theory and methodology (rather than, more vaguely, that criticism may be improved by some knowledge about language), it is obviously untrue. If we can conceive of the possibility of an adequate theory of literature, quite clearly a theory of language can be no more than a part of that more inclusive theory – a theory of language can only be a part of the theory of any specialized variety of linguistic performance, irrespective of whether the texts concerned are "literary" or not. And of course the assertion is behaviourally untrue also: most of the world's most respected critics haven't a clue about formal linguistics.

To take the second question, very briefly. There is an implication in the critical work of some linguists that linguistic analysis is an available mode of criticism. Let it be stated yet again that linguistic description is not critical study; that the use of techniques or terminology drawn from linguistics is no guarantee whatsoever of discovering, or saying, anything specially interesting about texts as literature. Particularly, linguistic description can suggest nothing distinctive about literature: there is no "linguistic criticism" if by

of Literature, Boston, 1967; Glen A. Love and Michael Payne, eds, *Contemporary Essays on Style*, Glenview, Ill., 1969; Donald C. Freeman, ed., *Linguistics and Literary Style*, New York, 1970.

that is meant a recognisably different, viably alternative, kind or mode of criticism. Linguistics in this context must either serve as an ancillary apparatus or lose some of its identity.

After we have disposed of the most ambitious proposals, what claim for linguistics in literary studies remains? Three areas of advantage can be asserted. The first and most important is also the humblest and simplest:

1 Some formal, overt knowledge about how language works is indispensable basic information for the student and critic of literature. (An *educational* claim.)
2 Certain areas of literary study demand close engagement with the mechanics of language (e.g. metrics); linguistics provides specific information and analytic technique. (A *technical* claim.)
3 Linguistics is an advanced theoretical discipline which provides certain insights into the nature of literature and criticism. (A *theoretical* claim.)

My first proposal is a weakened and redirected version of Whitehall's claim. Whereas he suggested that linguistics is the foundation of criticism, I am maintaining that critical practice can be improved by knowledge about language. Linguistics is a theory of how language works: how it is acquired, how it communicates meanings, what kinds of structure it employs, and so on. Literary criticism is an account of the use of language in some particular types of text. It would be surprising if knowledge of language in general did not enhance understanding of specific instances of language use.

A very few major critics seem to know about the nature of language by instinct, without the benefit of formal linguistics: William Empson, I would claim, is one notable example. As one reads such people one learns something about language, as well as about the texts being discussed. How should a literature department educate its students if it is to produce critics with these qualifications? We must admit at once that there is no easy way to inculcate a grasp of fundamental linguistic principles. It has long been known that speakers are naturally innocent of the character of their linguistic behaviour; that consciousness of the process of language is generally achieved only as a result of professional training. Teachers of linguistics know that it is a discipline which generates great enthusiasm among students who achieve intermediate or advanced competence; an exceedingly satisfying subject once the student "gets on top of it" – formally pleasing, neat, of obvious intellectual importance and social relevance. The drawback is that the concepts and techniques involved are strange at the initial level, and highly complicated and detailed once sentences above the artificially simple are to be accounted for conscientiously. There seems to be no satisfactory way of introducing students to the general framework of linguistics without forbiddingly detailed specific exemplification. A further problem is that contemporary linguists are obsessed with the theoretical implications of their discipline to the extent that a large proportion of books and articles nowadays are abstrusely meta-theoretical. Beginning students are likely to make little of the most important books in the field: I suppose Chomsky's *Aspects of the Theory of Syntax* is the classic instance: an extremely difficult (and badly written) book which is nevertheless so important that it is impossible to proceed further than a term into an introductory linguistics course without referring students to it.

My major recommendation (a difficult one to fulfil, in the light of the above observations) is that a place for general linguistics should be found in literary education. Under this recommendation, the student is supposed to have his critical statements improved by knowing about language in a profound, general but perhaps unspecific way. He knows the language expertly; but he only needs to know *about* language in rather general terms – just enough to meet the conditions of accuracy, sensitivity to linguistic functioning, and clarity of exposition. As a concrete example of what he needs to know and what he doesn't, let me cite the case of "stress" as an indispensable piece of knowledge; or, the student ought to know what an "embedding transformation" is, but he need not acquaint himself with the dispute about the validity of the notion of Verb Phrase Complementation. It is clearly possible to write interestingly and responsibly about recurrent images in Shakespeare, sub-culture reference in Malamud or John Braine, romantic parody in Jane Austen, or T.S. Eliot's allusions, without a very advanced linguistic apparatus. This would not seem to be the case with studies of rhythm in Hopkins, sound-texture in Keats, syntax in *Paradise Lost* or in Henry James, metaphoric structure in Wallace Stevens, ungrammaticalness in Cummings, style in Flaubert. Here we move on to the second of my three claims for a linguistic contribution to literature, the *technical* claim. I would think that such studies simply cannot be undertaken except by someone with an advanced descriptive competence in the relevant dimension(s) of linguistic structure. Any worthwhile statement in any of these fields must be based on a detailed, analytic awareness of the texture of language. You cannot talk usefully about sound-structure, for instance, without knowing a lot about the acoustic and articulatory levels of speech, and a good deal about the psychology of perception. Without such special knowledge, only a meaningless impressionism is possible.

At this point I would wish, ideally, to give a catalogue of linguists' successes in discussing various aspects of the linguistic structure of literary texts: triumphs in the analysis of metre, phonetic structure, metaphor, departures from grammaticalness, or whatever. Good progress has been made in prosodic theory and analysis; and some of the papers in Sebeok's volume, and in Chatman and Levin's anthology, suggest the beginnings of insights into other, relatively technical, areas. Again, linguists are starting to provide the basis for an understanding of the nature and effect of grammatical deviation in poetry. To take one more example of technical study, I can see promise of a linguistic contribution to the description of what might be called "interlevel" effects in poetry. By this I mean concords and dissonances between different levels of linguistic structure (syntax and vocabulary, sound and semantics, etc.). In *Essays on Style and Language* (1966) Peter Wexler and I made some preliminary notes on what we called "grammetrics", the interrelation of syntax and metre, in French and English poetry. W.K. Wimsatt's essay "One Relation of Rhyme to Reason" in *The Verbal Icon* (1954) is also an exercise in interlevel analysis. But on the whole, the most that I can do at this stage is indicate (as above) the areas in which technical contributions of linguistics to literary studies might be expected, and hope that this short paragraph may serve as an efficient plea to linguists to undertake detailed work on the verbal texture of literature.

3. Theoretical considerations

I want now to refer to some theoretical insights which arise from the juxtaposition of general linguistics and literary criticism, and to some theoretical problems and programmes raised by this juxtaposition.

Despite I.A. Richards' efforts to place it on a scientific footing, modern literary theory remains depressingly uninformative about the nature of literature. The pronouncements of aestheticians – for example Monroe C. Beardsley – are often wide of the mark because the aesthetician tends to generalize across the boundaries of different art media, neglecting the qualities which distinguish literature from, say, the visual and musical arts. If we turn from aestheticians to critics, we find that their general comments on the definition of literature are characteristically no more than apologies for their own practical methods. This is particularly true of the theoretical discussions of New Critics such as Cleanth Brooks: a caveat against this style of criticism is, I think, generally acknowledged.

There is a damaging romanticism about the New Critical stance: this verbal object, the poem, is an "urn", an "icon", a "monument", a thing with clear-cut edges which you can place in front of you and admire in its self-sufficiency. I am of course referring to the doctrine of the "autonomy" of the work of literature, a creed usually associated with W.K. Wimsatt, but in practice a good deal more widespread. The dangerous romanticism consists not only in believing that a particular literary text is a separate thing (a belief which I will examine directly) but also in believing that literature *as a whole* is a separate *kind* of thing: belief in what Richards dismissed as "The Phantom Aesthetic State". Richards' commonsense strictures should be adequate counter-argument; here is a sample from his *Principles of Literary Criticism:*

> When we look at a picture, or read a poem, or listen to music, we are not doing something quite unlike what we were doing on our way to the Gallery or when we dressed in the morning. The fashion in which the experience is caused in us is different, and as a rule the experience is more complex and, if we are successful, more unified. But our activity is not of a fundamentally different kind. To assume that it is, puts difficulties in the way of describing and explaining it, which are unnecessary and which no one has yet succeeded in overcoming.

In general, a view of the qualitative distinctiveness of verbal art leads to a feeble-minded reverence in students and critics, a foolish belief that to "analyse" is to desecrate or destroy; alternatively, it leads to an aggressive dismissal of all "scientific" approaches as being irrelevant to a thing of "value". These views are of course both reactionary and precious; they serve only to inhibit progress in critical theory (and often, care in critical practice).

Perhaps even more unhelpful, though, is the "tough-minded" autonomism of the school of Wimsatt. In the two famous articles written in collaboration with Beardsley, "The Intentional Fallacy" and "The Affective Fallacy" in *The Verbal Icon* Wimsatt proffers an apparently logical demonstration of the critic's obligation to ignore all evidence except that of the text "itself". Particularly, we are to reject an author's statements about his work, not to trust them as clues or criteria in explicating or evaluating texts; and we are to discount our own responses to a text (*pace* Richards), preferring rather a confrontation with the objective features of the text. This is sound advice. But the argument, both in the two articles concerned and in the injunctions of their popularizers, has run wild. Many students who have been exposed to Wimsattian doctrine are led to believe that the teaching enjoins no reference to *anything* external to "the text" – a Calvinism which is blatantly ridiculous. The theory holds that each text – poem, novel or whatever – is unique (so that comparisons are improper) and self-sufficient: everything that can be said about it has to be learnt by concentrated study of the text itself and only the text. But the practice of criticism proves this attitude to be unrealistic. Who can imagine a good study of Keats by someone who had not read his letters? or a critic of T.S. Eliot whose secret was that he had ignored the critical essays? an eminent Yeatsian who knew nothing of the poet's aesthetic theories? Who would regret Richard Ellman's biography of Joyce? or the existence of Hopkins' correspondence? It is of course to be admitted that "the text" provides the best evidence of its own structure: but it cannot be seriously claimed that texts are utterly independent of contexts, or that their contexts are not relevant to understanding them.

These are practical considerations. There are also excellent theoretical reasons why we should refuse to regard a text as autonomous. To start from the obvious: texts may be either the same or different; when they are different, they may be closely similar or very distant; when they are closely similar, each one is nevertheless unique. By "unique" here I mean "having different sentences". But a crucial point is that being unique is not equivalent to being autonomous. The uniqueness of texts derives from a natural characteristic of language: the linguistic knowledge which speakers possess enables them to produce and understand an infinite number of sentences they have never encountered before. It is likely that, when we read a poem for the first time, each of its sentences will be new to us This does not mean that we face the poem in a state of total innocence – that the poem has no relation to any existing knowledge or experience we might have. In a sense, we know these unfamiliar sentences already: if they are grammatical sentences of English, they are wrought from materials which we and the poet share. The poem is, in a most important sense, a link between poet and audience: it derives from the linguistic knowledge that is common to both parties. In this way, a poem is neither a free creation by the poet nor his own exclusive property: it belongs to the language. With this argument in mind, we have to say that the critic is wrong who regards practical criticism as a "from scratch" activity entailing learning, by analysis, the qualities of a brand-new creation; likewise, the linguist who claims the status of discovery procedures for his techniques is making a false assumption. In both cases, "analysis" of the language of a text can do no more than confirm and articulate what the reader already knows. The fact is that, if a poem is read by someone who knows the same language as its author, every sentence is as much the property of the reader as of the poet: the poet does no more than exploit linguistic resources that the reader also has at his command. There is no sense in which a poem might be, linguistically, isolated.

In modern criticism, the doctrines of textual autonomy and uniqueness have encouraged us to stress the idiosyncratic nature of poems-as-communicative-events. If, say, a particular metaphoric structure is discovered and accounted for in a poem of Wallace Stevens, the critic will hesitate to extend these observations to some other poem; or the syntax of *The Waves* will receive an explanation allegedly independent of that of sentence-patterning in *To the Lighthouse.* But the sociolinguist, like the structural anthropologist, takes an overview. A culture is assumed to have a vast overall pattern, a complicated network of familial, group, economic, political, sexual, linguistic, relationships. It is further assumed that cultural patterning is reflected in, and reinforced by, systematic linguistic patterning. Thus the influence of cultural context on the shape of linguistic performance in any specific instance is thought to be more profoundly understood if it is itself contextualized: if it is placed in relation to other relevant language-culture connections. This seems to me a proper and profitable approach to language and its sociocultural dimensions, and one which is adaptable to literary studies.

Recognition of the general principle which is involved provides a way of integrating literature and culture in a manner which is not antagonistic to close textual criticism. It is often implied that the critic has to choose between "textual" (i.e. verbal) and "contextual" study. In the light of the theory sketched above, the choice seems to require a false opposition. In fact, we can quite easily envisage a linguistic study of literature which dovetails very smoothly into a study taking account of generic categories, genetic factors, or the relation of poetry to other art and non-art media.

The above discussion of style concentrates on the cultural motivations for linguistic variety. It rests on a theoretical premise which seems indispensable to stylistics (though not to criticism generally): we must assume that a distinctive use of language reflects distinctive extra-linguistic circumstances. There is a second assumption of stylistics upon which linguistics can shed some light. All stylistics (but not all criticism, of course) apparently rests on a distinction between "form" or "expression" and "content" or "meaning"; the correlation between style and cultural context is not wholly deterministic – it is always assumed that a meaning "could have been put in different words". Or if it is deterministic, at least it is believed that "the same meaning" occurring in different situations is "expressed" in distinctive linguistic arrangements. Of course, this supposition is very rarely stated explicitly in stylistic studies, and it is anathema to poetic theory. New Critical doctrine asserts as a fundamental principle that the medium is the message: that poems are definitely not paraphrasable. Evidently, the kind of practical criticism which is typified by New Criticism needs this principle; equally evidently, stylistics in the sense intended here is committed to a quite different, and antagonistic, aesthetic. For this reason, there is no point objecting to a form/content distinction in stylistics on the grounds that poems cannot be paraphrased. By the same token, it is confusing to apply the label "stylistics" to just any form of criticism which pays close attention to language – "stylistics" ought to delimit one specific area of literary studies, and its dependence on the form/content division will help us to define this area.

However, the terms "form", "content", "meaning" and "expression" are notoriously difficult to pin down and stabilize. "Form" and "expression" have a range of senses and additionally, in the derivatives "formal" and "expressive", evaluative connotations; "content" involves a misleading spatial metaphor; as for "meaning",

Ogden and Richards wrote a book on the multiplicity of its meanings nearly half a century ago, and we are still a very long way from deciding which sense of the term to settle for. As it happens, there is a related distinction in recent linguistics which may help us understand the form/content distinction more easily (though it does not cover all of the ground which is mapped by stylistics).

The major revision to transformational-generative theory since it was first expounded in 1957 has been the formulation of a distinction between *deep structure* and *surface structure* in syntax. It is proposed that every sentence is characterizable on both of two levels, and that an adequate structural description *must* so characterize a sentence. Briefly, the surface structure consists of a sequence of lexical and syntactic formatives strung together in certain structural relationships; thus:

the + new + grammar + give + s + all + the + answer + s

Such a surface structure may be phonetically (or graphically) represented: that is to say, it may be spoken or written down, the above sequence of elements being preserved. Notice that this sequence reflects only rather indirectly certain underlying syntactic relationships. For instance, the Noun Phrase *the new grammar* is structurally related to the sentence *the grammar is new*, but that fact is not deducible from the surface structure of the longer sentence which contains the *NP*. Similarly, we have in the long sentence two affixes *-s*. Superficially, there is no way of distinguishing them; but of course we know that the first means "verbal affix, used when Subject is singular", the second "nominal affix, used when the noun is plural". I have, in fact, just given information about the deep structure of the sentence: about certain aspects of the meaning of the sentence which are not clear from the surface structure. Chomsky summarizes the distinction in this way: "The deep structure contains all the information relevant to semantic interpretation; the surface structure, all information relevant to phonetic interpretation."[5] Now deep and surface structure are rarely isomorphic, so

5. For another exposition of the distinction between deep and surface structure, see Paul M. Postal, "Underlying and Superficial Structure", *Harvard Educational Review*, 34 (1964), 246-66, reprinted in R.C. Oldfield and J.C.

that we can have pairs of sentences with the same surface structure but different deep structures ("different meanings") or sentences with different surface structures but the same deep structure; respectively, examples 1 and 2-5 below:

1 (a) I saw him in the street.
(b) I saw him in the street.
(1 (a) means "I saw him when I was in the street", 1 (b) "I saw him when he was in the street".)
2 (a) He took off his hat.
(b) He took his hat off.
3 (a) It is clear that this distinction is important.
(b) That this distinction is important is clear.
4 (a) The prisoner who has escaped is dangerous.
(b) The escaped prisoner is dangerous.
5 (a) He unlocked the car and drove off.
(b) He unlocked the car and then drove off.
(c) When he had unlocked the car, he drove off.
(d) After unlocking the car, he drove off.
(e) He drove off after unlocking the car.
(etc.)

In some reasonable sense, the members of each of the sets 2-5 have the same meaning – they are *paraphrases* of the other member(s). We can say that the same deep structure is realized in different surface structures within each set; the differences could be called "stylistic", and a transformational grammar allows us to describe such differences as variations of "expression" leaving "content" intact.

I shall not state in detail the technique for this kind of description. Informally, every sentence has a deep structure comprising one or more underlying strings, each string having a determinate, unambiguous, syntactic and semantic composition. These strings may be represented as simple sentences, as long as it is remembered

Marshall, eds, *Language*, Penguin, 1968, pp. 179-201. The primary sources for this distinction are J.J. Katz and P.M. Postal, *An Integrated Theory of Linguistic Descriptions*, Cambridge, Mass., 1964; N. Chomsky, *Aspects of the Theory of Syntax*, Cambridge, Mass., 1965.

that they are so represented for the purpose of exposition only – they are not really fully-fledged sentences. So the deep structure of the sentence *The new grammar gives all the answers* might be shown as *The grammar gives all the anwers* and *The grammar is new*. Example 3 is *It is clear* and *This distinction is important*; Example 4 *The prisoner is dangerous* and *The prisoner has escaped*. Example 5 consists of *He unlocked the car* and *He drove off.* The underlying strings establish the meaning of the finished sentence; the process from deep structure to surface structure involves the application of transformational rules, which amalgamate the strings in various ways (see 3-5 above), or rearrange the elements in a string (see example 2), or perform other operations, *without changing the meaning established in the deep structure*. Thus a formal linguistic definition is provided for at least one aspect of the notion of "paraphrase". On this basis, stylistic analysis consists of identification of the underlying strings in sentences, and a statement of the "transformational histories" of sentences (the routes between underlying and superficial structures). Examples of stylistic analysis in terms of the deep structure/surface structure division are found in Richard Ohmann's article "Literature as Sentences".[6]

It is clear that the approach leaves untouched one large area of the study of stylistic paraphrase: the discussion above refers only to stylistic choices at the level of *syntactic* alternatives, and pays no attention to alternatives in *lexical* expression of "the same meaning". In the model of syntax preferred here, particular lexical items are chosen and inserted in the underlying strings, so that lexical choice is settled *before* the transformational processing which I have associated with stylistic choice. In view of this problem, the model obviously needs some minor adjustment. But before we can decide how to carry this out, we need to consider a very problematical issue: are there such things as synonyms? Common sense says yes: *cat, pussy, feline quadruped; pleasant, affable, friendly, engaging; strong, powerful, tough; beautiful, attractive, handsome,* etc. But many philosophers and linguists have disputed the existence of synonyms; in general, it has been said that a word is a new word in every different context, and therefore, speaking of lexical choice,

6. To be found in the anthologies of Chatman and Levin, and Love and Payne referred to in note 4.

you cannot choose to say the same thing in different words – different lexical items, or different contexts, guarantee non-reproducibility of messages. (Notice the convergence of this argument with the New-Critical thesis of non-paraphrasability of poems.) I would take the view that there *are* synonyms: that some sets of words share a basic core of meaning and differ only in some secondary semantic components. These secondary components are stylistically contrastive. Now this is of course a commonplace of traditional semantic assumptions, recognized in the distinction between "denotation" and "connotation". But the referential view of meaning which those terms imply is not valuable to descriptive linguistics. At present, transformational-generative grammar has no method of presenting semantic information in a form which might be assimilable to stylistic analysis on such lines. We can only look forward to a more sophisticated semantic theory than we possess at present.[7]

University of East Anglia — Roger Fowler

7. Important modern work in semantics includes J. Lyons, *Structural Semantics*, Publications of the Philological Society, 20, Oxford, 1963; J.J. Katz and J.A. Fodor, "The Structure of a Semantic Theory", *Language*. 39 (1963), 170-210; U. Weinreich, "Explorations in Semantic Theory", in T.A. Sebeok, ed., *Current Trends in Linguistics*, The Hague, 1966, 395-477; G.N. Leech, *Towards a Semantic Description of English*, London, 1969.

This paper is the outcome of a British Council Lecture Tour of five universities in The Netherlands which Professor Fowler undertook in 1969. The arguments presented here are worked out in greater detail in his book *The Languages of Literature*, London, 1971.

VICTIMS AND HISTORY AND AGENTS OF REVOLUTION:
An Approach to William Styron

Richard Gray

Most post-war writers in the American South have, as Gore Vidal once remarked, settled for a more or less minor status – for achievement within stringent, self-imposed limitations. What they do, they do incomparably well: but theirs remains an idiosyncratic vision which avoids most of the problems confronting men living in a public world – the problems, to use those portentous words, of history and society, tradition and modernity – and accepts the relative simplicity of the single, separate life. Not so William Styron: far from avoiding the big issues, he has always sought to grapple with them. Since the time he started writing, indeed, it seems to have been his conscious aim to perpetuate the great tradition in Southern literature; and to assume the throne left vacant by William Faulkner by producing something which, in terms of both its themes and its historical scope, could merit comparison with *The Sound and the Fury, Look Homeward, Angel* and *All the King's Men.* Small wonder, then, that Norman Mailer, that supreme egotist and self-publicist, should see Styron as a kind of twin, and rival. Styron, it appears, wants to write the great novel of our time just as much as Mailer does. Small wonder, either, that Styron's first published book, *Lie Down in Darkness,* should have been treated with almost universal respect and had epithets like "brilliant," "major," and "tragic" showered upon it. *Lie Down in Darkness,* as befitted its author, had ambition written over its every page – it represents a deliberate stab at greatness; and the fact that Styron could back his ambitions up with an extraordinarily seductive style more or less guaranteed its initial success. It was almost too easy, thanks to the prodigious brilliance of its language and the intricacy of its narrative structure, to read more into the book than was actually there.

Not that *Lie Down in Darkness* is a poor or uninteresting novel. Far from it: it is, I believe, a fascinating and to some extent a perceptive one because – whether Styron intended it or not – it presents us with such an honest account of the author's own predicament. It is, in a way, profoundly autobiographical; and since the area of autobiography it deals with bears upon Styron's problems as a Southern writer it is worth looking at briefly, I think, before we go on to examine the later and more successful work. *Lie Down in Darkness* concerns itself with one family, the Loftis family living in Port Warwick, Virginia. In actual clock-time it covers the events of one day, during which the body of the older daughter, Peyton Loftis, is brought back from New York for burial. But in describing this particular day, the author reaches back continually into the past to investigate the circumstances leading to Peyton's death, which came at her own hands; and in the process the book becomes an intensive exploration of the family's almost effortless self-destruction. The father Milton Loftis is, we learn, a romantic who has never found a satisfactory object for his romantic longings in his wife, Helen, who wants simply to mother him. So his feelings, unrewarded there, have flowed into a latently incestuous relationship with Peyton; while Helen has turned for comfort to a second daughter, the helplessly crippled Maudie. "I think we've got a Freudian attachment,"[1] Peyton Loftis says of her father and herself – and it is this attachment, really, which precipitates the disaster. It is the immediate cause of rivalry between mother and daughter. More important, it leads eventually to the failure of Peyton's own marriage (which mirrors that of her parents), her neuroticism (which mirrors Helen's), her compulsive drinking (which mirrors Milton's), and her suicide (which, of course, mirrors the self-destructiveness of all the Loftises). Like the characters in Sartre's *Huis Clos* the various members of the Loftis family constitute one another's Hell; their home life is a kind of prison-house from which they are unable and, because of their mutual dependence, unwilling, even, to escape.

Put in this way, *Lie Down in Darkness* sounds rather like a Freudian closet drama: one of those psychological thrillers that were in fact quite popular during the period when the book was first published. What this leaves out of account, however, is how Styron's manner of telling the tale affects our reception of it. The over-all framework of return which he uses for the narrative, the complex layers of memory through which the characters speak to us, above all the powerful sense of re-enactment attaching itself to

1. P. 235. *Lie Down in Darkness* was first published in 1951. References are to the New York, 1957 edition.

almost every thought and gesture: all this makes us feel that the dark backward and abysm of the old world lies just below the surface of landscape and consciousness, waiting for an appropriate moment to reappear. Further, it makes the Loftis family seem just as much imprisoned in time as they are by each other – or, to be more accurate, imprisoned in times passed. They are obsessed with memories, of an age now disappeared and opportunities missed, and yet they cannot understand them; that is, establish a definite and objective relationship with them. And because of this their lives tend to become peculiarly subtle illustrations of a saying attributed to Ben Jonson: that those who cannot cope with the past are condemned to repeat it, all their lives.

To repeat the past can involve a number of things. It can mean allowing one's immediate ancestors to dictate one's actions and judgements: this, really, is what Milton Loftis tends to do – and what Peyton does as well, by trying to re-enact both her own relationship with her father and her mother's relationship with her father in her disastrous marriage. It can also mean behaving like a character out of one of Poe's tales; like a somnambulist driven by forces beyond his personal control, distilling within the blood the inherited obsessions of an entire race. And this too is a part of the Loftis make-up. What I would like to emphasise, however, rather than either of these possibilities, is a third form that imitation of the past can assume. This is, not just to surrender to the preoccupations and special patterns of yesterday, but to try to reproduce its life-style, to essay being a man of the old world in a completely new one. This inevitably brings its own complications with it. For to divorce articles of belief from the context which has previously given them meaning is, really, to set up a parodic relationship between imitator and imitated. It is to wear the right uniform at the wrong moment; to declare oneself an anachronism and so play the fool – and this is what Milton, Helen, and Peyton Loftis are all doing. They are all fools, enacting a gross pastiche of their predecessors, and the tragic consequences of their behaviour only serve to emphasise, I think, just how total their commitment to their folly is.

Take Milton Loftis, for example. On the evidence of appearance alone, we could easily take him for a true Southern hero. He is the scion of an old if declining family, a graduate of the University of Virginia, an officer and subsequently a lawyer. All this, however, only goes to show us just how deceptive appearances can be. Milton is also a coward and a drunkard. He is emotionally dependent, first upon Helen and then on Peyton; worse still, for him, he is financially dependent too, since his law practice is almost worthless and the house where he lives (that familiar emblem of authority in Southern culture) belongs to his wife. It seems appropriate, somehow, that one of the most glorious moments of his life should involve a wild parody of heroic action; when, drunker even then usual, he runs with the crowd across the football field after a college match carrying a Confederate flag. For Milton is nothing more than a parody himself, a comic travesty of the traditional Southern gentleman; just as, in another way, Helen Loftis is a parody of the Southern lady, her fragility and gentleness all dissolved into neuroticism, and Peyton a brutal parody of the Southern belle. He, and they, are shadows without substance, the products of what one of Styron's other characters calls "a *husk* of a culture"[2]; and together their grotesque postures testify, not so much to the continuity of past and present as to a terrible entanglement – in which the present generation can neither reject the shibboleths of its ancestors nor give them any genuine meaning.

This brings us to the autobiographical nature of the book. For the question Styron seems to be asking in *Lie Down in Darkness* is briefly this: when the old institutions become irrelevant and the old myths obsolete, and when our habits of thought and feeling continue nevertheless to be shaped by them – how then do we change the situation? How can we create new institutions and new myths when our usual means of altering things – our minds and our hearts, dictating the scope of our actions – are among the things to be altered? How do we will an act of defiance if our wills have been conditioned by the very forces we would defy? I have stated the problem over-simply, of course, in order to make it clear. Styron does not think that a complete break with the past is either necessary or possible. But a more active and detached relationship with it *is* necessary, Styron implies, if we are not to suffer the fate of Milton Loftis – and how is this to be achieved?

Styron never answers this question during the course of the

2. P. 363.

book, nor is any satisfactory solution ever implied; and the reason for this, I think, is very simple. For all his perceptiveness in locating the problem he, William Styron the creator of the Loftis family, is as caught up in that problem as any of his creations are. He depends, to the point of parody, on the earlier literary tradition of the South just as Milton, Helen, and Peyton Loftis all depend on its broader cultural tradition. The most immediate and important debt Styron owes is (predictably enough, perhaps) to William Faulkner. In an interview published shortly after the first appearance of *Lie Down in Darkness* Styron readily admitted that he had begun it following a thorough re-reading of Faulkner's work; and we hardly need this admission, I believe, to see how close the similarities are. For the book amounts almost to an elegy, or imitative tribute, to the father-figure of modern Southern literature. There, in the portrait of the Loftises, is the dissolving family familiar to us from *The Sound and the Fury:* the alcoholic father, the neurotic, selfish mother, the idiot child, and the older child who wanders around a strange Northern town for much of one day, clutching a timepiece, and then shortly afterwards commits suicide. There, also, are the Negro characters performing the function of chorus: commenting on the Loftises just as they do on the Compson family, and coming together at the end of the action to round it off on an unexpectedly hopeful note. The narrative framework of Styron's book, involving a family's journey to inter a coffin, is modelled on *As I Lay Dying;* Peyton Loftis is modelled on Temple Drake in *Sanctuary*, another Southern belle turned nymphomaniac; Milton Loftis's father is modelled on the platitudinous Mr. Compson. And so on. "Son you don't have to be a campfollower of reaction," old Mr. Loftis tells Milton when he is still a young man, "but always remember where you came from"[3]; and Styron's trouble really, like Milton's, is that he takes this advice to extremes. The result is a story which has an almost overpowering feeling of *déjà vu* about it; that is full of echoes and vague remembrances. Is Styron himself aware of this dimension of the novel? It is difficult to say; although my guess, based on the available evidence, is that he probably is. Does he know what he could do to change it? That is an easier question to answer, because it is clear from the world he imagines that he does not. *Lie*

3. P. 47.

Down in Darkness never escapes, for more than a moment, out from under the shade of William Faulkner and Faulkner's contemporaries. It represents a cul-de-sac; and the gravity of its language, the brilliance of its structure – the impeccable nature, even, of its own self-reflexiveness – should never blind us to the fact that nearly everything in it is borrowed.

The two books Styron wrote during the next nine years register no significant advance on *Lie Down in Darkness,* at least as far as this problem of liberation from the past is concerned. His novella *The Long March,* for example, merely describes the same predicament as his first novel does, only this time in simpler terms; using the army as the institutional frame which tends to fix the movement of life and inhibit choice. And his second full-length novel, *Set This House on Fire,* does not so much find a solution as impose one. Cass Kinsolving, its hero, suffers almost up until the last page just as Milton Loftis does, then assures us on the last page, and several years later, that through his suffering he finally found a way out:

> "Now . . . I wish I could tell you that I had found some belief, some rock, and that here on this rock anything might prevail – that here madness might become reason, and grief joy, and no yes. And even death itself death no longer, but resurrection. But to be truthful . . . I can only tell you this: that as for being and nothingness, the only thing I did know was that to choose between them was simply to choose being, not for the sake of being, or even the love of being, much less the desire to be forever – but in the hope of being what I could be for a time. This would be an ecstasy."[4]

This, despite the initial modest disclaimer, is pure bombast: Styron's attempt to make up in sheer verbal energy for what he clearly lacks in terms of substance, genuine conviction – and, if we take the rest of the novel into account, for his failure to realise the solution predicated in credible, human terms. Norman Mailer used this particular passage to buttress an attack on the entire book; and he was, I think, quite right to do so. For at best what Styron

4. Pp. 500-501. *Set This House on Fire* was first published in 1960; *The Long March,* in 1956.

says here exists as an expression of need: a cry for emancipation which, like Milton Loftis's, remains more or less trapped in the vocabulary and values of the very systems it wishes to defeat.

Which brings us to *The Confessions of Nat Turner*: Styron's fourth book and the one, I think, in which he has begun to find the answers he needs – both to his own problems as a Southern writer of the second, post-War and post-"renaissance" generation, and to the larger questions facing anyone who inherits, however unconsciously, a particular way of organising and figuring experience. Its subject is that ultimate victim of the past, and the roles and mythologies the past bequeaths, the American Negro slave. Its method, as Styron puts it, that of a "meditation on history"[5]; since the story is based on an actual slave revolt which occurred in Virginia in 1831 and the supposed "confessions" made by its leader, Nat Turner, after his defeat and eventual capture. In this way, Styron places himself squarely at the centre of the Southern tradition: and not, as in *Lie Down in Darkness,* merely to commemorate that tradition but so as to develop it, carry it a stage further. History – the relationship of past to present in the writer's own experience and in the lives of his characters – is as much the motivating force in this book as it is in Faulkner's work, say, in John Crowe Ransom's or Robert Penn Warren's. The only difference is that it is now what James Baldwin has called the "common history" of white and black which comes under scrutiny; and this change, far from being a superficial one, signals other changes of approach and interpretation which enable Styron to achieve a radically fresh understanding of familiar material. In a sense the *Confessions* represents the most significant attempt made over the last twenty years to fashion something new out of the creative inheritance of the South: which is why I would like to look at it in some detail – at the controversy it has aroused, the problems it investigates, and at the fresh territory which it has begun, however tentatively, to map out.

When *The Confessions of Nat Turner* was first published in 1967, it was greeted with almost unanimous critical acclaim; just as *Lie Down in Darkness* had been. The consensus seemed just about complete, Southern historians like C. Van Woodward joining with

5. "Author's Note" to *The Confessions of Nat Turner* (New York, 1967).

black writers like James Baldwin to heap praises on the book, and then suddenly, less than a year after publication, opinion took a sharp and surprising turn. The immediate occasion and in a way the symbol of this change was the appearance, early in 1968, of a collection of essays called *William Styron's "Nat Turner": Ten Black Writers Respond.* Flatly contradicting most earlier commentators, the ten contributors to this book charged Styron with almost every literary crime under the sun. He had written an undramatic and unexciting novel: that was one accusation. More to the point: in the interests of his own condescending, and essentially hostile, attitude towards Nat Turner he had distorted history. Taking the 1831 text of the *Confessions* (written by one Thomas Gray, and supposedly dictated by Turner while he was awaiting execution) Styron, the ten black writers claimed, had omitted certain details and added others – and all completely without justification. These were serious charges; and they were made the more serious by the fact that, as Styron himself had suggested already, the theme of black revolt in the *Confessions* was and is of more than antiquarian interest. The shadow of Nat Turner hovers so ominously behind the figures of Malcolm X, Stokely Carmichael, and Eldridge Cleaver, as an example, warning and inspiration, that to comment on him is in some sense to comment on them, and on racial oppression and revolution in general.

Just as they intended, the ten black writers aroused a storm of controversy; and, I think, they went right to the heart of the book – what Styron was really trying to do, and the problems this involved. Styron has described the *Confessions* as a "meditation on history." Precisely, his critics now replied: but in a meditation on history, how much scope should be given to the "meditation" and how much to the "history"? At what point does historical interpretation topple over into historical romance, myth into fantasy; and hadn't Styron passed that point? Their questions had more than just an immediate application, of course. For the approach Styron had chosen for the *Confessions* was no different, in essentials, from the classic Southern strategy of an imaginative reenactment of the past. In questioning Styron's use of it, consequently, they were by inference questioning his abilities as a *Southern* writer. In examining his presentation of history – history as an idea, that is, and as a series of events occurring in a specific society – they were, eventually, measuring his work against other works of the historical imagination such as *Absalom, Absolom!*, *All the King's Men, Antique Harvesters* and *Ode to the Confederate Dead.* That is why their arguments merit serious consideration: because even if we disagree with them they force us, in the course of disagreeing, to consider first principles.

A good example of this – of how, to put it another way, Styron's ten black critics tend to ask the right questions even if they do not always come up with the right answers – is offered by their criticism of the language Styron puts in the mouth of his slave characters; and, more particularly, in the mouth and mind of Nat Turner. Styron, as most of the contributors to *Ten Black Writers* point out, deploys two kinds of language in his portrait of Turner: the one a "Sambo" or "nigger" dialect which Turner shares with all the other slaves and uses in conversation, the other a mellifluous, incantatory rhetoric which is more or less unique to the protagonist and is supposed to describe the movement of his thoughts. Both, they argue, involve imposing a mask on the character. Turner is given an idiom (or, rather, idioms), and by inference an identity, that is not really his at all: which, if anything, must be seen as the product of certain, specifically "white" preconceptions.[6]

In a way this criticism is perfectly accurate – and useful, because it draws our attention to an aspect of the novel which most of its earlier reviewers preferred to ignore. Styron's Nat Turner does, for example, talk in a way which makes him sound very much like Twain's "Nigger Jim" or Joel Chandler Harris's Uncle Remus. What it fails to take account of, however, is Styron's motives for making his hero speak and think like this – motives which he actually explains to us in the course of the narrative. Here, for instance, is Nat Turner himself giving one reason why he talks the way he does:

> "I'se twenty, massah," I replied, "twenty-one come de first day October." It is good for a Negro, when trying to ingratiate himself with a strange white man, to convey an impression of earnest simplicity and this may often be achieved by

6. See, e.g., *William Styron's "Nat Turner": Ten Black Writers Respond*, ed. by John H. Clarke (Boston, 1968), pp. 43, 81.

> adding to such a reply as mine phrases like "Das de truth" or "Das right." I think that I must have tacked on then a sweet and open "Das de truth."[7]

The message is plain. It is, really, a moral necessity for Turner and his fellow-slaves to speak the way they do, because that is the only way they can defend themselves against the fear and suspicions, prompted by guilt, of their white oppressors. Language is something they use as a shield, a form of self-protection which gradually becomes second nature to the protected. Elsewhere Styron offers another explanation, that it is a matter of cultural necessity as well: since on a broader, historical level the Negro dialect can be seen as an example of those cruelly impoverished types of culture imposed by the white man upon the black – after his original African traditions had been taken away from him and only an embattled species of Christianity, and a hopelessly defensive kind of group identity, offered by way of a replacement. At once "a form of self preservation" (as Styron puts it at one point in the book) and a proof of "the cultural barrenness of black life" in the South (as the Negro writer Richard Wright described it in his autobiography, *Black Boy*), "nigger talk" is consequently placed for us even while it is being used; it becomes part of the armoury of Styron's criticism (of slavery and racial oppression in general) rather than something for which Styron himself should be criticised.

Turner's other idiom, the one Styron gives him whenever he is left alone to remember and meditate, is intended, really, to counter this: by offering a linguistic equivalent of a movement towards self-realisation, in energetic denial of those processes of de-culturisation and de-personalisation which helped create the "nigger" and his speech. The model here, I think, is what has often been called the "real language" of Negroes; something evolved out of African rhythms and phrasing and white vocabulary – and to be found nowadays, for example, in "jive talk," black spirituals, or the performance of a good black preacher. By definition, this is a difficult language to reproduce in print because it depends on what professional linguists call a "para-language" as much as anything else; it draws its energies, partly, from such things as

7. P. 235.

gesture and physical expression, those resources of oral communication which can supplement or even give substance to the written word. Despite the difficulty, though, Styron had to find some way of reproducing it if another, more active and unusual side to Turner's life was to be suggested. Which is what, surely, he is trying to do in passages like this:

> Cloudless sunlight suggesting neither hour nor season glows down upon me, wraps me with a cradle's warmth as I drift toward the river's estuary; the little boat rocks gently in our benign descent together toward the sea. On the unpeopled bank the woods are silent, silent as snowfall. . . The breakers roll to shore, the lordly tide swells back beneath a cobalt sky arching eastward toward Africa.[8]

This is not, needless to say, a colloquial style. Nor, as several contributors to *Ten Black Writers* have argued, does it involve any attempt to impose the author's own, self-evidently "white" rhetoric on his black characters either. Styron's aim is, simply, to create the sense of an emergent language. The opulent vocabulary, the hypnotic rhythms and inversions, the lush sonorities of phrasing and the pulsing, emphatic movement of the passage as a whole: everything points towards a voice intoning rather than just speaking. Every resource at Styron's disposal is geared towards catching the buck, drive, and lilt – the total effect – of a "genuine" Negro speech.

This criticism, in *Ten Black Writers,* of Styron's handling of Negro idioms is carried over into his treatment of the Negro personality as well; and naturally enough, since it is language after all which creates characters in the novel. Again, Styron's ten black critics say something that previous commentators had somehow managed to avoid saying: which is that the Negro characters – even Nat Turner himself, to some extent – are accorded a diminished and comparatively marginal status in the *Confessions.* They act largely as a chorus, observing and commenting on their white masters' behaviour; and, even worse, as a chorus composed almost entirely of "Sambo" or nigger minstrel stereotypes.[9] But again

8. P. 421.
9. See, e.g., *Ten Black Writers,* pp. 7-8, 16, 22, 56-58.

what is really a conscious device is read as unconscious hostility. Styron is attacked for his ignorance and even, by some of his critics, for his instinctive hatred of an entire race: whereas it is clear, I think, if we look at the novel closely, that the dehumanisation of the black man is one of Styron's subjects rather than his premise. He is actively inviting us to consider how a system can eat away at character – pervert a man just as much as it can pervert his speech – which is why something like, say, the peripheral status of the slave is explained for us in the course of the narrative, placed by the action and the occasional side:

> It is impossible to exaggerate the extent to which white people dominate the conversation of Negroes... white people really see nothing of a Negro in his private activity, while a Negro . . . has often to suffer for . . . his ubiquitous presence by being called a spy.[10]

The point, as Styron makes it here, and elsewhere in the story, is that within the kind of social structure epitomised by the aristocracy of the Old South the less privileged person *is* dismissed to the periphery. The message communicated to him by his situation is that he matters only to the extent that he makes possible the life-style of his oppressors; and the most pernicious aspect of this, Styron argues, is that he is often inclined to believe the message himself, because there is nothing in his customary life to contradict it.

This reading of slavery and the impact it has on the personalities of the enslaved has wider implications which I will go into shortly: although it will be fairly obvious at once, I suppose, that it helps relate Nat Turner to Milton Loftis, Cass Kinsolving, and Styron's other fictional victims. But what is worth pointing out before that, I think, is that Styron owes the immediate stimulus for such a reading to a professional historian – and to a book which he, Styron, had reviewed for the *New York Review of Books* several years prior to the publication of the *Confessions.* The book, *Slavery: a Problem in American Institutional and Intellectual Life* by Stanley Elkins, is one of the most important treatments of the entire subject to appear in the past few years. In it,

10. Pp. 54, 62.

Elkins argues that the "Sambo" character really did exist, and he compares life on a slave plantation to life in a Nazi concentration camp in order to suggest the conditioning circumstances which made such a character possible. Both the plantation and the concentration camp were, Elkin claims,

> . . .closed systems from which all standards based on prior connections had been effectively detached. A working adjustment to either system required a child-like conformity. . .all lines of authority descended from the master. . . The individual, consequently, for his very psychic security, had to picture his master. . . as the "good father" even when. . . this made no sense at all.[11]

Only those slaves who lived "outside the full coercion of the plantation-system" escaped the full impact of this conditioning; and Elkins even cites Turner as one of the exceptions who proves the general rule. For Turner, he points out, developed an awareness of alternative sources of authority simply by learning to read and becoming apprenticed to a craft. This is a hint that Styron has taken up in drawing a distinction between his protagonist and most of the other slave characters: the kind of distinction implicit, for example, in the fact that Turner alone is given two idioms. It is not that, as many of his black critics suggest, Styron is attributing his own loathing of Negroes to his principal character. It is simply that he is describing somebody very similar to the kind of person Richard Wright describes himself as being in *Black Boy*: a man who, by one means or another, has become painfully aware of how rules are mapped out for his race – and whose very awareness of this fact has created a feeling of "eternal difference" between him and them. Of course, this is an arguable interpretation of slavery or racism and its psychological effects on the oppressed, but it is one drawn out of hostility to the slave system rather than any kind of sympathy with it. More to the point, perhaps, it depends upon as closely reasoned an idea of history – the involvement of the past with the present, and the public with the private

11. *Slavery: A Problem in American Institutional and Intellectual Life* (Chicago, 1959), pp. 128-129. Styron's review appeared in the *New York Review of Books* (Sept. 26, 1963).

life – as we are likely to find in any Southern book.

These, I think, are the two things we need to bear in mind about the *Confessions* in order to see it as a worthy exponent of the Southern tradition: that it is an attempt, not merely to record times passed, but to rediscover them in the light of contemporary concerns – and that it does this, not by a policy of deliberate distortion, but by reinterpreting the known and making calculated guesses about the unknown. For when all is said and done, what *is* known about the actual revolt led by Nat Turner? Very little beyond the fact that there was a revolt, it failed, and Turner was executed. All the records by which the story has come down to us (and Styron) are suspect, from the 1831 text of the *Confessions* written by Gray, which was intended mainly as an awful warning to slaveholders; through the narratives provided by both Abolitionists and apologists for the South later on in the nineteenth-century; to the more recent accounts of Southern historians, like Ulrich Phillips, and Marxist ones, such as Herbert Aptheker. Every man has his own axe to grind. Every one has consequently tended to explain things in terms of his own reading of society and human nature; and, in those many areas where the truth is not known or the meaning ambiguous, has been tempted sometimes to invent. This accounts for many of the so-called "facts" which Styron is criticised for neglecting or altering: they are not facts at all, merely details from somebody else's myth. He has been attacked, for example, for omitting any mention of Turner's wife, and for claiming that the Nat Turner rebellion was "the only effective, sustained revolt in the annals of American Negro slavery." But the attack itself is built on shaky ground; since the wife was an addition to the story made by later, Northern historians (motivated, needless to say, by feelings of genuine sympathy), and the belief that there were ever any serious revolts besides Turner's is based on evidence concocted by Herbert Aptheker – out of memories of strikes, plots scotched in the hatching, and rumours of rebellion. There is nothing to prove that Turner was married, any more than there is anything to prove that he was not. It is not certain that there are parallels for the Turner rebellion (indeed, it has never been certain since slaveholders tended to confuse fear of revolts with their existence) and, equally, it is not certain that there are not. In these respects, as in so many others, the story of Nat Turner is disputed territory where different voices have tried, and still do try, to establish their own versions of the truth. And Styron is simply following precedent in operating freely within the limits of discretion so allowed him – in recognising, in fact, that his own meditation on history is quite as defensible as anyone else's as long as it sticks to the authenticated facts.

Styron's critics are right about one point, though. The crucial thing in the *Confessions* is not its author's portrait of the larger historical background, nor even his presentation of Nat Turner by itself. It is, rather, his description and development of one special kind of relationship; the relationship, that is, between black man and white woman and, in particular, between Nat Turner and Margaret Whitehead, the daughter of a local plantation owner. This is the aspect of the book to which Styron's critics have taken more exception than anything else: accusing him, among other things, of racism – and of being plagued by what W. J. Cash once christened "the rape complex."[12] And, as I see it, they have been right at least to emphasise its importance. For whatever finally we may think of the novel it is this relationship, I believe, which offers us the key to its meaning – the best clue we have as to Styron's reading of history here, and consequent reappraisal of Southern literary conventions. And I would like to develop the point I am trying to make by suggesting the possibility of another analogy; a comparison with a comtemporary black writer and radical. For in its analysis of the sexual implications of an oppressive and exploitative society the *Confessions* is, I think, very similar to a book to which it might otherwise seem to bear no relation at all: *Soul on Ice* by Eldridge Cleaver. I have two chapters of Cleaver's book in mind especially, *The Allegory of the Black Eunuch* and *The Primeval Mitosis,* where Cleaver argues that a clear and definable connection exists between the given structure of any society and the personal lives and sexual drives of its members. Cleaver's theory is developed largely in terms of its negative implications, as manifested in what he calls a "Class Society":

> The Class Society projects a fragmented sexual image. Each class projects a sexual image coinciding with its class-function in society. And since its class-function will differ from

12. See W. J. Cash, *The Mind of the South* (New York, 1941), p. 84.

> that of other classes, its sexual image will differ also . . . The source of the fragmentation of the Self in Class Society lies in the alienation between the function of man's Mind and the function of his Body.[13]

What is particularly relevant here is the special relationship which Cleaver claims is fostered in the American version of a "Class Society" between the oppressed black man and the privileged white woman. The black man, or "Supermasculine Menial" as Cleaver calls him, is reduced by the American system to the status of a work-house donkey, a body without a mind; while the white woman, to whom Cleavers refers – in typically sardonic fashion – as "the Ultrafeminine" is placed on a pedestal, a frail mind or sensibility without a body. Each, Cleaver argues, perceives in the other what he or she lacks. The "Supermasculine Menial," for example, soon senses that the "Ultrafeminine" is his opposite and necessary complement – and so, in a way, his "psychic bride":

> She is his dream girl . . . She exerts a magnetic attraction upon him. Also, since . . . standards . . . are set by the elite, the Ultrafeminine personifies the official standard of feminine beauty . . . imbued with the official standard . . . the Supermasculine Menial develops an obsessive yearning . . . for sexual contact with the Ultrafeminine.[14]

Effectively, Cleaver is describing a situation here in which the white woman is dangled in front of the black man as a kind of tempting object; he longs to possess her because to do so would, as he sees it, be to recover wholeness and demonstrate his freedom. Cleaver puts the matter with his usual feeling for the right, brutal and memorable, phrase: in this context, he says, rape assumes a special, symbolic status. It comes to seem like "an insurrectionary act."[15] Only seem like an insurrectionary act, though; the black man, Cleaver goes on, may believe that he is asserting his freedom in lusting after a white woman, but really all he is doing is demon-

13. P. 127. *Soul on Ice* was first published in 1968. References are to the London, 1970 edition.
14. P. 136.
15. "On Becoming", in *Soul On Ice,* p. 25.

strating his servitude. Despite anything he may think to the contrary, his longing for a white "dream girl" only proves that he is still imprisoned within a fragmented sexual being, and still controlled by the standards of beauty and value his society engenders. The "Supermasculine Menial," simply shows that he is a "Supermasculine Menial," in fact, by lusting after the "Ultrafeminine." Even this paradoxical situation is not the whole truth, however. By a final twist of logic Cleaver suggests that, while the black man is certainly deluded in seeing the white woman as a direct means to freedom, he may still recover his freedom in possessing her. And this simply because in possessing her he may realise the emptiness of his dream, and the scope and causes of his illusion. The point is not a difficult one, although it adds to the complexity to the total situation. The fulfilment of the desires of the "Supermasculine Menial," Cleaver is saying, will inevitably be followed by disillusionment; and this in turn may be followed by a moment of illumination, in which the limited and conditioned nature of his earlier ambitions is revealed to him. Understanding the nature of his previous self, and the forces which shaped and constricted it, the black man may finally enter into his full manhood.

Returning to the *Confessions*, the main point can, I think, be made at once. Nat Turner, as William Styron presents him, is clearly a close relative of Cleaver's "Supermasculine Menial": a being who is caught within the confines of a closed system of society, and defined by the narrow possibilities of a repressed and fragmented self. He can neither objectify his feelings in terms of the world around him; nor achieve the more fundamental satisfaction of knowing what the full range of his feelings is and, consequently, what he himself might be. His life is really a series of withdrawals, from the outer world of action into the inner world of frustrated fantasy. In a way Turner recognises this himself but what he does not realise is that, initially at least, this inner world is as much of a prison for him as the outer one is – because the two are inseparable. The situation is a complex one, full of ironies which reach their climax, I think, at the actual moment of rebellion. For though Turner now seems to be acting in defiance of white society, really he is only betraying his continued allegiance to the dream it dictates. His definitive act during the revolt, the murder of Margaret Whitehead, involves not so much a rejection of white ideals as a positive attempt to embrace and realise them:

> "Ah how I want her," I thought, and unsheathed my sword. . . she tripped forward her arms outthrust as if to welcome someone beloved. As she stumbled. . . I heard her. . . ragged breathing, and it was with this sound in my ears that I plunged the sword into my side.[16]

It takes very little stretch of the imagination, I think, to see that for Turner at this moment his violence is a means of fulfilling his earlier fantasies, more like a rape of his white "dream girl" than anything else. That the rape is itself internalised, and so quite literally a part of the dominant illusion, only adds a further dimension to the irony: Turner cannot, in effect, see his actions for what they are any more than, before this, he has been able to see Margaret Whitehead for what she is. Like Cleaver's "Supermasculine Menial" he remains trapped, an innocent victim, even while performing what is apparently an "insurrectionary act".

Captured

16. Pp. 413-414. For the preceding dreams of rape see, pp. 232, 265, 347.

Nat Turner has very little time left for the further stage which Cleaver describes, leading from disillusionment to revelation. Still, the self-analysis which occupies his last days, and which accounts for the retrospective standpoint of the book, does offer him the possibility of a new direction. Turner manages a full look at the worst and this, in a fashion characteristic of tragedy, enables him to see that there may be a way to the better. Not only that, he begins to take that way. For how else are we to interpret the language of his meditations which (as I mentioned earlier) owes less to his white masters and the culture they have imposed on him than it does to his own groping efforts towards self-realisation? The very manner of Turner's meditations suggests, I think, that he is beginning to find a trustworthy means of shaping his own experience, and so of defining his own being. And the suggestion is confirmed right at the end of the novel, with Nat Turner's death. At this moment, just as Turner is about to leave his prison cell for the gallows, an echo of an echo comes to his mind – the recollection of a phrase heard long ago in childhood, which seems to have acquired a new significance thanks to his experiences. It supplies the last line of the narrative proper:

> Oh, how bright and fair the morning star. . .[17]

The initial source of this phrase is, of course, the Bible and Turner's own religious upbringing: but it is surely not stretching a point too far to say that it may also contain an echo of the last paragraph of Thoreau's *Walden,* an echo or association which is crucial to its meaning. For it reminds us, I think, just as the closing lines of *Walden* do, that the book we have been reading is about the "dark night" which precedes the "new dawn" announcing the liberation of the self. It tells us, as clearly as any figurative expression can, that what we have witnessed is that stripping away of illusion, painful but inevitable, which must preface the discovery of a new identity – and the beginning of a new life.

Nat Turner dies, though, before he can actually begin life anew; just as Thoreau disappears from view even before he has left Walden Pond, evading any questions we may ask about what hap-

17. P. 428.

pened to him when he returned to society. In practical terms, the process of self-emancipation described in the *Confessions* – like the one described in *Walden* or *Soul on Ice* – is left unfinished, equivocal; and the real, which is to say the only completed, liberation occurs not in the life of the protagonist but in the consciousness, the mind and spirit, of the writer. The freedom won in the book, and by the book in a sense, is an imaginative rather than an active, political one – to which the writer's craft, his own act of writing bears witness. Perhaps it will be obvious enough already just how, in the *Confessions*, Styron achieves this freedom: by developing for the first time beyond his tradition – the tradition of the South, that is, and, in particular, the tradition of William Faulkner – adding to the existing monuments, rearranging them and so endowing them with an original value. For the familiar ghosts of Southern literature – the great plantation, the gentleman-farmer, the plantation lady and the Southern belle: they are all there as usual. But they have all been made unfamiliar now, severed from their old connections. This time it is the underdog who presents them to us, the victim whose suffering had made all their elegant games possible. We see them with altered vision, as if the past were being redeemed and revalued for us as we read – as if, to borrow a line from Eliot's *Dry Salvages*, we had had the experience before but somehow missed its meaning.

Of course, a simple change in narrative point-of-view, however significant it may be historically, does not go all the way to account for this metamorphosis. Even more important, in a sense, is the use Styron makes of the accepted structures of Southern writing. His general attempt to re-write history – by engaging event with myth, yesterday with today, and by establishing what is essentially a symbiotic relationship between his characters and their environment – is familiar up to a point. We have, after all, seen other characters who have tried to re-enact the past (among them Faulkner's Quentin Compson and Wolfe's Zachariah Joyner)[18] and many other writers (Southern writers and historical

18. I.e. in, respectively, *Absalom, Absalom!* (New York, 1936) and *The Hills Beyond* (New York, 1941). Other examples of this figure in Southern literature include the narrators of Allen Tate's *The Fathers* (New York, 1938) and *Ode to the Confederate Dead, Mr. Pope and Other Poems* (New York, 1928) and of Robert Penn Warren's *All the King's Men* (New York, 1946).

writers generally) who have seen it as their main purpose to reconcile their ideas or beliefs with the received facts and legends of history. The difference in Styron's case, however, and it is a crucial one, is that these strategies are now being used not for nostalgia's sake nor even to demonstrate the virtues of precedent, ceremony, and ritual but so as to further the cause of a carefully formulated, highly sophisticated form of radicalism. Traditionalism in Styron's hands becomes, effectively, an agent of revolution, the kind of plea for immediate, drastic, and even violent change that we are more inclined to associate with political writers such as Cleaver, or visionaries such as Emerson and Thoreau, than with the likes of Robert Penn Warren, Thomas Wolfe, and William Faulkner. One way of charting the course Styron has taken, in fact, is to say that Faulkner and his generation could never have written something like the *Confessions,* if only because it is the sort of book which measures itself in terms of its distance from them and their work. It predicates a certain tradition, in other words, a particular orthodoxy from which it has developed and with which it can establish a definite, objective relationship; and that tradition is made up as much from the novels, plays, and poems of the "renaissance" as from the broader, social and cultural patterns of the South. Without necessarily endorsing the aims of the *Confessions*, though, or sharing in the impulses which led Styron to write it, Faulkner and his contemporaries would, I believe, have understood the novel: they would have seen how it has grown out of their own work and, in growing, taken on a separate, distinct life of its own. The *Confessions* uses its given inheritance and then transcends it so as to present us with a broadly inclusive, yet cross-grained and self-evidently personal portrait of all our lives in history; and that, as Styron's predecessors would probably have recognised, is really the best that can be said about any Southern book.

This article, first published in *DQR* in 1975, became part of chapter 6 in the author's study of "Modern Writers of the American South", *The Literature of Memory*, London, 1977.

SHAKESPEAREAN TRAGEDY: HAMLET*

Although I have allowed the phrase "Shakespearean tragedy" to appear in my title, I can only give very little time to such big questions as the nature of Tragedy in general or of Shakespearean tragedy in particular. Frankly, although we have to use the phrase, there is no such thing as Shakespearean Tragedy; there are simply a number of tragedies by Shakespeare, interconnected, it is true, but each attempting something different, and employing different dramatic means. As for Tragedy, although we all know what plays we include under that head —*Oedipus, Phèdre, King Lear* — there is very little that we can usefully say about the nature of "the tragic experience". I will only say two things, the first is obvious: great tragedy faces honestly and clearly, and makes us face, what is most deeply disturbing in our common fate: not only pain, separation and death, but pain and frustration associated with, indeed often springing from, the most necessary, even the highest, forms of human potential. The second is recognized in experience, but not often clearly formulated. It is that tragedy is both desolating and life-enhancing. The point was made many years ago by W. Macneile Dixon in his little book, *Tragedy*, when he objected to Aristotle's famous remark that tragedy "through pity and fear ... effects a proper purgation of these and such like emotions". Dixon's comment was: "Pity and fear — how do, or how can, these emotions provide the lofty satisfactions of tragedy? There is a gap in the argument. [Aristotle] would have this medicine restore us to the normal, to health, but surely it is an elixir, not a remedy, and the function of tragedy is to exalt, not to cure us". I think this paradoxical effect is partly a matter of the energy of the artist's creating mind. But, also, our own concentration on a particular figure or a particular situation, as we respond to the energies

*This lecture was delivered by the distinguished scholar and critic, L.C. Knights, at the University of Groningen and the Vrije Universiteit of Amsterdam, October-November 1978.

DRAMA
in
DQR

shaping a particular work, engages us too fully to allow generalised or self-regarding lamentation. In meeting the demand for our deepest personal involvement the "merely personal" is taken up into a more-than-personal meaning: when our everyday selves are overwhelmed, we find — if only by glimpses — more of ourselves. I hope this doesn't sound too blandly academic. A great tragedy is far from consoling; and it is only when we allow ourselves to *feel* it, to be overwhelmed by it — when, as Keats said of his reading of *King Lear*, we have burnt our way through it — that we can see how the death-centred makes for life.

There is one more preliminary thing to say. It is a commonplace that great works of art have multiple meanings. Within definable limits they "mean" something different to each individual reader or spectator, as they must necessarily and more markedly to each generation of readers. They are "infinitely explorable" and even when we guard against the temptation to impose contemporary interests simply because they are contemporary, they have an uncanny power to "grow" as fresh minds and imaginations apprehend them.

Hamlet, we know from experience, is a great tragedy. As we watch or read, it grips and enthrals us. It also exhibits with peculiar fulness that tricky possibility of multiple meanings that I have referred to. If the critic sees himself represented anywhere in the play it is surely in the person of the Second Gravedigger as he ponders the riddle propounded by his fellow, "Who builds stronger than a mason, a shipwright, or a carpenter?"

> *First Gravedigger.* Ay, tell me that and unyoke.
> *Second Gravedigger.* Marry, now I can tell.
> *First Gravedigger.* To't.
> *Second Gravedigger.* Mass, I cannot tell.

The subtitle of the Olivier film version of the play was, "The tragedy of a man who could not make up his mind". The American critic, Stephen Booth, parodies this when he calls it, "the tragedy of an audience that cannot make up its mind". ("On the Value of *Hamlet*", in *Reinterpretations of Elizabethan Drama*, ed. Norman Rabkin). In the play, as he sees it, expectations are set up and their satisfaction is delayed or defeated; the audience is invited to go in one direction and finds it is going in another; there is coherence and incoherence. Even on the nature of the hero the play gives grounds for conflicting and contradictory estimations, from Goethe's "lovely, pure, noble and most moral nature, without the strength of nerve that makes a hero", or Dover Wilson's "the most adorable of heroes", to Salvador de Madariaga's description of the prince as a ruthless, and foul-mouthed, Elizabethan egoist.

What, then, can the critic usefully say about such a play, especially within the confines of a lecture of fifty minutes? Well, he can give some extremely good advice: see the play as often as possible (even an indifferent performance can tell you something), read it and re-read it (sometimes aloud) and, forgetting the professors, make up your own mind. However, it needs no ghost come from the grave, nor a critic come from England, to tell you that. The only other thing he can do, and it is the course I propose to follow here, is to indicate what seem to him the main lines of force governing the construction, the qualities of mind and feeling most insisted on by poetry and action, and leave his auditors to absorb what they will, testing it in their next encounter with the play. No one can tell you "the meaning" of *Hamlet*; and its meaning for you will go on changing as your lives change.

It would be easy to spend an hour talking about the mastery of Shakespeare's opening scenes. *Hamlet* is no exception. Consider the first ten lines or so of Act I, scene i.

Barnardo. Who's there?
Francisco. Nay, answer me. Stand and unfold yourself.
Bernardo. Long live the king!
Francisco. Bernardo?
Bernardo. He.
Francisco. You come most carefully upon your hour.
Bernardo. 'Tis now struck twelve, get thee to bed, Francisco.
Francisco. For this relief much thanks, 'tis bitter cold,
And I am sick at heart.
Barnardo. Have you had quiet guard?
Francisco. Not a mouse stirring.

It is superbly done, and with great economy. In those few lines we are aware of darkness, intense cold, and a complete stillness, broken only by the sharp exchanges of the men; there is a sense of foreboding, uncertainty and nerves at stretch, — all of which, as so often in Shakespeare, will carry forward to more than some immediate cause. In its sense of darkness, the impenetrable, the opening strikes the keynote of the play, and we should remember it when, in the very next scene, we watch a well-lighted indoor scene in which the world's business is briskly transacted.

From this first scene, with its Ghost, onwards, our attention is constantly directed towards death. It's not only that eight persons are killed in the course of the play's action: death is talked about — "From the first corse till he that died today" — brooded on, made the subject of jest and speculation. The play insists on it, and any full imaginative engagement must surely make us feel that Fortinbras' words at the end,

> O proud Death!
> What feast is toward in thine eternal cell,

refers to more than the heap of bodies on the stage, As C.S. Lewis has well said (in his British Academy Lecture, *Hamlet: the Prince or the Poem?*), whereas in the other tragedies plenty of people are concerned with dying, "no one thinks, in these plays, of being dead. In *Hamlet* we are thinking about it all the time, whether in terms of the soul's destiny or of the body's". It is against this background of dark uncertainty — one that doesn't allow of any shilly-shallying: "There is no shuffling; there the action lies in his true nature" — that the characters are shown as making their choices and asserting their values.

That, I think, is obvious. What is not so often noticed is the presence and pressure not only of the surrounding unknown, but of the dead past. In the first scene, between the first and the second appearance of the Ghost, there is a discussion of some sixty lines concerning the warlike preparations now going on in Denmark. Sixty lines is rather a lot, especially from a dramatist who knew the value of economy; and I suggest that one purpose of this inset history is to make us aware of something in the nature of the society to which all the characters belong. It is, quite simply, a story of violence meeting violence in a kind of chain reaction: Old Fortinbras ("prick'd on by a most emulate pride") challenges Old Hamlet; Old Hamlet kills him; Young Fortinbras plans to recover his father's lands "by strong hand / And terms compulsative": that is why he has "Shark'd up a list of lawless resolutes", and why, in turn, there is this "post-haste and rummage" in Denmark. It seems deliberate, for it is echoed in the speech that the First Player delivers to give Hamlet "a taste of his quality". That speech is about Pyrrhus' killing of Priam — Pyrrhus, son of the dead Achilles, another son avenging his father — and the killing is described in some detail: if this is "aroused vengeance" it is pretty horrible. And finally, leaving out for the moment the ancestral voice that calls on Hamlet to revenge, there is another avenger, the son of a murdered father, who fully endorses the morality of an eye for an eye: Laertes'

What would you undertake [the King asks him]
To show yourself your father's son in deed
More than in words?
Laertes. To cut his throat i' the church.
King. No place, indeed, should murder sanctuarize;
Revenge should have no bounds.

Since the speaker of the last lines is King Claudius, Shakespeare's judgment on revenge could hardly be clearer; but it is to revenge that that very ambivalent figure, the Ghost, commands Hamlet.

But this is to anticipate. We have still to bring into view the moral opacity of the world of which Hamlet is conscious from the beginning, — a metaphorical darkness, both in the sense of corruption, and in the sense that the characters are opaque to each other. We all know Hamlet's first soliloquy, "O! that this too too sullied flesh would melt ...". The world is "an unweeded garden / That grows to seed; things rank and gross in nature / Possess it merely". His revulsion of course springs from the very quick remarriage of his mother (he doesn't yet know of his father's murder): there's no need, here, to invoke an Oedipus complex — what he mourns is the apparent meaninglessness of human affection. Apart from Horatio, there is *no one* in his world whom he can trust. What is presented on the stage is a world where there is very little real communication; words are used, not to communicate but to conceal, to manipulate, or to keep at a distance. Nothing is clear and open; everything is dark and opaque. And since there is so little openness, there is naturally a great deal of prying and spying. To quote C.S. Lewis again: "The characters are all watching one another, forming theories about one another, listening, contriving, full of anxiety .... The world of *Hamlet* is a world where one has lost one's way", Hamlet, to sum up this rather lengthy introduction, is surrounded by darkness, and he is virtually alone. As the speaker of Pasternak's poem, "Hamlet", says:

I am alone; all round me drowns in falsehood:
Life is not a walk across a field.

How alone Hamlet is we can see if we now look, rather quickly, at the play's first movement, Act I, scene i to Act II, scene ii.

I,i.	The battlements. The soldiers tell Horatio and Barnardo about the Ghost. The Ghost makes its first appearance.
I,ii.	The King in Council transacts state affairs. Hamlet is informed of the Ghost's appearance.
I,iii.	Laertes gives moral advice to Ophelia, and Polonius gives moral advice to both his children.
I,iv, v	On the battlements (or, for v, somewhere outside the main building of the castle). Hamlet encounters the Ghost.
II,i.	Polonius instructs Reynaldo to spy on Laertes, and learns from Ophelia of Hamlet's disturbed state.

What you have here is a series of contrasts. Three scenes are, presumably, inside, and three are outside. On the one hand is the public, social and, apparently, firmly estabished world of King Claudius' court, — a world of imposing surfaces and considerable self-assurance. ("Hath there been such a time, I'd fain know that, / That I have positively said ''tis so', / When it proved otherwise?", as Polonius is to say later.) On the other hand there is an altogether different kind of world. Shall we say tentatively that the difference is between a *closed* (or apparently closed) world and an *exposed* world? Let us look at this first sequence in a little more detail, whilst on the way picking up some hints of the play's later development.

I have already spoken of the first scene. The second, which opens with a king and his councillors transacting public business, is certainly an effective contrast to the first. But just as the first scene had, as it were, a dimension added to it by a deliberate reference to public affairs, so this second scene is shot through with disturbing implications. As the focus of attention moves from Claudius, who dominates the opening, to Hamlet, who dominates the close, it begins to appear that the world of settled forms is not as solidly established as it seems. Nothing could be further from the soldiers' tensed-up apprehensiveness in "the dead vast and middle of the night" than Claudius' unruffled efficiency in dealing with a world where there may be difficulties, but there are certainly no doubts. His own accession and marriage to his brother's widow, the warlike preparations of Young Fortinbras and the embassy to Norway, Laertes' petition to return to Paris — all are dealt with coolly and in order: "Now follows what you know .... So much for him .... Thus much the business is". The chairman of the firm is well in control of the meeting. Even the inconvenient fact of death — since Hamlet insists on calling attention to it — can be disposed of without fuss as "what we know must be ... as common as the most vulgar thing to sense". Mourning that goes beyond the timetable, so to speak, is

> a fault to Heaven,
> A fault against the dead, a fault to nature,
> To reason most absurd, whose common theme
> Is death of fathers, and who still hath cried,
> From the first corse till he that died to-day,
> "This must be so".

The king perhaps goes on a trifle too long; but certainly in a world of such reasonableness no one need pause to reflect that the first corpse was Abel's, killed by his brother, or to bring home to himself with any vividness that even a king may go on progress through the guts of a beggar.

A main purpose of this second scene is, I take it, to establish a solid-seeming world. Not that we, the audience, are allowed to take it entirely as it takes itself. If the first scene has really touched our imaginations we are not likely to forget the surrounding darkness; and although this awareness may only be on the fringes of our consciousness, there is something in the *tone* of Claudius' first speech — not only the oily rhythms but the glib patterning of his public rhetoric — that prompts us to some questioning of this assured appearance. The questioning is sharpened by Hamlet's conspicuous aloofness from the rest, and by his ambiguous answers and asides. And of course, with his first soliloquy and the news of the Ghost brought by Horatio, questioning gives way to something more positively critical, even though we are not yet sure of the weight to be given to Hamlet's all-embracing disgust and world-weariness. For the moment I only want to notice that in two scenes Shakespeare has established a firm dramatic pattern. Thrown into relief against a world of undefined fears is an apparently everyday world going about its business. And against this, in turn, is an isolated figure who is clearly the bearer of a consciousness far more extensive ("I have that within which passeth show") than that of any of the persons who surround him.

Hamlet of course is the central consciousness of the play, — though that does not mean that our interest is centred on him alone — and at the end of scene ii our curiosity and interest are clearly directed to what will happen when he meets the Ghost: —

> My father's spirit in arms! all is not well:
> I doubt some foul play: would the night were come.

These are almost the last words of the scene. But instead of sweeping us straight on to the expected encounter, Shakespeare delays the action for a domestic scene exhibiting the *mores* of the Polonius family. Laertes, off to Paris, says goodbye to his sister and gives her some good advice; Polonius performs the same service for his son — though *his* little sermon is couched in more general terms: it is, I am afraid we have to assume, a summing-up of what the old man has learnt from his life; and then, alone with Ophelia, he reinforces the lesson of her careful brother. All this is obviously necessary for the plot: we learn that Hamlet has declared himself in love with Ophelia; Polonius commands her to have nothing more to do with him; and the breaking off of this relationship will have consequences that we shall see. But as usual, besides what is done, there is the manner of the doing. Laertes' and Polonius' coarse *certainty* about the ways of the world is brought to bear, vigorously and at length, on Ophelia's *uncertainty*. Neither can see in Hamlet's attention to the girl anything more than an attempted seduction. It doesn't seem too much to say that what we have here is a picture of experience poisoning innocence, and any good production would bring out the poignancy of Ophelia's reply to her brother's worldly-wise definition of Hamlet's love as "trifling ... a fashion and a toy in blood": — "No more than so?", she says. But neither father nor son knows anything about love: "Affection!", says Polonius, "Pooh!". In essential ways Ophelia is as isolated in her world as Hamlet is in his. Her only guide-line is the apparently authoritative command to listen to the voice of the past — the crudely generalising voice of experience — and to deny life. Perhaps Shakespeare wants to suggest to us that the voice of experience is not always an entirely reliable guide. He is certainly suggesting something that we need to keep in mind, since as we shall see, he himself did.

The scene, then, has considerable weight, and we should remember from it rather more than Polonius' celebrated maxims. Both Polonius and Laertes represent the ethos of that Denmark that will soon appear to Hamlet as "a prison", — and it's pretty unpleasant. In relation to the dramatic pattern that is beginning to be established we can say that they express the crude and easy *certainty* of the worldly-wise, — something that will appear as rather more than a mere foil for Hamlet's doubt and uncertainty. Polonius, like Laertes, has a great belief in the well-tried formulas of his world — "these few precepts in thy memory / Look thou character" — and they are mostly directed to ways of *not* risking the self in any kind of genuine expression: "Give thy thoughts no tongue ... Give every man thine ear, but few thy voice". On the art of succeeding without too much risk Polonius may perhaps be taken as an authority. The limits of his kind of awareness of the world Shakespeare indicates clearly by the ironies.

> Costly thy habit as thy purse can buy,
> But not expressed in fancy; rich, not gaudy;
> For the apparel oft proclaims the man.

This in a play in which at least six of the major characters wear an apparel — metaphorically speaking — that does *not* proclaim them! The supreme irony is however reserved for Polonius' peroration. "This above all: to thine own self be true ...." What does it mean, to be true to the self? What, for that matter, is the self? Although these are questions that Hamlet might ask, Polonius certainly will not see the need to ask them. And it is this kind of obliviousness that makes the dialogue of brother and sister, of father and daughter (if we call it a dialogue) represent an almost complete breakdown of communication, for whatever else Polonius and Laertes may be doing they are certainly not communicating with Ophelia. And in this, which is one reason why the scene is put just where it is, they are representative figures of Hamlet's world. And perhaps this brings out something of what I meant to convey when I quoted Pasternak's poem: "I am alone; all round me drowns in falsehood".

The hero of this play is, then, very much a solitary consciousness confronted by darkness, by words that don't give clear answers. There is the darkness out of which we emerge, and to which we return, in the words of Gerard Manley Hopkins, the "Womb of all, home of all, hearse of all, night". There is, metaphorically speaking moral darkness, ranging from murder and betrayal and treachery to obtuseness and superficiality. There is also the opacity of persons to each other. We often don't know what, or how much, to believe; and it is perhaps worth remarking here that in *Hamlet*, more than in any other Shakespearean tragedy, crucial events (and the nature of those events) are given in reports that there is no way of checking by what we actually see or by the reports of other characters: examples are the Ghost's report of the manner of his death, and of his own qualities, Ophelia's account of Hamlet's distracted visit to her and Gertrude's description of the manner of Ophelia's death, and Hamlet's own account of his mother's sensuality. If there were time we should pay more than passing attention to the Ghost. Eleanore Prosser, in her book, *Hamlet and Revenge* has shown that in the light of Elizabethan beliefs the apparition of Hamlet Senior fails all the tests for "an honest ghost". But there is no need to bring in scholarly information here; all we need to do is to attend to the play; and I should claim that what the Ghost says and commands, the way he says it, and the consequences of what he says, make it clear that there is no question of any straightforward endorsement. Hamlet did well to question its credentials.

How does Hamlet face this world? Our interest in *that*, and it is very much an *engaged* interest, is what carries us forward through the play. He is given plenty of opportunities of explaining himself to us, in six major soliloquies, or virtual soliloquies. [I,ii, "O that this too too sullied flesh ..."; II,ii, "Oh what a rogue and peasant slave ..."; III,i, "To be, or not to be"; III,ii, " 'Tis now the very witching time of night"; III,iii, "Now might I do it pat ..."; IV, iv, "How all occasions do inform against me ..."]

Most of these have a common characteristic: they all consist of violent over-simplifications: there is indeed often an element of play-acting — you see it in the language — as Hamlet tries on one role after another, none of them very satisfactory. Cumulatively they present an impressive image of a trapped consciousness, so that we can apply to Hamlet the words that Claudius uses of himself: "O limed soul, that struggling to be free / Art more engaged". If you think this is arbitrary, I would ask you to read aloud such things as the Hecuba speech (after the first meeting with the Players), or the "Now could I drink hot blood" one (after the success of the Mouse-trap), and contrast them with the free run, the darting enjoyment and intelligence displayed when Hamlet meets Rosencrantz and Guildenstern, before he has begun to suspect them, or his greeting of the Players and the subsequent theatre talk.

There is, however, one soliloquy to which the term over-simplification very obviously does not apply. I mean of course the famous soliloquy in III,i, which occurs between the planning of the Mouse-trap play and its performance, and which is thrown into relief by the fact that it is spoken in the context of Polonius' little plot to make Hamlet reveal himself to Ophelia. Of the "To be or not to be" soliloquy it is difficult to speak, partly because it is so well known that the words tend to slip over the surface of our minds without engaging; partly of course because it *is* difficult. Some things however can usefully be said. One is that the speech will never yield its meaning to paraphrase, simply because, like other Shakespearean speeches at moments of high tension, it represents not "thought" but thought still emerging from the matrix of feeling. The difficulties are clear from the start.

> To be, or not to be, that is the question,
> Whether 'tis nobler in the mind to suffer
> The slings and arrows of outrageous fortune,
> Or to take arms against a sea of troubles,
> And by opposing, end them, to die to sleep ....

We can of course take "To be or not to be" as referring to Hamlet's contemplated action against the king: is that to be, to take place, or not? On that reading, "that is the question" refers both backwards and forwards, so that "whether 'tis nobler ... to suffer ... or to take arms" is parallel to, and an expansion of, the alternatives offered in "To be, or not to be". But it is also possible to take the opening phrase absolutely, as arising from the depths of Hamlet's consciousness, and referring to the problem of what it means in any full and absolute sense "to be". That, I take it, is the hidden centre of the play: that, as Hamlet says, is the question, — and it is so whether we believe that the blows of fortune must be endured, or whether we think it better actively to combat evil, a course which, as he goes on to say, is likely to involve his own death. From this point on, thoughts of killing the king, of suicide, of the attractiveness of death, which is yet feared, and of the horrors of life, are carried on a current of deep feeling with many eddies, but of which the main direction is clear. As John Vyvyan has said, in his book, *The Shakespearean Ethic*, "Throughout the long soliloquy, every idea is negative". It doesn't matter that in Hamlet's mind the thought of suicide merges with the thought of killing the king: what matters is the quite unambiguous sense of health giving way to disease, of a loss of purpose and a lapsing from all positive direction. What the soliloquy does in fact is to bring to a head our recognition of the dependence of thought and decision on deeper levels of consciousness, and to make plain beyond all doubt that the set of Hamlet's consciousness is towards a region where no resolution is possible at all. The soliloquy, we recall, is immediately followed b y the encounter with Ophelia, where Hamlet wounds the person actually present to him by substituting for her a fantasy projection of female sexuality: it is a telling comment on what we have just heard, for as Vyvyan says, the dialogue with Ophelia "is really a continuation of the death theme; indeed, it is more, it is part of the long-drawn act of spiritual suicide".

As I see it, *Hamlet* is a moving dramatic image of a man, a consciousness, that is trapped, partly by circumstances, the people around him, the evil and obtuseness that make the whole world seem an unweeded garden, but partly also by the set of his own consciousness, his obsessive preoccupation with all those negatives of death and evil which therefore find a mirror or echo in himself, the "o'ergrowth of some complexion", the "dram of evil" that infects the whole "noble substance". If this is so it certainly explains something of thc play's universal appeal. *Hamlet* is an imaginative exploration of attitudes that represent very real possibilities for all of us.

At this stage we had better remind ourselves that *Hamlet* is not a moral problem, it is a play; and our sense of the moral issues involved depends on our full engagement with the particular structure of action that Shakespeare puts before us. The play's last movement (to which I now turn) is as close-knit and purposeful as the opening movement to which we gave so much attention. In Act IV, after the success of the Mouse-trap, Hamlet's interview with his mother and the killing of Polonius, Hamlet is shipped to England. From the end of Act IV, scene iv to Act V, scene i — that is, for three scenes — Hamlet is absent from the stage, but he is kept very much in our minds, and I mean by something much more than the messages received by the King and Horatio to say that he has returned to Denmark. IV,v and IV,iii, interrupted only by a short scene in which Horatio reads aloud Hamlet's letter about his escape, are concerned with the madness and then the reported death of Ophelia, the return of Laertes and his determination to revenge the death of his father. By the end of IV,vii, all is set for the final action, the treacherous duel in which Hamlet, so Claudius and Laertes agree, can finally be disposed of.

The plotting is masterly, but caught up as we are bound to be in the action, the quick movements of events, the play asks our attention for a good deal more. I said that although Hamlet is absent from the stage he is kept in our minds by more than the talk about him or the messages received from him: he is kept in our minds by Ophelia and by Laertes. Ophelia is deranged in fact, as Hamlet had half-pretended to be, by the murder of a father whom her world had agreed to dispose of "in hugger-mugger" — another corpse, like the elder Hamlet's, "which bewept to the grave did not go" — by the verbal sexual assaults of someone close to her affection, as we see plainly enough from her songs, and by the fact that, like Hamlet, she is emotionally isolated and thrust back on herself: her madness too is an emphatic instance of that failure of real communication that is so marked a feature of the play. Ophelia's mad talk and her snatches of song, however, are not only touching in their bewildered helplessness. I do not mean that her words are a code to be broken, only that these stray wisps of thought and feeling are in fact subtly related to the body of the play. Her distribution of different flowers to the King and Queen and Laertes has long been seen as significant, though I am not sure that all the overtones have been recognized. Fennel and columbines, flattery and cuckoldry, are clearly for the King; the rue she keeps for herself is herb of grace, or sorrow; as given to the Queen — "with a difference" — it is repentance. But what of the rosemary, used, we are told, as a symbol of remembrance both at weddings and funerals? "There's rosemary, that's for remembrance; pray you, love, remember." That, surely, is for Laertes, whose last words before he left her had been, "Remember well What I have said to you", namely, that love was dangerous. And behind this we may perhaps hear, though Ophelia cannot, the further echo of the Ghost's command to Hamlet, "Adieu, adieu, adieu! remember me". Perhaps indeed we may say that in this play there has been too much remembering of the wrong kind — the remembering of commands to repeat the sterile patterns of the past — and too little remembering of the right kind, the kind, for example, that allows the expression of grief for the dead in natural human mourning. "I would give you some violets," says Ophelia — violets are for faithfulness — "but they withered all when my father died." They had of course withered long before then.

As for Laertes, I have already spoken of him as contrast and parallel for Hamlet. In his fiery impetuosity he is not only a foil for the Prince, he is also, as John Vyvyan says, "Hamlet's deadly twin". He embodies that total commitment to revenge to which Hamlet has tried to bend his will:

> To hell, allegiance! vows, to the blackest devil!
> Conscience and grace to the profoundest pit!
> I dare damnation. To this point I stand,
> That both the worlds I give to negligence,
> Let come what comes; only I'll be revenged
> Most throughly for my father.

Those who think that Hamlet had only to obey the Ghost's commands in order to right the wrongs of Denmark should perhaps ask themselves whether they would really wish Hamlet to reduce him to that.

When we next see Hamlet it is in the graveyard, where the two Clowns are preparing Ophelia's grave. Hamlet's long exchange with the gravediggers and his meditation on death envisaged as mere physical corruption, are of course followed by the sudden shock of his recognition that the burial is Ophelia's, then the maimed rites of her funeral, and the quarrel and boasting of Hamlet and Laertes beside her grave. What you can call the thematic importance of this scene is very obvious indeed: it is a variation on the theme of death that runs throughout the play:

> Imperious Caesar, dead and turn'd to clay,
> Might stop a hole to keep the wind away.

But there is more to it than this. Even the conversation of the Clowns, about when a half-sought death is to be counted as suicide, is not intended simply to raise a few laughs at their malapropisms. It is partly, I suppose, a reminder of the way life goes on, fairly indifferent, in spite of tragedy. But it is the indifference that is the point. The Clowns and Osric come from opposite ends of the social scale; but like Osric, they have their own pedantry; their words no more engage with reality than his, and the quasi-legal logic-chopping is no more relevant to the real suffering of Ophelia than the Queen's elegiac distancing of her death, or the priest's cold religious legalism, or, we may add, the ranting of Hamlet in, or beside, Ophelia's grave. In a play so largely about the failure of real communication, these particular variations should not go unnoticed.

There remains the problem of the play's end. I am aware that there is something almost ludicrous in reducing to a problem an experience of tragedy so deeply moving. But in Shakespeare's tragic art mind and feeling go together; feeling, allied with intelligence and understanding, leads us towards that more inclusive grasp of things for which we use the name imagination. And in the play's last scene there seems some ambiguity and uncertainty of feeling that we must at least try to resolve.

The scene opens with Hamlet's rehearsal to Horatio of how he escaped the King's plot on his life, and sent Rosencrantz and Guildenstern on their way to an unsuspected death in England, "not shriving them allowed" — "Why man, they did make love to this employment; They are not near my conscience". In all this he sees "a divinity that shapes our ends", and "heaven ordinant", though these phrases seem to refer to a pagan Fortune rather than to have any kind of Christian meaning. I don't suppose many readers or spectators before Tom Stoppard have felt much concern for the fate of these "baser natures" who came "between the pass and fell incensed points / Of mighty opposites". But in serving to remind us of how completely Hamlet is dedicated to revenge, no matter what the cost to anybody like Rosencrantz and Guildenstern, it is an odd prelude to what follows. Hamlet, you remember, — it is part of the King's plot — is challenged to a duel with Laertes. Accepting the challenge, he is left alone for a few minutes with Horatio.

Horatio. You will lose this wager, my lord.

Hamlet. I do not think so. Since he went into France, I have been in continual practice. I shall win at the odds; but thou wouldst not think how ill all's here about my heart - but it is no matter.

Horatio. Nay, good my lord —

Hamlet. It is but foolery, but it is such a kind of gain-giving as would perhaps trouble a woman.

Horatio. If your mind dislike any thing, obey it. I will forestall their repair hither, and say you are not fit.

Hamlet. Not a whit, we defy augury. There is special providence in the fall of a sparrow. If it be now, 'tis not to come — if it be not to come, it will be now — if it be not now, yet it will come — the readiness is all. Since no man, of aught he leaves, knows what is't to leave betimes, let be.

Those last words have a noble, haunting quality, and we certainly respond favourably to them; but to say with C.S. Lewis that Hamlet has now found the way that he had lost, seems to me to oversimplify something very complex. Hamlet's words, taken in isolation, move us to admiration for the way in which "the 'I' in the individual" (Turgenev's phrase) has yielded to a more impersonal opennes to life and fate. But in context, when we respond, as we must, to the varying pressures that the play has built up, the varying movements of sympathy and recoil, then I think we must take the lines, not as indicating that Hamlet has come through his ordeal and is now wholly self-possessed, but as the paradoxical recognition of a truth glimpsed in defeat.

It is the same at the end, when Hamlet — his imposed task finally accomplished, though at the cost of six lives besides Claudius' and his own — receives from Horatio on the one hand and from the newly arrived Fortinbras on the other, a final tribute, each of which corresponds to something we have deeply felt in the progress of the play.

Horatio Now cracks a noble heart. Good night, sweet prince,
And flights of angels sing thee to thy rest!

And

Fortinbras Let four captains
Bear Hamlet, like a soldier, to the stage;
For he was likely, had he been put on,
To have proved most royally: and for his passage,
The soldier's music and the rites of war
Speak loudly for him ...
Go, bid the soldiers shoot.

Since Shakespeare is asking us to extend our imaginations rather beyond their usual bounds, no simple formula will serve us here. Hamlet both is, and is not, the "sweet prince" of Horatio's touching valediction. So too, although we may agree with Fortinbras that there was that in Hamlet that could "have proved most royally", I don't see that we can agree with Helen Gardner when she tells us that "the soldiers' music and the rites of war", and the final volley, endorse the play's presentation of an heroic Hamlet. One mustn't cheapen things, and sometimes it is too easy to invoke irony to suit one's own tastes. But Shakespeare was a master of a very serious, non-belittling, irony — as you see not only at the end of *Richard II* and *1 Henry IV* but at the end of a great tragedy like *Coriolanus*. And in *Hamlet* it is, after all, Fortinbras who is left in command: Fortinbras who we were told in the first scene was "of unimproved mettle hot and full", and whose values have been so clearly shown as directly opposed to all that was best in Hamlet's own code. To all that was best, but not all: for Hamlet, at the mercy of pressures and circumstances that the play has revealed, had tried to turn himself into conventional man. That, even more than his own death, is his tragedy. But even as we say that we must beware of moralizing an experience, which calls for judgement, centainly, though it is Hamlet himself or Shakespeare speaking through Hamlet, who clarifies whatever standards of judgment we may feel bound to apply. But we are called on for something more than that: we are called on to stretch our imaginations in facing fully a very "special case". To which it is necessary to add rather quickly that it is a tragedy so universalized by the pressure of Shakespeare's art that we cannot stand aloof from it and merely watch it: too many aspects of our own lives are reflected there.

There is now a final word. *Hamlet*, like all great tragedies, makes us confront not a problem but a mystery. A problem can be solved; a mystery can only be faced and, in its tragic implications, endured. But in facing and enduring comes that strange quickening of the sense of life that I began by speaking of. It is, I think, more than stoic endurance, though the ability to endure is indeed strengthened in us by the great tragic dramatists. It is, rather, a sense of human potential discovered in defeat. At all events we can only speak of *Hamlet*, or even of *King Lear*, where, at the end, "All's cheerless, dark and deadly", — we can only speak of these plays as pessimistic if we ignore the creative vitality of the mind and imagination that made them.

L.C. Knights

LITERARY CRITICISM AND LINGUISTIC DESCRIPTION

Ever since linguistics began to take an interest in the language of literature, the relation between critic and linguist, in the English-speaking world, has tended to be an uneasy one of mutual distrust rather than mutual respect. True, linguists have been increasingly active in this area, and there have been one or two successes, such as the conversion of I. A. Richards to the value of linguistic analysis through the study of Shakespeare's "Sonnet 129" by Jakobson and Jones.[1] Yet the literary critic is still typically cast in the role of the coy bride-to-be, who rejects the advances of the linguistic bridegroom, and his promises of a fruitful union between the two disciplines. In the USA, the course of this unhappy liaison has been charted (from an antilinguistic point of view) by W. Youngren, in his book *Linguistics, Semantics, and Criticism,*[2] and in the United Kingdom, it can be traced most openly in the dispute between F. W. Bateson (for the critics) and R. Fowler (for the linguists) in the pages of *Essays in Criticism,* 1967-8,[3] a dispute sparked off by a review in that journal of Fowler's volume *Essays on Style and Language.*

My aim here will be to argue that the linguist-critic disputes over the linguistic analysis of literary texts have resulted from false

1. Richards (1970: 549) describes Jakobson and Jones's analysis of Shakespeare's "Sonnet 129" as "what may very likely prove a landmark in the long-awaited approach of descriptive linguistics to the account of poetry".

2. Youngren (1970: 141): "This brief survey of recent attempts to apply linguistics to criticism will do to show not only the failure of these writers to come up with anything useful, but also the candour with which they have criticised each other...".

3. The main contributions to this debate are reprinted as Chapters 4-6 in Fowler (1971).

assumptions, by members of both parties, about the theoretical relation between the two disciplines. I shall try to dispel this confusion, and to clarify the way in which linguistics may be said to contribute to the study of literature, by addressing myself to the following questions:

(a) What is the nature of literary critical statements about a literary text?

(b) What is the nature of linguistic statements about a literary text?

(c) In what sense can linguistic statements be said to *explain* or *support* critical statements?

To illustrate the argument, I shall take as an example of literary critical discussion a well-known essay by F. R. Leavis on the poetry of Keats, concentrating on Leavis's treatment of the first stanza of the "Ode to a Nightingale";[4] this discussion I shall relate to the sort of statements one can make about the stanza from a stylistic point of view.

I shall not attempt to rehearse here the various arguments about the merits or demerits of "the New Stylistics".[5] The formulation of the above questions, however, disposes of one unnecessary source of acrimony: the tendency to think of linguists and critics as two separate breeds of scholar, separated by their differences of temperament and methodology. As soon as we think of "linguistic statements" and "critical statements" rather than "statements by linguists" and "statements by critics", we realise that "critic" and "linguist" are two roles that may be assumed by the same person: any critic who turns his attention to linguistic detail can scarcely avoid acting as a linguist (however tentatively or imperfectly); likewise, any linguist who turns his attention to the interpretation and evaluation of a work of literature can scarcely avoid acting as his own critic (however tentatively or imperfectly). The question

4. Leavis (1936), Chapter 7 "Keats", especially pp. 244-50.

5. The term "The New Stylistics" (which forms the title of the introductory chapter of Fowler, 1975) is a useful one for referring to the cumulative body of writings applying the techniques of linguistics to literature over the last twenty years. As Fowler points out, however, this term does not designate a unified "school of thought". Fowler's chapter gives a brief review of the characteristics of "the New Stylistics", and of the history of its relationship with literary scholarship. Earlier treatments of the same subject are given in the introductions to Fowler (1966) and Fowler (1971).

is: how do linguistic statements and critical statements interrelate, and what is the purpose of their interrelation?

1. *The Nature of Critical Statements*

It will be generally agreed that the function of literary criticism is to *interpret* and *evaluate* literature, or a literary work. In *interpreting,* the critic arrives, both from linguistic evidence, and from knowledge of extralinguistic background, at an assessment of the meaning of a work, by showing the interrelations between the meanings of its parts and elements. In *evaluating*, the critic uses his interpretation in arriving at a verdict about the merit of the work. Interpretation and evaluation are often in practice difficult to separate; we might, indeed, subsume the two activities under the single heading of literary *appreciation.* The two activities seem, indeed, to fuse in the use of "aesthetic terms" (such as *elegant, sad, delicate, stately, unity, atmosphere, enchantment, expressive, buoyant*) which make up an important part of the vocabulary of literary criticism.

The notion of "aesthetic term" I understand in the sense that has been explained by the philosopher Frank Sibley.[6] Sibley regards aesthetic terms as terms which require, for their correct application, taste, discrimination, and judgment. Thus to call a painting "elegant", "forceful", "evocative", etc. is to exercise discriminatory judgment in a way that is not required for the description of a painting as "pale in colour", "executed with thick brush strokes", "composed of straight lines", etc. The description of a painting's mere visual appearance can be carried out by the use of non-aesthetic terms. Sibley points out that a critic often feels the need to explain, or in some sense justify, his use of aesthetic terms, by the use of non-aesthetic terms. Thus he may argue that a piece of music is "lugubrious" *because* it is written in a minor key and moves at a slow tempo. But this use of the word *because* requires careful scrutiny: one cannot do more than partially define an aesthetic term by means of non-aesthetic terms, nor can one predict with certainty, from the observation of non-aesthetic qualities in a work, the applicability of an aesthetic term.

6. Three papers by Sibley (1959, 1965, 1968) explore the nature of aesthetic concepts and the meaning of aesthetic terms and statements.

Thus a slow piece of music written in a minor key may well strike one as "grand", "sublime", or "stately", rather than "lugubrious". The most one can do is to establish a *typical* dependence of an aesthetic term on a particular non-aesthetic term or combination of non-aesthetic terms ("A sad piece of music is typically slow and in a minor key"). Another important point made in Sibley's account of aesthetic concepts is that "the particular aesthetic character of something may be said to result from the *totality* of its relevant non-aesthetic characteristics".[7] What this implies is that aesthetic appreciation and its "explanation" in terms of non-aesthetic description must be undertaken anew for each work studied: one cannot mechanically generalise on the aesthetic value of non-aesthetic features from one work to another. This point of view finds an echo in the critic's instinct to regard each work as a particular unity, which must be explicated in its own terms.

The activity of criticism, of course, involves much more than the appreciation of the character of a work by means of aesthetic terms. A critic may use aesthetic terms to support a pure value judgment (e.g. because a drawing is "balanced" and "graceful", he may argue that it is "good"); a critic's endeavour to persuade the reader of a work's artistic character may involve paraphrases or metaphorical explanations of its meaning, etc. But whatever else may be involved in criticism it can scarcely be denied that criticism typically involves an attempt to support an aesthetic judgment by *reasoned argument*, and that an important part of this argument is the appeal to non-aesthetic terms as a justification for the use of aesthetic terms. In certain schools of English literary criticism, notably the "Cambridge critics" in England and the "New Critics" in the U.S.A., the type of argument which relates aesthetic appreciation to the observed properties of the text is particularly prominent. We may say that an explanation or justification of aesthetic statements in terms of non-aesthetic statements is a "reasoned argument", even though the argument can go no further than pointing out non-aesthetic properties which are *typically* associated, rather than *invariably* associated, with a particular aesthetic effect.

7. Sibley (1965: 138).

2. *The Nature of Linguistic Statements*

How does the distinction between aesthetic terms and non-aesthetic terms (or, correspondingly, between aesthetic statements and non-aesthetic statements) relate to the argument about the value of linguistics to literary criticism? I have discussed Sibley's account at some length, because it is used by Youngren as a means of refuting the claim that linguistics can somehow make the arguments and judgments of the critic more precise. Youngren's contention is that linguists (likewise the philosophical critic I. A. Richards) have wrongly claimed that their formulations can be used to define, in more precise logical, or objective terms, those things which the literary critic is attempting to elucidate or describe. But since, as Sibley shows, there can be no non-aesthetic definition of aesthetic terms, this endeavour (according to Youngren) is a wholly misguided one, based on a "theoretical mistake".

There is no point in resurrecting here the various claims that linguists have made about the value of linguistics as a precise or objective "underpinning" of literary criticism. Such claims have sometimes been made with ill-advised confidence, implying that criticism suffers from excessive impressionism and subjectivity, from which it might be rescued if the objective formulations of the linguist could explicate, or even entirely displace, the subjective statements of the critic. I have no desire to defend such claims. Yet Sibley's account of aesthetic and non-aesthetic terms can, I believe, be used to defend the proper role of linguistics in critical theory. My argument depends on first of all clarifying the role of linguistics as that of making non-aesthetic statements about a literary text. In other art forms (such as painting and music) non-aesthetic statements often take the form of statements about the sensory properties of the work (colour, lines, tones, harmonies, melodic progressions, etc.). Such statements can (leaving aside certain philosophical reservations) be directly verified by observation. For literature on the other hand, the medium of a work is linguistic rather than directly sensory. Therefore a non-aesthetic statement about a literary text is, at least in the first instance, a linguistic statement: a statement, for example, about the meaning of a word, about the grammatical structure of a sentence, about a phonological pattern of repetition. To make linguistic statements about a text, one has to have, of course, an adequate linguistic metalanguage; and such a metalanguage gains precision and clarity to the extent that it is based on an adequate linguistic theory. Linguistic statements, so conceived, are not "objective" in the sense that applies to statements about sensory data; indeed, it is debatable whether they should be considered "objective" in any sense; but they are well-defined if the linguistic theory within which they have meaning is well-defined, and justified by empirical criteria. (Linguists can be expected to agree in the main that a phoneme is a phoneme without the exercise of "taste" and "personal judgement"). Therefore there is a valid distinction to be made between the aesthetic statements of criticism and the descriptive statements of linguistics. Sibley's distinction between aesthetic and non-aesthetic concepts can be applied to the distinction between linguistic statements and literary critical statements about a text, and can replace the in some way misleading subjective/objective distinction which has sometimes been applied in this connection.

3. *The Relation between Critical and Linguistic Statements*

Further, we can use this conclusion to justify (although in more guarded terms than has been common) the role of linguistics in critical theory. Criticism involves giving reasons in favour of a given aesthetic appreciation, and since such a reasoned argument can take the form of "explaining" aesthetic terms by means of non-aesthetic terms (which are subject to independent validation), linguistic statements can be regarded as "explanatory" (in the limited sense of "explanatory" already discussed) of critical statements.

In putting this distinction into practice, however, we come across a number of difficulties. One difficulty is that critical discussion is of a "mixed" genre, which involves aesthetic observations and linguistic observations intermingled with many other elements. We have to distil the aesthetic statements which have linguistic relevance from the other factors before we can embark on the task of explaining or supporting them linguistically. It must also be acknowledged that a complete explication of aesthetic terms by means of non-aesthetic terms is out of the question. If Sibley is right in holding that the aesthetic character of a work depends on a *unique* combination of the non-aesthetic features composing the work, all the linguistically inclined critic can do is to point to a number of the non-aesthetic features most prominently contributing to the aesthetic effect.

At the linguistic end, there is a parallel difficulty: a complete linguistic analysis, comprising all the linguistic statements that can be validly made about a text with a given theoretical framework, is a practical impossibility, and in any case most of the linguistic statements that can be made (such as the statement that the word *of* occurs 9 times in the "Ode to a Nightingale") have no conceivable aesthetic relevance. Therefore in practice, a critic's statements about a text are confined to the location of a few *prominent* features of language, and the linguistic analysis that might be used for a more detailed explanation of the critic's observations must in practice confine itself to a selection of the more aesthetically relevant features. We must also notice that linguistic statements can be of a lower or higher order of abstraction: a statement to the effect that there is a pattern of repeated fricatives in a given line is ultimately dependent on a statistical statement about a relative frequency of certain phonemes in this or that part of the poem, or in the language generally.

Without too much simplification, however, we can draw a distinction between three levels of exegesis: the *linguistic level* of non-aesthetic discussion (Level O), the *literary critical level* of aesthetic discussion (Level 2), and an intermediate level (Level 1) which I shall call the *stylistic level*. The stylistic level is the level on which linguistic statements that can be made on Level O (often at a relatively high level of abstraction) are selected for their relevance to the aesthetic discussion on Level 2:

Aesthetic appreciation ↕	Level 2	literary critical
Selection of features relevant to Level 2 from Level O	Level 1	stylistic
↕ Linguistic analysis	Level 0	linguistic

The selection of features for attention on Level 1 need not be based solely on aesthetic considerations. A general theory of stylistics should provide purely formal criteria for identifying features which are likely to have aesthetic implications. For example, the theory of *foregrounding*[8] leads us to assume that a linguistic deviation, or a pattern of repetition, or an abnormal clustering of features, is worth special consideration. In this way, the linguistic analysis may bring to light features which might be overlooked in a critical assessment, but which might, on further investigation, prove to have an important aesthetic function. Thus the diagram above may be interpreted as analogous to Spitzer's "philological circle",[9] in that it implies a "to-and-fro" motion between linguistic analysis and critical appreciation, in which non-aesthetic discussion explains or supports aesthetic discussion, and aesthetic discussion is further elucidated and enriched in the process.

Having attempted to justify the role of linguistics within a general framework of stylistic exegesis, I am aware that scepticism about the value of linguistic analysis cannot be dispelled by theory alone: "by their fruits you shall know them" is a slogan that might fittingly represent the most common objections of critics to linguistics. "Show me an example where stylistics actually tells me something useful, and I shall believe".[10] But often, I think, this sort of question has been posed in the wrong way. A critic, on his home territory of Level 2, finds himself at odds with a linguist who sticks relatively firmly to Level O. He finds that the linguist does not give him any new insight into the aesthetic functions of language, and therefore rejects his painstaking analysis as useless. I feel that in such a situation, both the critic and the linguist may be at fault for not realising that their true meeting ground is neither on Level 2, nor on Level O, but on Level 1. The linguist should realise that "objectivity" and "precision" are not goals in their

8. On the theory of foregrounding, see Mukařowský (1964) and, for a more popular account, Leech (1969: 56-9).

9. Spitzer (1948: 19-20).

10. This attitude is illustrated in the quotation from Youngren in note 2 above, and the following from Bateson (1968: 182): "Ultimately it is, I suggest, because of this verbal immobility, this failure to recognize that in literature language is for the reader a mere preliminary to style – and style itself is a preliminary to the literary response in its fullest sense – that the critic finds so little nourishment in modern linguistics in any of its forms. *Not here, O Apollo, are haunts meet for thee.*"

own right; the critic should realise that linguistic analysis should not be read as if it were criticism manqué.

4. *Leavis on Keats's "Ode to a Nightingale"*

To elucidate the different, but complementary roles of criticism and linguistics, I turn now to an account of Keats's "Ode to a Nightingale" by F. R. Leavis. I shall try to use linguistic observations not to undermine Leavis's account of the poem, but to add to it, as it were, a further dimension of analysis. I suspect that Leavis himself would see little point in this procedure; but it may be of value to other critics, particularly those who are deeply concerned with understanding the linguistic means by which a writer achieves an aesthetic effect, and with the philosophical respectability of critical argument. Leavis's own position can be judged from the following:

> In criticism, of course (one would emphasize), nothing can be proved; there can, in the nature of the case, be no laboratory-demonstration or anything like it. Nevertheless, it is nearly always possible to go further than merely asserting a judgment or inviting agreement with a general account. Commonly one can call attention to this, that, or the other detail by way of making the nature and force of one's judgment plain.[11]

Whereas Leavis is content to "call attention" to certain features of the text, I shall want to go further, and to analyse certain structural aspects of the text, confining myself in the main to the first stanza. I shall concentrate on two particular aesthetic judgments that Leavis makes about the poem:

(a) That it has a "fine organization":

> The rich local concreteness is a local manifestation of an inclusive sureness of grasp in the whole. What the detail exhibits is not merely an extraordinary intensity of realisation, but also an extraordinary rightness and delicacy of touch; a sureness of

11. F. R. Leavis, *Education and the University* (London: Chatto and Windus, 1943; 2nd ed. 1948), p. 74.

touch that is the working of a fine organization. The Ode, that is, has the structure of a fine and complex organism. . . (p. 245).

(b) That this "fine organization" manifests itself in an interplay or balancing of contrasting emotional movements:

In the first stanza, there is a balance of the "death-wish" enunciated in the first four lines against the "life-wish" of the remaining part of the stanza. These are not static moods, but dynamic "motions".

. . . the Ode is, in fact, an extremely subtle and varied interplay of motions, directed now positively, now negatively. . . It starts Lethe-wards, with a heavy drugged movement ("drowsy", "numb", "dull") down to "sunk" . . . In the fifth and sixth lines, with the reiterated "happy", the direction changes, and in the next line comes the key-word, "light-winged". The stanza now moves buoyantly to life, the fresh air, and the sunlight ("shadows numberless") – the thought of happy, self-sufficient vitality provides the impulse. The common medium, so to speak, in which the shift of direction takes place with such unobtrusive effectiveness, the pervasive sense of luxury, is given explicitly in the closing phrase of the stanza, "full-throated ease" (p. 246).

5. *Linguistic Support for Leavis's Appreciation*

Leavis's reference to language confines itself mainly to a noting of words whose symbolic and emotive connotations point to shifts and developments in the unfolding theme. But if a poem is a "fine and complex organism", one would expect to find not just its vocabulary, but its organization on various linguistic levels, working towards the same end. I shall therefore consider aspects of the structure of the stanza mainly on three levels: on the level it will be convenient to call *phonemic* (i.e. that of individual speech sounds); on the *metrical* level,and on the *syntactic* level. I shall finally add a comment or two about contextualisation. On all these levels, I shall try to show that the "change of direction" noted by Leavis after line 4 is reflected in changes of linguistic pattern.

My heart aches, and a drowsy numbness pains
My sense, as though of hemlock I had drunk,
Or emptied some dull opiate to the drains
One minute past, and Lethe-wards had sunk:
'Tis not through envy of thy happy lot,
But being too happy in thine happiness, –
That thou, light-winged Dryad of the trees,
In some melodious plot
Of beechen green, and shadows numberless,
Singest of summer in full-throated ease.

i. *The Phonemic Level*

The transcription I shall use for this analysis assumes that a careful and deliberate style of recitation is appropriate to the *Ode*:[12]

maı hɑ:t eıks ənd ə drɑuzı nʌmnəs peınz 1
mɑı sɛns, əz ðəu əv hemlɒk aı həd drʌŋk, 2
ɔ: ɛmptıd sʌm dʌl əupıət tə ðə dreınz 3
wʌn mınıt pɑ:st, ənd li:θi:wədz həd sʌŋk; 4

---

tız nɒt θru: ɛnvı əv ðaı hæpı lɒt 5
bət bi:ıŋ tʊ: hæpı ın ðaın hæpınɛs, 6
ðət ðɑu, laıt-wıŋıd draıæd əv ðə tri:z 7

- - - - - - - - - - - - - - - - - - - -

ın sʌm mələudjəs plɒt 8
əv bi:tfən gri:n ənd ʃædəuz nʌmbəlɛs, 9
sıŋəst əv sʌmər ın ful-θrəutıd i:z 10

I have marked here not only the major stanza-division after line 4, but a minor division after line 7, since, as Leavis hints, and as further analysis will bear out, the end part of the stanza reasserts, to some extent, the mood of the opening lines: "The common

12. The transcription follows Gimson (1962). The force of the analysis does not, however, depend on the choice of a particular system of transcription. Nor is what I have to say about the sound patterning of the stanza likely to be affected by the choice of a particular historical, dialectal, or stylistic variant in English pronunciation as a "model" for the recitation of the poem. In this context, whether I ought to have attempted a reconstruction of the early nineteenth-century pronunciation of Keats is an interesting debating point, but no more.

medium, . . . in which the shift of direction takes place with such unobtrusive . . . effectiveness, the pervasive sense of luxury, is given in the closing phrase . . . 'full-throated ease'." These two divisions correspond to the most important divisions within the rhyme scheme: *abab cde cde.*

The "drugged" movement towards Lethe in the first four lines is dramatised by a density of certain sounds and sound-combinations:

(a) Frequency of nasals: There are as many as 18 nasal consonants in the first four lines, the greatest number (6) being in the first line: *m*y, a*n*d, *num*b*n*ess, pai*n*s.

(b) Frequency of sibilants (/s/, /z/): there are 12 such consonants in the first four lines, again the highest number (4) being in line 1: ache*s*, drow*s*y, numbne*ss*, pain*s*.

(c) Especially noteworthy are sequences of postvocalic consonants, where either the first consonant is a nasal (nu*mbn*ess, pai*ns*, se*ns*e, dru*nk*, etc.) or where the second consonant is a sibilant (a*ches*, se*nse*, drai*ns*, -war*ds*, etc.)

(d) More generally, stressed positions are frequently occupied by long syllables, containing long vowels, diphthongs, or consonant clusters. Notice, in particular, the first line's heavy syllables *heart, aches, drows-, pains.*

One does not have to be a blind believer in sound symbolism to accept that the density of these particular phonemic features in some degree reinforces the mood expressed in the lines. Nasals and sibilants are both continuant consonant-types, favouring prolonged articulation (their power to suggest seductive lassitude is recalled, for instance, in Tennyson's "The moan of doves in immemorial elms,/ And murmuring of innumerable bees" and Spenser's "Sweet-breathing Zephyrus did softly play"). The consonant clusters and long vowels contribute, in addition, to a slow, lingering, consonant-clogged movement in the opening lines. There is a particular density of these features in line 1, which strongly establishes, from the start, the dominant pattern of sound.

In the next section of the stanza, these features are markedly less frequent, and instead we have the thrice-repeated word *happy* (noted by Leavis), a word containing two very brisk syllables with the simple structure CV, the consonant being plosive and the vowel being short in both cases. (Compare, for example, the length of this disyllable with that of the antonymous monosyllable *pains* in line 1.) This contributes to a lightness of rhythm in lines 5-6, which may be seen as a phonetic correlate of Leavis's reference to the "buoyant" movement towards "life".

Another indication of the change of mood is the contrast between the six-times repeated vowel /ʌ/ in the opening quatrain, and the thrice-repeatedd /æ/ in 5-6: the former belonging with the soporific associations of the words *dull* and *numb*, the latter with the opposed associations of the word *happy*. It is worth observing that /æ/ does not occur at all before line 5, and that it occurs only once later, in the final tercet (*shadows*).

The last three lines show a return to the predominance of nasals, sibilants, and the /ʌ/ vowel of the opening lines, but now the consonant clusters of the opening lines are rare. However, the phrase *full-throated ease* not only recalls the opening mood by sounding a "note of luxury", as Leavis suggests, but also, through the length of its constituent syllables, brings a final return to the initial slowness of rhythm.

The distribution of these features is shown by the following table, in which changes in relative frequency show the transition at line 5, and the partial resumption of the opening pattern in line 8:[13]

13. In the table, affricates and diphthongs count as single phonemes. The percentages in the right-hand column, giving the general frequency in English of certain phonemes and phoneme classes, are taken from D. B. Fry's phoneme count, as reproduced in Gimson (1962: 143 and 214).

	Lines 1 - 4	Lines 5 - 7	Lines 8 - 10	General % age frequency in English
Total number of phonemes	111	75	70	
No. of nasals /m/ /n/ /ŋ/	18	7	11	
(% age of all phonemes)	(16.2)	(9.3)	(15.7)	(11.95)
No. of sibilants /s/ /z/	12	3	8	
(% age of all phonemes)	(10.8)	(4.0)	(11.4)	(7.27)
No. of nasal + consonant occurrences	9	2	2	
(% age of all phonemes)	(8.1)	(2.6)	(2.9)	
No. of consonant + sibilant occurrences	5	0	0	
(% age of all phonemes)	(4.5)	(0.0)	(0.0)	
No. of occurrences of /ʌ/	6	0	3	
(% age of all phonemes)	(5.4)	(0.0)	(4.3)	(1.75)
No. of occurrences of /æ/	0	4	1	
(% age of all phonemes)	(0.0)	(5.3)	(1.4)	(1.45)

The rough indications of relative frequency provided by the percentages of this table give reasonably clear support to the claim that the tercet (lines 5-7) contrasts with the opening quatrain in terms of all the features considered, and that the second tercet (lines 8-10) returns to the pattern of the quatrain with respect to all features considered except that of consonant clustering.[14]

These observations are consistent with Leavis's interpretation of the stanza, if we accept that what he calls the "pervasive sense of luxury" shows itself in the reemergence, in the final tercet, of the

14. It would be pointless to look for statistical significance here, since the psychological effect of a stylistically prominent feature depends, I assume, crucially on its interaction with other features having parallel aesthetic functions. I agree with Halliday (1971: 344) that for literary stylistics "a rough indication of frequencies is often just what is needed: enough to suggest why we should accept the analyst's assertion that some feature is prominent in the text, and allow us to check his statements".

mood established in lines 1-4, minus the dragging effect of the consonant clusters. The data suggest, however, a slight rethinking of Leavis, whereby lines 8-10 are seen to merge and reconcile the different "motions" of lines 1-4 and lines 5-7. There are two reasons why this should make sense in terms of the thematic development of the poem. Firstly, the end of the stanza does not present a mood opposed to the opening "lethargy", but rather a reinterpretation of that "lethargy", as the poet's ecstatic response to the nightingale's song. Secondly, both the languor of the opening lines, and the related "luxury" of the final lines can be seen, in the context of the whole poem, as offering an ultimately illusory promise of self-realisation – hence it is appropriate, in retrospect, that the last lines, expressing a purely hedonistic delight in the nightingale's song, should be tinged with the negative associations of the first quatrain.

(ii) *The Metrical Level*

Of most interest on the metrical level is the interplay between the binary iambic rhythm x / x / x / . . . and the trisyllabic "dactylic" rhythm / x x / x x . . . It is a commonplace of traditional metrics that a trisyllabic rhythm (anapaest, dactyl, etc.) is conducive to liveliness, light-heartedness, even levity; presumably because there is a tendency (if one assumes a version, however weak, of the isochronous stress theory) for tempo to increase in proportion to the number of unstressed syllables per stress. Apart from at the beginning of the first line, where the strong stresses on the adjacent long syllables *héart áches* set the stanza off with adagio emphasis, there is no disturbance of the iambic rhythm in the first quatrain. This, combined with the pervasive phonemic texture noted above, gives the quatrain a steady, languid movement in keeping with the mood it expresses, as shown pre-eminently in line two:

x / x / x / x / x /
My sense, as though of hemlock I had drunk.

But this rhythm is progressively interrupted in the last six lines, by the intrusion of trisyllabic (dactylic) patterns:

/ x x / x x
light-winged Dryad of . . .

The trisyllabic rhythm takes over triumphantly in the last line, which may be recited as dactylic throughout:

/ x x / x x / x x /
Singest of summer in full-throated ease.

The "note of luxury" sounded in the last phrase is reinforced metrically, by the secondary stress on *-throat-*, which produces a rallentando effect comparable to that of the final cadence of a piece of music.

The buoyant, affirmatory mood is developed further in the next stanza of the poem, which, according to Leavis, "reverses the movement of the first", moving from an initial life-affirming mood to a final life-negating mood. In keeping with this, the foot-reversal at the beginning of the first six lines of the second stanza continues the dactylic motif from the end of stanza 1:

/ x x / O for a draught. . .	/ x x / x / Dance and Provencal song. . .
/ x x / Cooled a long age. . .	/ x x / x O for a beaker. . .
/ x x / x Tasting of Flora. . .	/ x x / Full of the true. . .

The métre, then, has its own way of drámatising the "interplay of motions", and in particular, the change of mood and direction which takes place between the quatrain and the sestet of the first stanza.

(iii) *The Syntactic Level*

The first thing to notice, syntactically, is that the quatrain and sestet of stanza 1 each constitute a single sentence. The major syntactic break of the stanza is therefore at the end of line 4, where Leavis notes that the "Lethe-wards" movement ends. The structure of the first sentence is *progressive*, in that it consists of five clauses, each succeeding the other by a simple conjunctive link of subordination or coordination:

My heart aches, (CLAUSE A)
and a drowsy numbness pains my sense, (CLAUSE B)
as though of hemlock I had drunk (CLAUSE C)
or emptied some dull opiate to the drains one
minute past, (CLAUSE D)
and Lethe-wards had sunk. (CLAUSE E)

It is not fanciful to suggest that this sentence-structure is a syntactic enactment of the movement "downwards", towards Lethe, as indeed is emphasised by its final word *sunk*. Psychologically, the sentence enables its interpreter to follow the line of least resistance: the end of each clause is, in Sinclair's terms,[15] a point of repose or release, a potential sentence-ending, for no clause contains anticipatory structural signals requiring interpretation in terms of a later clause. But at line 5, an element of *regressive* structure, of anticipatory tension, enters the syntax: *'Tis not* . . . looks forward, for its resolution, to the *but*. . . in the following line. A more striking case of syntactic suspense occurs in lines 7-10, where the subject of the final clause, *thou*, anticipates its verb, *singest*, which does not occur until nearly three lines later. Thus a syntactic expectancy is built up, to find its release in the last line, which in this respect, as well as metrically, becomes the climax of the sestet's "affirmatory" movement.

We may correlate this mounting tension and its resolution with a progressive clarification of the contextual implications of the stanza in the last six lines. The first-person pronouns *my* and *I* are the only pronouns to occur in lines 1-4, which describe the poet's consciousness in a purely inward-looking, self-regarding way. In contrast, the only pronouns to occur in lines 5-10 are *thy, thine* and *thou*: the poet is now looking outwards, and addressing, the external source of his ecstasis: the nightingale. But the identity of the poem's "thou" is only gradually revealed; from the enigmatic references of lines 5-6, we move to the identification of "thou" with the "light-wingéd Dryad" in line 7, and finally with the "singer" of line 10. The hidden addressee's nature, and hence identity, is at least clarified. The effect is of a progressive shift of focus from the poet towards nightingale.

Thus in these three respects – metrically, syntactically, and

15. Sinclair (1966: 72-4).

contextually – line 10 is the culmination of a tendency or movement which takes place in lines 5-10. By the end of the stanza, the "pervasive sense of luxury", although still present in the phonemic patterning, has undergone a transformation into something vital and positive.

Although this analysis has been necessarily selective, it has illustrated, I hope, how Leavis's general critical judgment and interpretation of the poem can be supported, and to some extent deepened and clarified, by a more systematic scrutiny of its language than he himself felt it necessary to attempt.

First, close analysis bears out Leavis's impression of a "fine organization", revealed in the way that patternings and tendencies on different linguistic levels work towards a common effect. Second, the balancing of the two contrasting parts of the stanza, representing the two main tensions of feeling in the poem, is also borne out by linguistic detail. Third, analysis can show how those expressions which Leavis picks out as thematically significant are actually highlighted by linguistic means. In the case of *happy*, the phonemic make-up of the word, in contrast with the pervasive phonemic texture of lines 1-4, reinforces its mood-changing effect. Again, the key-note value of *light-wingéd* is foregrounded (a) by its innovatory status as a poetic neologism; (b) by its dactylic stress pattern (when in attributive position, as here); and (c) by the pattern of assonance (/ai/) and consonance (/t/ and /d/) which links it with the following word *Dryad*.

More generally, the linguistic analysis gives tentative clues to the explanation of vague aesthetic terms such as "balance" (in the opposition between lines 1-4 and 5-10 in this stanza), and "climax" (in the working of metrical and syntactic features, in alliance with the sense of the stanza, towards a resolution in the final line). In accord with Leavis's emphasis on "dynamic 'motions' ", the analysis deals in dramatic concepts such as intensification and the heightening of tension, and not merely in the static, structural relations with which linguistic studies of poetry tend to be associated. Even that most general of aesthetic terms, "unity", may gain some meaning from the observation of how, in this stanza, contrasting linguistic features predominate in opposed parts of the whole, and are reconciled in a final synthesis: just as some phonemic prominences of the opening quatrain return in the final tercet, so the rhythmic rallentando on *full-throated ease* recalls the metrical tempo of the quatrain, and the release of syntactic tension in line 10 brings back the tensionless character of the opening sentence.

6. *Conclusion*

My aim in this article has been to refute Youngren's contention that linguists are making a "theoretical mistake" in claiming that linguistic analysis has an explanatory value for criticism. I have argued, and have tried to demonstrate, that the mistake lies only in claiming too much, and that linguistic stylistics has a proper role in providing a more secure basis for critical arguments from the text. My analysis of part of Keats's Ode goes some way, I hope, towards the fulfilment of this role, but is obviously incomplete and defective in various respects. In conclusion, I would like to add some further comments on the explanatory role to which I think stylistics should aspire, noting the ways in which my present analysis has fallen short of it.

First, let us distinguish again between the three chief sorts of statements which can be made about a literary text, or text-portion, *T*. A statement may be made about some linguistic property, some stylistic property or some aesthetic quality of *T*. A linguistic statement is either simple (e.g. "*T* is a relative clause") or quantitative (e.g. "*T* contains 5 relative clauses"). A stylistic statement is derived from linguistic statements about *T*, and generally asserts some respect in which *T* is in some relative or absolute sense abnormal ("*T* contains an unusually high frequency of short vowels", "*T* contains such-and-such a regular pattern of repetition", "*T* is ungrammatical in such-and-such a respect"). The applicability to *T* of an aesthetic statement (such as "*T* is lively"), cannot be demonstrated, but can be given a reasonable justification in terms of the stylistic properties of *T*. But, the relation between aesthetic properties and stylistic properties is not one-to-one, and therefore we cannot make such assertions as "the liveliness of *T* is due to the high frequency of short vowels". Instead, we must say that a given stylistic property s_i is potentially an exponent of a range of aesthetic values $a_m \dots a_n$, and that a given aesthetic property a_i is expounded by the coincidence of a set of stylistic properties $s_m \dots s_n$ within whose range it lies. Thus the aesthetic value of a stylistic property must be considered variable.

and as dependent on other coexisting stylistic properties "sympathetic" to that value. Aesthetic statements require the exercise of taste or discrimination by their user because the user has to evaluate the relative strengths of the stylistic properties (both of form and of meaning) contributing to this or that effect, and moreover has to choose between aesthetic terms with overlapping meanings (e.g. *languid, lethargic, lingering* might be, with slightly differing degrees of appropriateness, applied to the first four lines of the Ode).

Between the two most relevant levels of statement, aesthetic and stylistic, there is a third, interconnecting type of statement which asserts that in *T*, a given stylistic property s_i contributes to the expression of a given aesthetic property A_j. The main shortcoming of the preceding analysis is that the reader has been asked to take such statements (e.g. the statement that frequency of nasals, consonant clusters, etc., contribute to "languor") on trust. This is justifiable, to an extent, on the grounds that judgements of such statements tend to vary little from person to person, and have roughly the same status as the judgements of grammaticality, etc., on which linguistic descriptions are based. Ultimately, however, such statements have to be validated in terms of general theories of the psychological effects of stylistic features. Such theories, or "rhetorics", although at present poorly developed, are open to empirical investigation. Thus, a rhetoric of metre has to include an account of the varying aesthetic effects of iambic, dactylic, and other metrical patterns; a rhetoric of syntax has to include an explanation of the psychological effects of progressive as opposed to regressive syntactic structures. A more general concern of these rhetorics must be the investigation of linguistic mimesis: the phenomenon of form imitating or enacting content.[16]

Such considerations may seem to make the goal of a satisfactory stylistic explanation of critical judgements seem remote. Yet, even with their imperfections and limitations, the present techniques of stylistics allow us to strengthen the basis for critical

16. A recent article by Epstein (1975) makes a promising start in the task of classifying and evaluating different kinds of linguistic mimesis.

argument, and reduce the critic's reliance on "mere assertion of judgement".

University of Lancaster Geoffrey Leech

Bibliography

Bateson, F.W. (1968), "Language and Literature", *Essays in Criticism*, 18, 164-82.

Epstein, E.L. (1975), "The Self-Reflexive Artefact", in Fowler (1975), pp. 41-68.

Fowler, R. (1966), ed., *Essays on Style and Language*, London.

Fowler, R. (1971), *The Languages of Literature*, London.

Fowler, R. ed., *Style and Structure in Literature*, Oxford.

Gimson, A.C. (1962), *An Introduction to the Pronunciation of English* London.

Halliday, M.A.K. (1971), "Linguistic Function and Literary Style: An Inquiry into the Language of William Golding's *The Inheritors*" in S. Chatman, ed., *Literary Style: A Symposium*, New York, pp. 330-65.

Jakobson, R. and L. Jones (1970), *Shakespeare's Verbal Art in "Th'Expense of Spirit"*, The Hague.

Leavis, F.R. (1936), *Revaluation*, London.

Leech, G.N. (1969), *A Linguistic Guide to English Poetry*, London.

Mukařowský, J. (1964), "Standard Language and Poetic Language", in P.L. Garvin, trans. and ed., *A Prague School Reader on Esthetics, Literary Structure, and Style*, Georgetown, pp. 17-30.

Richards. I.A. (1970), "Jakobson's Shakespeare: the Subliminal Structural of a Sonnet", *Times Literary Supplement*, 28 May, pp. 589-90.

Sibley, F. (1959), "Aesthetic Concepts", *Philosophical Review*, 68 (1959), 421-50.

Sibley, F. (1965), "Aesthetic and Nonaesthetic", *Philosophical Review*, 74 (1965) 135-39.

Sibley, F. (1968), "Objectivity and Aesthetics", *Proceedings of the Aristotelian Society*, Supp. 42, 31-54.

Sinclair, J. McH. (1966), "Taking a Poem to Pieces", in R. Fowler (1966), pp. 68-81.

Spitzer, L. (1948), *Linguistics and Literary History*, Princeton University Press.

Youngren, W. (1970), *Semantics, Linguistics and Criticism*, New York.

This article was written after the author had given a paper on this subject to a number of audiences during a tour of Dutch universities in January 1976.

A DUTCH GRAMMARIAN'S ENGLISH: A REASSESSMENT OF POUTSMA

1. The traditional image

In his excellent review of Quirk *et al* (1972) in *DQR* F. G. A. M. Aarts (1975) employs the term "The Great Tradition" as a common denominator for the outstanding traditional grammarians of the first half of this century. Perhaps I may be permitted to borrow another title from F. R. Leavis, and plead for (at least a partial) "revaluation" of one of the Dutch exponents of this tradition, H. Poutsma, and his monumental work *A Grammar of Late Modern English.*[1] As far as the other continental traditionalists are concerned, a revaluation of O. Jespersen is hardly called for; he is the one exponent of the Great Tradition who is referred to quite regularly in current linguistic writings.[2] As for E. Kruisinga, his revaluation may be well under way with the extremely well-documented study by A. J. van Essen in *Levende Talen* 315 and 317 (December 1975 and April 1976). My reason for concentrating on Poutsma is not, however, the fact that he might seem the only one left to revaluate, but the fact that I sincerely feel he has been rather severely underrated, on the whole, so that a reassessment might be in the interest of the "common pursuit" of present-day linguistics.

The most important opinion-forming voice in this country on

1. The division of Poutsma's *Grammar of Late Modern English* into Parts, Sections, Volumes, Halves etc. is rather bewildering. Part I first appeared in 1904, in one volume. Part II comprises three volumes: Section I,A (1914), Section I,B (1916) and Section II (1926). A revised and greatly expanded second edition of Part I appeared in 1928, in two volumes (Part I First Half, and Part I Second Half). References in this article are to the first edition of the various volumes comprising Part II, and to the *second* edition of Part I (as constituting, presumably, Poutsma's more sophisticated views).

2. References to Jespersen can be found in practically all important present-day linguistic writings. Kruisinga and Poutsma I have found referred to only in Bolinger 1952, Rosenbaum 1967, Nilsen 1972, 1973, Kuiper 1972, and Akmajian & Heny 1975, (and, of course, Meys 1975).

the relative merits and demerits of the three Great Traditionalists *par excellence*, Poutsma, Jespersen, and Kruisinga, has of course been that of R. W. Zandvoort (see particularly Zandvoort 1932, 1952, and 1958). From Zandvoort's writings there can be no doubt that he ranks Kruisinga the highest of the three. About the relative position of the other two on his "rank-scale" he is not quite so explicit, but from Zandvoort (1958) it would appear that he puts Jespersen below the two Dutch grammarians: "If, in my distribution of praise and blame, I should seem to have been rather severe on Jespersen, it is because I thought there was a balance to redress. In the minds of many students of English Jespersen's work has somehow come to overshadow that of Poutsma and Kruisinga: not altogether deservedly, I think." As far as Poutsma is concerned, however, the above remark seems to spring from chauvinistic rather than linguistic considerations, for, beside the words of praise which are certainly there, his criticism of Poutsma is quite devastating. Thus Zandvoort criticizes Poutsma for working with an antiquated, partly diachronic, partly synchronic framework, and for being too much concerned with the written – particularly literary – language. More importantly, Zandvoort pictures Poutsma as "anything but a theoretician" (*op. cit.*, p. 86), whose "useful spadework" (*op cit,* p. 88 – the characterization is Poutsma's own, though) mainly consisted in diligently recording countless examples of all sorts of constructions from literary sources. In Aarts (1969), too, we find an assessment of the three great traditionalists. Aarts does not share Zandvoort's predilection for Kruisinga: "he does not now strike us as a particularly original thinker" (p. 12). His evaluation of Poutsma, however, does not differ much from Zandvoort's: "Upon the whole one cannot help feeling that Poutsma would have been a more significant grammarian, if he had been less of a collector and more of a theoretician" (p. 12).

I would not dream of disagreeing with Zandvoort (and Aarts) in their criticism of Poutsma's inconsistent mixing of synchronic and diachronic elements, and of his preoccupation with the written, literary language. However, I believe their image of Poutsma as a great collector but poor theoretician needs to be corrected. For, in spite of these shortcomings, *A Grammar of Late Modern English* nevertheless contains a wealth of shrewd grammatical observations deriving from a basically consistent conception of the structure of the living, contemporary language. Moreover, it seems to me that, considered in the light of the current linguistic scene, many of Poutsma's views have stood the test of time rather better than Kruisinga's. In what follows I shall try to justify this contention on a number of points.

2. Explicitness, "transformational techniques", and grammatical argumentation

One of the main shortcomings of traditional grammars in the eyes of transformationalists is of course their "impressionistic, non-rigorous, exemplificatory, informal" (etc.) presentation of the rules of the language, in short, their lack of "explicitness". It is undeniable that transformational linguistics, with its concomitant formal apparatus, has enriched our insight in structural aspects of language enormously. Apart from Otto Jespersen, in his *Analytic Syntax* (1937), no Great Traditionalist has produced anything even remotely comparable to the transformational format in the sense of a system of formal rules. Nor does Jespersen's formal system prevent him from being inexplicit on many aspects of sentence structure. Thus, to take just one example, on the relative ordering of the various elements within the "auxiliary complex" (i.e. the intricate interplay of the elements "tense", "modals", "aspect", "passive", "negative", "interrogative", "emphasis", etc., which is shown in a crystal-clear way in the transformational format) *Analytic Syntax* has little more to offer in terms of formalization then "v" for "lesser verb (separated from the main verb)" and "V" for, alternatively, the whole of the verbal predicate, or the remainder of the verbal predicate when some lesser verb happens to be separated from the main verb (cf. pp. 6 and 91-93). In *A Modern English Grammar* (Part VII, p. 61 ff.) basically the same system is used, introduced by the remark "Thus we have frequent collocations like *has come, is taken, is coming, will come, does come,* even with two or three 'lesser vbs': *has been taken, will be coming, will have been taken.*" In Kruisinga's *Handbook of Present-day English*[3] the internal structure of the auxiliary complex is not gone into at all. In the opening sections on word-order (Part II,3, pp. 317-318) Kruisinga only talks about the relative position of subject and verbal predicate, making a distinction only

3. All references are to the fifth edition (1932).

between normal and inverted order. In fact the most explicit of the three Great Traditionalists, although he does not use any formalism, turns out to be Poutsma, who remarks (Ch. VIII, 29, pp. 414-415) that "when the predicate consists of more verbs than one, they are arranged thus:

	a.	*b.*	*c.*	*d.*
two verbs	: finite verb,	participle, or infinitive.		
three verbs	: finite verb,	infinitive,	participle.	
four verbs	: finite verb,	infinitive,	participle,	participle."

It is clear that this scheme, in combination with remarks elsewhere in *The Grammar of Late Modern English* about word-order in negative and interrogative sentences, is a great deal more precise than Jespersen's or Kruisinga's account. Notice that the interesting generalization in this scheme, that possible third and fourth verbs are always "participles", entails vagueness on a less general level; i.e. the scheme does not explicitly indicate that when there is a modal as well as the progressive and perfective aspects (for example) the order must be as in:

The police may have been investigating the case.

and not, as in:

*The police may have being investigated the case.

On the other hand it is interesting to observe that the choice of the more general label "participle" allows the scheme to apply to passive sentences as well (cf. the sentence *The case may have been investigated by the police*).

Transformationalists frequently – and fruitfully – employ assumptions about transformational relationships between sentences to bring out structural characteristics which might not be so apparent if the same sentences were considered in isolation. Thus a favourite "transformational technique" to try and establish whether the structure of some sentence A is like that of some superficially similar sentence B (or not, as the case may be), is to put both of them through the same set of transformations to see which ones work for each of them, and which ones don't. Unlike Kruisinga, Poutsma sometimes fairly systematically employs this kind of transformational technique (in a non-formalized way, to be sure). As an example, consider the way in which Poutsma puts the sentence *Yesterday I offered your brother a shilling for his knife* systematically through the same "emphasis transformation" involving "anticipatory *it*" six times, each time emphasizing a different element, and notice especially the interesting distinction which this "transformational technique" then permits him to make:

1) It was yesterday that I offered your brother a shilling for his knife.
2) It was I that (who) offered your brother a shilling for his knife yesterday.
3) It was your brother to whom I offered a shilling for his knife yesterday.
4) It was to your brother that I offered a shilling for his knife yesterday.
5) It was a shilling that I offered to your brother for his knife yesterday.
6) It was for his knife that I offered your brother a shilling yesterday.

It will be observed that the subordinate clauses in the above sentences, some of which are awkward enough, are of a different description. In 1), 4), and 6) they are subordinate elements introduced by the conjunction *that*; in 2), 3) and 5) they are substantive clauses introduced by an independent ('condensed') relative pronoun (Ch. II, 12a, pp.140-141).

Similarly, consider how Poutsma illustrates his observation (Ch. L, 12b, pp.213-214) that "verbals" (Poutsma's term for the nonfinite verb-forms) express "a time-sphere anterior to that of the action or state expressed by the finite verb with which they are syntactically connected (. . .) by means of the auxiliary *to have,* formerly also *to be.*" The addition after the comma is one of Poutsma's diachronic lapses!)

Compare:

i. I know that he was here a minute ago.
   with I know him to have been here a minute ago.

ii. I thank you that you did all this for me when I was away.
   with I thank you for having done all this for me when I was away.

iii. As he was born on May 3rd 1905, he has now completed his twentieth year.

with Having been born on May 3rd 1905, he has now completed his twentieth year.

The two "points of grammar" illustrated above from Poutsma are also dealt with amply as well as adequately in Kruisinga's *Handbook,* as a matter of fact (Part II,3, pp. 505-509, and Part II,1, pp. 396-401 respectively). A comparison between their treatments will reveal, however, that Kruisinga does not make such systematic use of the kind of transformational technique illustrated above. Such a comparison will also bring out another difference, and that is that, although the "collector" Poutsma has of course a much larger corpus of utterances at his disposal, he nevertheless uses sentences of his own making much more freely than Kruisinga does, to illustrate particular points. Thus nearly all of the illustrative sentences in Ch.XLV, which contains some of Poutsma's most important and insightful observations, are apparently of his own making. Kruisinga, on the other hand, though working with a much smaller corpus, generally bases his discussion of grammatical phenomena almost exclusively on the corpus-utterances themselves. Poutsma, then, is less strictly "corpus-bound", another feature which agrees well with current linguistic insights (cf. Aarts (1975), p. 101).

A possible consequence of the transformational technique referred to above is of course that, once in a while, some transformation will not "work". The result is an ungrammatical sentence. We see that Poutsma is fully prepared to accept this consequence of the kind of grammatical reasoning he has adopted, and he sometimes uses the (by now) familiar asterisk to mark such ungrammatical products of transformations that have "misfired". Thus in Ch.XLV: **He made his losses good, *He called the military out,* etc. (p. 25); **He had to listen to a long speaking to, *The accounted for facts,* etc. (p. 34); **That he would come was told me, *To go out was allowed me* (Ch.XLVII, p.130) (As far as I have been able to ascertain ungrammatical utterances nowhere figure in Kruisinga's *Handbook*). The use of ungrammatical sentences in grammatical argumentation is not of course in itself necessarily a virtue. In fact, to my mind many linguists have been overdoing things a bit in this respect the past few years, (sometimes even comparing various ungrammatical sentences with one another to establish degrees of ungrammaticality) and I have a suspicion that over-exposure to ungrammatical utterances might well lead to serious impairment of one's linguistic judgement. However, when employed with moderation, as in Poutsma, this technique makes for more flexibility in grammatical argumentation, somewhat similar in its effect to the use of negative integers in mathematics, and it can be a powerful means for bringing out the structural scope of a given linguistic unit. Nor do we always have to actually *use* an ungrammatical sentence in the argument, as can be seen from Poutsma's comparison of *seem* and *appear* on the one hand, and *get, grow* on the other (Ch.XLV, 4, p. 6). He first points out that at first sight these might seem to belong to the same category; both pairs of verbs may occur with or without *to be* preceding the adjective: *He seems (to be) happy, He grew (to be) happy.* But then he brings out the difference: "...while such a sentence as *He seems* (or *appears*) *to be happy* admits of being expanded into *It seems* (or *appears*) *that he is happy*, (...) no such expansion is possible with sentences containing *to get, to grow*".

As a final characteristic which seems to put Poutsma closer to current views in linguistics than Kruisinga, one might consider the fact that on the whole Poutsma tends to accept more readily that certain structures, though different in form, may be used to convey basically the same semantic content (cf. again the transformationalist view that certain structures can be considered transforms of others). Thus if, in Ch.XLVII (The Passive Voice), we replaced "conversion" and "converted into" everywhere by "transformation" and "transformed into", the chapter would sound very much like a transformational treatise. Even so, having first established that certain structures may be to all intents and purposes equivalent, and hence interchangeable, in the majority of cases, Poutsma will then characteristically go on to specify the conditions under which differences between the two structures *can* be ascertained. By contrast, many transformationalists tend to accept rather too uncritically that "x" means the same thing as "y" without attempting to find out whether there might perhaps be differences too, an attitude which is rightly criticized in, for instance, Chafe (1970). Poutsma's more "transformational" outlook leads him to treat infinitive, gerundive, and participial complement structures as clauses, just like relative clauses, content clauses etc., corresponding to the transformationalist derivation of all of them from embedded sentences. By contrast, Kruisinga, who nearly always takes the view that, whenever there is a formal difference, there must be a corresponding semantic-functional difference, strictly limits the use of the term "clause" to the finite ones.[4]

So far I have been using the term "transformationalist" in a rather informal way. The correspondences pointed out so far are mainly with the more structurally-oriented "Chomskyan" transformationalism. However, the correspondences between Poutsma's outlook and the more semantically-oriented "post-Chomskyan" brands of linguistics (particularly Generative Semantics and Case-grammar) are perhaps even more striking. I should think a reading of the introductory survey to Part II Section II (Ch. XLV) and the further elaboration in Chs.XLVI, XLVII, and XLVIII, should be sufficient to dispel any notion that Poutsma was "anything but a theoretician". The points that are raised in these 150-odd pages are, many of them, issues which have been the focus of attention in linguistics of the last decade, and, what's more, most of the analyses which Poutsma suggests correspond in interesting ways to such as have been formulated, perhaps in more "explicit" ways, in the more recent linguistic literature. The central theme can be indicated by the title of Ch.XLVI,1: "the floating nature of transitiveness" (for comparison: Kruisinga devotes less than two pages to this issue; cf. *Handbook* II,3, pp.205-206).

Poutsma gives a whole array of shifts from transitive to intransitive and *vice versa,* corresponding to accounts of subject-selection etc. in terms of Case-frames by various Case-grammarians (Fillmore 1968, Gruber 1970, Hall-Partee 1965, Nilsen 1972, 1973, and others). In fact, Poutsma's terminology in dealing with these matters is often that of the Case-grammarians: "agent, recipient, instrument" etc. The sentence *the door opened* which figures in Fillmore's discussion (Fillmore 1968, p.27) of case-frames, is already used in Poutsma to make very much the same

4. He does, however, devote a few sections (Part II,1, pp.283-289) to a discussion of differences and similarities between verbals and subordinate clauses (in which, rather uncharacteristically, he also uses a few illustrative sentences of his own making).

point, i.e. that "the recipient of the action is at the same time thought of as its originator (. . .), although a moment's reflection makes us aware that the movement is in reality due to the operation of some outside agent: some person or animal, a puff of wind, etc." (Ch. XLVI, 19a, p.54). Among the various shifts from transitive to intransitive or *vice versa* Poutsma mentions, for instance "passive use without change of voice" (*The book sells well, the meeting adjourned*), "causative use" (*to fly a kite, to grow potatoes, to walk a horse* etc. along with suffixed forms like *blacken, deepen,* etc.), and the "addition of cognate or effective objects" (*to fight the good fight, it rained cats and dogs,* etc.). Very interesting is also the parallel that can be drawn between Poutsma's notion of "absorption" (of objects or prepositions) resulting in a change from transitive to intransitive or the other way around, and the idea of "incorporation" which we find in Case-grammarians like Gruber (1970) and Nilsen (1973).

3. Some specific "points of grammar"

My aim in the preceding section was to present an over-all picture of Poutsma's "proto-transformational" line of thinking as a theoretician. In the course of the discussion various "points of grammar" have already been touched upon to support my claim. In this section I shall point out some more parallels in Poutsma's work with certain transformationalist accounts. For reasons of space I shall not go into each of these issues in equal detail, leaving it to the reader to verify the facts for himself.

Related to Poutsma's views on the floating nature of transitiveness, and his conception of what constitutes a grammatical or logical subject, object, etc., are his ideas about "variable applicability of the predicate" (cf. Ch.LIII in Part II Section II, which can best be read in conjunction with Chs.II and III in Part I first Half). Poutsma's analysis of the relation between such sentences as *This question is difficult to answer* and *It is difficult to answer this question* corresponds essentially to the more explicit transformationalist accounts (cf. for instance Rosenbaum 1967, Postal 1971, 1974, Jacobs and Rosenbaum 1968, Burt 1971). At the same time it can be seen that Poutsma manages to resist the temptation to consider such structures always and everywhere identical. Thus Poutsma observes (Ch.II, 14, p. 144):

> . . .there may be a distinct semantic difference between a given construction and its alternative. Thus there is a material difference between *It is extremely easy to condemn other people* (Galsw. *White Monkey,* III, Ch.XII,281) and *Other people are extremely easy to condemn.*

Cf. also observation III on p. 145 (further elucidated in Ch.LV,81):

> In the case of the predicative adjective indicating no quality of the action denoted by the infinitive, but of the person or thing indicated by the subject (. . .), the alternative construction would, of course, be impossible. Thus *My horse . . . is quiet to ride* (Thack., *Van. Fair,* I, Ch. XXXII, 346) cannot be replaced by **It is quiet to ride my horse.*

Even more striking is Poutsma's analysis of constructions involving *happen, seem, appear,* and *certain, likely, sure,* etc., which again squares very nicely with the transformationalist accounts in such works as Rosenbaum (1967), Jacobs and Rosenbaum (1968), Akmajian and Heny (1975). Cf. what Poutsma says in Ch.LIII, 15, p. 368:

> Thus *It happened* (or *chanced*) *that they met that very day* may be turned into *They happened* (or *chanced*) *to meet that very day.* Similarly *It appeared* (*seemed*) *that they knew each other* may be converted into *They appeared* (*seemed*) *to know each other.*

(It almost seems as if by his use of "turn into" and "convert into" Poutsma is deliberately trying to avoid the term "transform into"). Although he is careful to observe first of all that "in many cases there is no appreciable difference between the condensed and the expanded construction", Poutsma also shows that there are cases in which there is some detectable semantic difference between the two alternatives, or where only one of the alternatives is possible. Thus he points out that we can only have the expanded construction when the main verb has future reference (as in *It so happens that the book will not be printed for another year*), an observation which I have not found in the transformationalist accounts.

Kruisinga's treatment of this matter is less convincing; cf.*Hand-*

book II,1, p. 167: "sometimes the stem is in no way the adjunct to a verb, but must be considered as the leading element of the verbal group in which the other verb plays the part of adjunct: *I happened to see him.* The same relation exists, though not so clearly, in such a sentence as *I went to see him.*"

To conclude this section, a few more "points of grammar" in which Poutsma, to my mind, shows himself to be a "proto-transformationalist" – something the reader might want to check for himself. Thus, for instance, the observation that *passive* and *reflexive* are incompatible has been a much-debated subject in transformational writings (cf. Lees and Klima 1963, Chomsky 1967, Postal 1971, Meys 1975). Lees and Klima (1963) attribute the observation to Jespersen (*A Modern English Grammar,* III,15,1.3 – 1927). It can also be found in Poutsma, Part II, Section II, Ch.XLVII,16 – 1926. The suggestion concerning *transitive and intransitive prepositions* in Emonds (1972) is in essence the same as what Poutsma proposes in Part II Section II, Chs LX,117 and XLV,27b. The transformationalist concept of *reduced relative clauses* is approached very closely in Poutsma's "undeveloped clauses answering to relative clauses" (Part I Second Half, p. 994). Notice that Poutsma's criterion for distinguishing these from appositions is possible expansion into full relative clauses.

4. "The Great Tradition" and the current scene in linguistics

In the preceding sections I have tried to show that, both in his general conception of synchronic grammatical theory, and in his treatment of particulars, Poutsma was a more important theoretician than he has generally been made out to be. Borrowing generously from many other grammarians, he was perhaps not as original a thinker as Jespersen, or even Kruisinga. But then, in a work of this size and scope, who could be entirely original? Quirk *et al,* too, admit having drawn freely and lavishly from other sources – and their grammar counts a "mere" 1120 pages versus Poutsma's 3400. In one respect Poutsma certainly excelled the other Great Traditionalists, and that is modesty, as is evident when one reads the prefaces to the various volumes. Perhaps it is this character-trait – which made him present himself as someone merely doing "useful spadework" – that can partly account for the fact that he has not generally received the appreciation he deserves.

It remains to give an answer to the question why, given the present linguistic scene, with its apparent preoccupation with explicitness and formal apparatus, and the resulting "deeper" insights in language, we should bother at all to dig up Poutsma's grammar, or any other "impressionistic" grammar of the Great Tradition. I think part of the answer has already been given by the man who may be considered to have revolutionized linguistics: Noam Chomsky. In Chomsky (1965) he writes that "traditional grammars give a wealth of information concerning structural description of sentences", and he argues that "the attempt to explore this largely uncharted territory can most profitably begin with a study of the kind of structural information presented by traditional grammars and the kind of linguistic processes that have been exhibited, however informally, in these grammars" (pp.4-5). Here the emphasis is still on *structure* rather than *meaning*. Since then, developments in transformational linguistics (in a wide sense) have shown a steady trend towards more semantically-oriented models of grammar, notably in Generative Semantics and Case-Grammar, and therefore towards a position that is very close to the traditional one, in which, after all, semantic considerations played a very important rôle. Thus the Case-grammarian Don F. L. Nilsen writes (after a reference to Poutsma's subcategorization of adverbs): "It can be seen from this one example that the traditional grammarians were well on their way to developing a solid semantically based grammar before attention was turned away by the structuralists and transformationalists who felt that grammars should have a syntactic rather than a semantic base" (Nilsen 1973, p.88).

I agree with Nilsen that we must look for the deepest level of representation in the semantic sphere. I also think the insistence in modern linguistics on explicitness in the framework of a formal calculus is of the utmost importance. But it is not self-evident that the formal systems that have been developed with the assumed primacy of the syntactic level of representation in mind are in fact adequate to cope with semantic deep structure. Confrontation with "The Great Tradition" may perhaps safeguard us, as I hope to have demonstrated in this article, against assuming too easily, from syntactic evidence alone, that "x" equals "y".[5]

Amsterdam — Willem J. Meys

5. On the basis of the kind of considerations expressed in this article the Department of English of the Municipal University of Amsterdam has staged a Candidate-Seminar devoted to a systematic comparison of the Great Tradition and current linguistic writings. Readers who are interested in this project, or would like to contribute to it in some way or another, can contact me at the following address: Engels Seminarium U.v.A., Lambert ten Katehuis, Herengracht 330-336, Amsterdam, tel. (020) 5253390.

BIBLIOGRAPHY

Aarts, F. G. A. M. (1969) *Approaches to English Grammar: from Henry Sweet to Noam Chomsky,* Nijmegen.

Aarts, F. G. A. M. (1975) "The Great Tradition, or Grammars and Quirk's Grammar", *DQR,* 5:2:98-126.

Akmajian, A., and Heny, F. (1975) *An Introduction to the Principles of Transformational Syntax,* Cambridge, Mass.

Bolinger, D. L. (1952) "Linear modification", *Publ. of the Mod. Lang. Ass. of America,* 67:1117-1144.

Burt, M. K. (1971) *From Deep to Surface Structure,* New York.

Chafe, W. L. (1970) *Meaning and the Structure of Language,* Chicago.

Chomsky, N. (1965) *Aspects of the Theory of Syntax,* Cambridge, Mass.

Chomsky, N. (1967) "Remarks on Nominalization", in Jacobs & Rosenbaum, 1970.

Emonds, J. (1972) "Evidence that Indirect Object Movement is a Structure-preserving Rule", *FOL* 8:4:546-561.

Essen, A. J. van (1975,1976) "Etsko Kruisinga, 1875-1975", *Levende Talen,* 315: 463-478, and 317: 125-142.

Fillmore, Ch. F. (1968) "The Case for Case" in *Universals in Linguistic Theory,* Bach, E. & Harms, R. T. (eds.), New York.

Gruber, G. (1970) *Studies in Lexical Relations,* Indiana Ling. Club.

Hall (Partee), B. (1965) *Subject and Object in English*, Cambridge, Mass.

Jacobs, R.A. & Waltram, P.S. Rosenbaum (1968), *English Transformational Grammar*, Mass.

Jacobs, R.A. & Waltram, P.S. Rosenbaum (1970) eds, *Readings in English Transformational Grammar,* Mass.

Jespersen, O. (1909-1947) *A Modern English Grammar on Historical Principles,* Heidelberg-Copenhagen.

Jespersen, O. (1937) *Analytic Syntax,* Gothenburg (reprinted 1969, New York).

Kruisinga, E. (1932) *A Handbook of Present-Day-English,* 5th ed., Groningen.

Kuiper, K. (1972) *Rules of English Noun Compounds,* Wellington.

Lees, R. B. & Klima, E. (1963) "Rules for English Pronominalization", *Language,* 39:17-29.

Meys, W. J. (1975) *Compound Adjectives in English and the Ideal Speaker-Listener,* Amsterdam.

Nilsen, D. F. L. (1972) *English Adverbials,* The Hague.

Nilsen, D. F. L. (1973) *The Instrumental Case in English,* The Hague.

Postal, P. M. (1971) *Cross-over Phenomena,* New York.

Postal, P. M. (1974) *On Raising,* Cambridge, Mass.

Poutsma, H. (1904-1928) *A Grammar of Late Modern English,* Groningen.

Rosenbaum, P. S. (1967) *The Grammar of English Predicate Complement Constructions,* Cambridge, Mass.

Quirk, R., Greenbaum, S., Leech, G., & Svartvik, J. (1972) *A Grammar of Contemporary English*, London.

Zandvoort, R. W. (1932) "Progress in Syntax", *English Studies* XIV, reprinted in *Collected Papers* (1954), pp. 76-95, Groningen.

Zandvoort, R. W. (1952) "A Critique of Jespersen's *Modern English Grammar", Etudes Anglaises,* V, reprinted in *Collected Papers* (1954), pp. 96-105. Groningen.

Zandvoort, R. W. (1958) "Three grammarians: Poutsma – Jespersen – Kruisinga", *Levende Talen* 193, reprinted in *Moderna Språk* (1958) and in *Collected Papers* II, pp. 85-96, Groningen.

CHAUCER, THE *NUN'S PRIEST'S TALE*, AND THE MODERN READER*

Chaucer's language does not present an immediate obstacle to the understanding of the modern reader, especially when we compare it with the language of genuinely difficult works like *Sir Gawain and the Green Knight*. Indeed, the danger with Chaucer may be less of not understanding than of not realizing that we do not understand, or of thinking that we understand when we do not. We may import into our reading linguistic preconceptions derived from later developments in the English language, and likewise we may miss shades of meaning that may have been obvious to Chaucer's contemporary audience. For this reason, we should always try to open our minds to the *differentness* of Chaucer's language, and to the possibility of differentness. For this reason, too, translations and modernizations of Chaucer can be regarded as pernicious, as well as useless and unnecessary. What they do is to interpose between us and the old language an opaque or at least a refractive medium, so that what we get is not Chaucer but some individual's limited understanding of Chaucer, and even more limited expression of that understanding. Translation and modernization also produce that effect of quaintness and naïveté which prevent us altogether from taking Chaucer seriously. The impression created is that Chaucer was trying to write "proper" English, and deserves credit for trying, but that he had the misfortune to live in a benighted age before the language was properly developed. Dryden put this view well, in his *Preface to the Fables*: "The words are given up as a post not to be defended in our poet, because he wanted the modern art of fortifying."

Modernizing, or fortifying, is a symptom of a widespread

*What follows is the text, with some modifications, of a lecture delivered in the Universities of Amsterdam and Groningen and in the Vrije Universiteit of Amsterdam during a visit to the Netherlands in March 1980. I am most grateful for the hospitality afforded to me on that occasion, and for the opportunity now to offer a souvenir of my visit.

disease in the criticism of older literature — the assumption that the old writer, Chaucer or whoever, was a forerunner or precursor, that he was doing quite well, as well as could be expected, what later writers did superlatively well. Often these claims are made with the best of intentions, as when *Troilus and Criseyde* was praised by Kittredge as the first "psychological novel" in English.[1] He wished to speak well of the work, to give it respectability by associating it with something that he knew his readers all approved of, as if the whole evolution of European literature had been designed to be consummated in the psychological novel. The effect, though, is to demean and diminish Chaucer's poetry, for in taking this line of least resistance we always find that we want to find rather than see what is there, hold Chaucer up to the mirror of our own civilization and culture rather than recognize in him a window through which we can look into the civilization and culture of another age.

Recognizing the differentness of Chaucer, the differentness of his language, of his habits of mind and of the culture that he lived in, is one step towards understanding his poetry, and we can be helped to appreciate the limitations of our modern approach if we acknowledge the historical relativity to which it is subject. The reader of Chaucer has always been "the modern reader", and he has always looked at Chaucer and found what he wanted or was preconditioned to find, what suited the cultural or moral or political preoccupations of his age. The fifteenth century found a great rhetorician and purveyor of *sentence*, the sixteenth century a type of the true Protestant reformer, the seventeenth century an example of untutored native genius who wanted art (in contrast with the seventeenth century), the eighteenth century a scurrilous practitioner of bawdy. The modern age has the advantage of seeing these interpretations in the perspective of history, but is none the less part itself of a larger historical perspective. Thus the modern age is the age of the individual, an age which appreciates the complexities of individual psychology: so Chaucer becomes a great creator of characters, a great delineator of the psychological complexities of his characters. The *Canterbury Tales* become "The Human Comedy", and the tales dramatic monologues primarily

1. G.L. Kittredge, *Chaucer and his Poetry*, Cambridge, Mass. 1915, p. 155.

intended to display the characters of their tellers,[2] while *Troilus*, as we have seen, becomes a psychological novel. But the modern age is also an age which longs for certainty: so Chaucer, if you have the tools to extract his proper meaning (and they are conveniently supplied by D.W. Robertson and his school), becomes the spokesman of the Augustinian doctrine of Charity and Cupidity, and in so doing is made the servant of a modern conservative neo-Christian orthodoxy. Ours is also an age, paradoxically, that cherishes radicalism and the subversion of orthodox values, and so the *Prioress's Tale* becomes a covert attack on the stereotyped and inhuman anti-Semitism of its age,[3] while the *Knight's Tale*, in a recent book, becomes a hymn to tyranny in the mouth of a cold-blooded professional killer.[4] Over-arching all, and making all these interpretations possible, is the modern worship of ambiguity and irony, at its highest a recognition that a poet is entitled to express contrary states of being, at it lowest a faint-hearted submission to the difficulties of understanding, whereby the reader's vagueness about what Chaucer means is elevated to the critical assumption that he did not mean anything in particular.

One would not wish to deny the particular validity of any of these readings as responses to elements that are present in Chaucer's writing; nor to deny that individual readers may often have had a much more generous understanding of Chaucer than they were permitted to express in the critical vocabulary available in their day. But they are only elements: they are not the key to Chaucer. We should be wary of critics who offer us keys to all understanding: anything that can be opened with such keys is probably not worth opening. With this warning in mind, it would be sensible now to focus the discussion more closely, and to examine some of the dilemmas of the modern reader of Chaucer as he confronts a particular work, the *Nun's Priest's Tale*, and tries to make sense of it and of what has been said of it.

2. Again, Kittredge is the most brilliant and persuasive exponent of this idea, both in *Chaucer and his Poetry* and in his earlier article, "Chaucer's Discussion of Marriage," *Modern Philology*, 9 (1911-12), 435-67.

3.R.J. Schoeck, "Chaucer's Prioress: Mercy and Tender Heart", *The Bridge: A Yearbook of Judaeo-Christian Studies*, 2 (1956), 239-55.

4. Terry Jones, *Chaucer's Knight: The Portrait of a Medieval Mercenary*, London, 1980.

The wisest words that have been spoken about the *Nun's Priest's Tale* are, appropriately enough, words of warning, and they were spoken by the wisest of all critics of Chaucer, Charles Muscatine: "The tale will betray with laughter any too-solemn scrutiny of its naked argument; if it is true that Chauntecler and Pertelote are rounded characters, it is also true that they are chickens .... Unlike fable, the *Nun's Priest's Tale* does not so much make true and solemn assertions about life as it tests truths and tries out solemnities. If you are not careful, it will try out your solemnity too."[5] These words have not been altogether heeded in the interpretation of the Tale over the past twenty years, and there is no one of the *Canterbury Tales* that has provoked so much hot air or been the subject of so much inflated speculation. A comic parody of a tale has somehow, perhaps appropriately, produced a comic parody of criticism. The poem is thus a test-case for the Chaucer critic: it is universally regarded as one of the best, if not the best, of the *Canterbury Tales*, and if criticism can find no way of explaining how and why it is the best, then it has failed in its task.

The dominant strain in modern criticism of the Tale has been the moral-allegorical. It began modestly enough with the interpretation of Donovan,[6] who used the traditional iconography of the cock and the fox, in bestiary and Scriptural commentary, to show that the Tale is "a sermon on alertness to moral obligation", in which the cock is the priest or preacher, whose crowing is the sounding of the canonical hours, the call to Christians to be wakeful, while the fox is the devil-heretic. The poor widow, meanwhile, is the Church, widowhood being the model for the control of the very passions to which Chauntecler succumbs, especially vanity and unprofitable sexuality ("Moore for delit than world to multiplye", 4535). Donovan took the ending of the Tale ("Taketh the moralite, goode men", 4630) as the stimulus to look for a homiletic interpretation, and he was immediately followed by

5. C. Muscatine, *Chaucer and the French Tradition*, Berkeley and Los Angeles, 1957, pp. 238, 242.

6. M.J. Donovan, "The *Moralite* of the Nun's Priest's Sermon", *Journal of English and Germanic Philology*, 52 (1953), 498-508. Chaucer quotations in what follows are from *The Works of Geoffrey Chaucer*, ed. F.N. Robinson, 2nd edn, London, 1957.

Dahlberg,[7] who confirmed and extended the iconographic interpretation, identifying the cock as the secular priest and the fox as the false flattering friar. "The cock priest, whose duty it is to awaken himself and others, may be in a state of sloth, where he is susceptible to the blandishments of the fox-friar and likely to lose his existence. Doctrinally speaking, a state like this amounts to the loss of free will and can be overcome only by reawakening." Dahlberg went on to identify not only the cock, the fox and the widow, but also to recognize in the *drye dych* which surrounds the farmyard an iconographic reversal of the *fons signatus* of Canticles, and therefore an emblem of the dry or desolate state of the Church in the world; to see in Chauntecler's *paramours* the reversal of the *sponsa* of Canticles, the holy bride of Christ; and to see in the colours of Chauntecler's plumage the associations of liturgical colours and the priestly life.

In 1962 D.W. Robertson laid his hands upon the work of his disciples and declared it good: the fox is the heretical *seductor* of the faithful, while the cock is the priest or prelate. He concudes: "The *Nun's Priest's Tale* is a story of a priest who falls into the clutches of a friar but who escapes just in time when he discovers the essential weakness of the friar's evil nature."[8] There is no doubt great satisfaction, even some exaltation of the spirit, to be obtained from confident pronouncements like this, in which literature, purged of its bewildering complexities and idiosyncrasies, emerges as essentially the statement of simple moral truths. But there must also be resistance to the tendency of exegetical criticism, whatever value it may have in alerting us to important levels of allusion, to reduce all literature to a common dead level of conventional expectation, where the difference between writers is only in the skill with which they disguise the universal platitudes which are the sum of their preachment. Does this Tale of incomparable brilliance and gaiety really end in such dust and ashes?

But there is more to come, more volumes of the *Patrologia Latina* tumbling about our ears. A recent article traces a connection between Pertelote's advice on the taking of purgatives and laxa-

7. C. Dahlberg, "Chaucer's Cock and Fox", *Journal of English and Germanic Philology*, 53 (1954), 277-90.

8. D.W. Robertson Jr., *A Preface to Chaucer*, Princeton, 1962, p. 252.

tives and the symbolic meaning of such remedies in relation to the whole spiritual being of man.[9] The article displays a wealth of erudition, and it would be harsh to say that the hanging of such erudition on non-existent pegs in Chaucer is a characteristic activity of modern scholarship. Perhaps such writing could be regarded as a kind of creative literature in its own right, unconstrained by literary pedantries such as a sense of contextual validity. It would be pedantry, for instance, to insist that Pertelote's advice about laxatives can hardly have much symbolic significance since it is recognizably bad advice, and Chauntecler's refusal to take it is one of his few sensible actions in the poem. Such naive pedantry would no doubt be countered by the adducing of irony, or at least of that version of irony which confirms the reader in his bemused sense that nothing means what it says and most things mean the opposite of what they say.

One last extravagance of moral-allegorical interpretation needs to be mentioned before we turn to other things. There are clear allusions in the course of the *Nun's Priest's Tale* to the story of the Fall, and a well-established critical view sees the Tale as an allegory of the Fall, and the farmyard chase at the end as a burlesque version of the chaos and disorder which follows on the Fall. In the hands of Speirs,[10] this interpretation was nicely judged, responsive to the allusion which is undoubtedly there, but conscious always of the informing spirit of comedy and the mock-heroic. In this later article, however, we have exegesis run riot.[11] The *moralite* of the Tale is "the recapitulation by Chauntecler of man's fall and redemption, and the theological meanings inherent in Chauntecler's repeating Adam's experience." So Chauntecler and Pertelote have their debate about dreams on a *beem*, which represents the Forbidden Tree and typologically the Cross; the flying down from the safety of the *beem* symbolizes the Fall, while the flying up for safety into the *tree* at the end symbolizes the resurrection. There is hardly a single piece of timber in the Tale which is not worked into this interpretation. Meanwhile the

9. Patrick Gallacher, "Food, Laxatives, and Catharsis in Chaucer's Nun's Priest's Tale", *Speculum*, 51 (1976), 49-68.

10. John Speirs, *Chaucer the Maker*, London, 1951, pp. 185-93.

11. Bernard S. Levy and George R. Adams, "Chauntecleer's Paradise Lost and Regained", *Mediaeval Studies*, 29 (1967), 178-92.

barnyard represents paradise, ruled over by a series of symbolic trinities — the widow and her two daughters, the three cows, the three sows — and the ram, which signifies Christ. Again, it might seem pedantic to remark that the ram is in fact an ewe (called Molly): to do so might seem to intrude upon some private act of self-communion.

How is one to deal with such interpretations? It is impossible to declare simply that they are wrong: nothing that is said about literature is strictly speaking verifiable, and therefore nothing is falsifiable. And yet we feel reluctant to allow ourselves to sink into a chaos of relativism, in which all interpretations are relatively true and more or less interesting. There must, we feel, be some principles, some criteria, by which we can test the validity of an interpretation, and discriminate between readings of greater and lesser truth and those of no truth at all.

There is of course such a test of validity, and it resides in the text, in the words of the text in their context and their ascertainable meanings, connotations and associations. What do the words say? is the question we should ask, not what should thay say if they are to support the interpretation that has already been decided on. Let us consider, for instance, the *povre wydwe*, universally interpreted by the moral-allegorical critics as the Church. Robertson makes this assumption, and supports it by the following process of reasoning. The widow is a *deye*, a dairy-servant; dairy-servants often engaged in other activities on the manorial estate, when needed, such as winnowing; winnowing is a symbol of the activity of the Church in separating the good souls from the bad (or the *fruyt* from the *chaf*); *ergo*, the widow is the Church.[12] Whatever the merits of this as a process of reasoning, or as a method of extracting the "true" meaning from a literary text, it runs clearly counter to what the words of the passage tell us. The description of the widow and her homestead has no suggestion of a representation of the Christian virtues of patient poverty, humility and temperance. Its tone is that of a genre-scene, a framed picture of rural virtue, and its effect is to provoke a charmed patrician smile as well as a genuine glow of sentiment. It is the ancestor of those Dutch landscapes in which all the unpleasant signs of poverty have

12. D.W. Robertson Jr., "Some Disputed Chaucerian Terminology", *Speculum*, 52 (1977), 571-81.

been safely stowed away, and it is full of elegant witticism at the expense of the widow; beneath it there is a sophistication of view which is sceptical of the value of enforced poverty. What virtue is in the temperance which is simply the necessary consequence of poverty? Such an understanding of the passage rests upon context: first of all, upon a large literary context, in which we would recognize the contrast between Chaucer's view of poverty and Langland's, or between this scene of romantically deodorized poverty and Langland's ruthlessly compassionate account of "the wo of this wommen that wonyeth in cotes";[13] second, upon a Chaucerian context, in which we see the resemblance between the life of the widow and the life of the frugal merchant of the *Shipman's Tale* on his business trip to Bruges, and the contrast with the life and drinking-habits of the chaste Griselda and Virginia;[14] and third, upon the context of the Tale, where we recognize the function of the description of the widow and her farmyard as an artistic contrast to the dizzy aristocratic splendour of Chauntecler. This last point is to be stressed: it is a matter of artistic or aesthetic contrast, not moral contrast. Chauntecler is a grand and splendid figure (as well as a cock), and the world would be the poorer without him. He would not have got into the scrape he did if he had been like the widow, perhaps, but he would not have got out of it either. To say that he *should* have behaved like the widow is rather like saying that Troilus should *not* have fallen in love: maybe things would have been easier for both of them, but all the world and all life would have been lost and all reason for writing about either.

It is possible to talk thus about the comparative validity of different readings of Chaucer. But there is of course an alternative reading of the *Nun's Priest's Tale* which has provoked into print a further numerous body of critics and which is the more difficult to refute and the more insidious because its initial premises are so plausible. Modern criticism has gained so much from the "dra-

13. William Langland, *Piers Plowman*, an edition of the C-text, by Derek Pearsall, London, 1978, Passus IX, line 83. See further, Claus Uhlig, *Chaucer und die Armut: Zum Princip der kontextuellen Wahrheit in den Canterbury Tales*, Mainz, 1974.

14. See *Shipman's Tale. Cant. Tales* VII.304; *Clerk's Tale, CT* IV.215; *Physician's Tale, CT* VI.58.

matic" interpretation of the *Canterbury Tales* — that is, from seeing the tales primarily as demonstrating in action the characters of their tellers — that there has been a temptation to push ingenuity in this kind of interpretation beyond the limits of good sense. On the whole, Chaucer has a care for the general congruence of tale and teller, but once a tale begins it is unusual to find clear-cut references to audience, teller or pilgrimage until the tale is over. And there are many discordant indications. These inbuilt restraints have not, however, deterred modern critics from wholesale dramatic interpretation, and a characteristic perversity has been to proceed from the detection of defects in a narrative through the application of irrelevant modern criteria to the conclusion that these defects must be attributed to the narrator, cleverly "framed" by Chaucer. In other words, a bad tale is made into a good tale by being seen as a good tale badly told by an inadequate narrator. That this can sometimes certainly be so — as in the case of a brilliantly bad tale like *Sir Thopas* — does not make the refutation of the position any easier.

The dramatic method has even been applied to the *Nun's Priest's Tale*, where it may seem that Chaucer has deliberately deprived us of anything to work on in the character of the Nun's Priest. In their determination to find the evidence that Chaucer fails to give us, critics have shamelessly conflated the hints in the Nun's Priest's Prologue with those in the Nun's Priest's Endlink, quite neglecting the fact that the latter is cancelled by Chaucer and the material in it used in the further characterization of the Monk in the Introduction to the *Monk's Tale.*[15] It is difficult to imagine Chaucer ever being exasperated by what modern criticism has done to him, but he would surely have been bemused, to say the least, by this procedure. Lacking all else, critics have fallen upon the very name Nun's Priest as the key to the meaning of the Tale, and have seen in the fact that the teller is a priest an opportunity to view the Tale as a parody of a sermon (conscious or unconscious, it hardly seems to matter which); and in the fact that he is attached to the Prioress a

15. See John M. Manly and Edith Rickert, *The Text of the Canterbury Tales*, 8 vols., Chicago, 1940, Vol. II, p. 422; Germaine Dempster, "A Period in the Development of the *Canterbury Tales* Marriage Group and of Blocks B^2 and C^2", *Publications of the Modern Language Association of America*, 68 (1953), 1142-59 (pp. 1147-51).

clue to the inner meanings of the Tale. "Every element in the story," says one critic, "bears some relation to the Priest's implicit aim — which is nothing less than to discredit the Prioress and establish his own intellectual and moral superiority to her."[16] The fact that this approach leads critics in totally contradictory directions — some, for instance, seeing Chauntecler as the representative of the admirable Priest and others seeing him as the representative of the un-admirable Prioress[17] — is only one indication of its perversity. It is, in fact, a sign-post to a wilderness, in which, with all the controls abandoned by which we would normally determine the validity of an interpretation, or the superiority of one interpretation over another, opinion only reigns.

In offering a way out of this wilderness, one would maintain that the satire in the *Nun's Priest's Tale* is Chaucer's own, and it is directed at all pretentiousness and particularly at the pretentiousness of intellect, the sanctuary from which satire normally operates. It could hardly be better exemplified than in Chauntecler's long and eloquent demonstration of the oracular significance of dreams, a conclusive argument which he then proceeds to ignore completely because he wishes to return to some unfinished business with Pertelote: indeed, it is his eloquence that *enables* him to return, for his self-esteem, bruised by Pertelote's reaction to his dream, badly needs the refurbishing which it gets from proving his intellectual superiority, particularly his intellectual superiority to the little woman. Grandeur and ridiculousness, the learned scholar and the randy cock, the human and the animal, are constantly juxtaposed in this Tale in a manner irresistibly comic. And yet even in the midst of all the hilarity there is meat for us to chew on. *Taketh the moralite*, we are told at the end of the Tale, but as we look at the threadbare morals we are asked to take note of — Keep your mouth shut, keep your eyes open — we feel that if this is the fruit, we would rather have the chaff. Chaucer is here directing us back into the Tale, as if to say that the real fruit of a tale is not in

16. Arthur T. Broes, "Chaucer's Disgruntled Cleric: *The Nun's Priest's Tale*", *Pubs. of the Mod. Lang. Assocn. of America*, 78 (1963), 156-62 (p. 157).

17. For the former, see Broes, *art.cit.*; for the latter, George J. Engelhardt, "The Ecclesiastical Pilgrims of the *Canterbury Tales*: A Study in Ethology", *Mediaeval Studies*, 37 (1975), 287-315 (pp. 296-300).

some little moral tag appended at the end, but in the body of the tale itself, in its reality as a narrative. He is criticizing all that kind of pedantry and bookishness which averts its gaze from the complexities, the mess, of reality and resorts instead to universalizing moral platitude. He is criticizing perhaps above all that sermonizing habit of mind (to which Chaucer critics are still susceptible, evidently) which turns fables of survival into allegories of salvation,[18] without respect to distinctions of category. The *Nun's Priest's Tale* has some very wise and witty things to say about human nature, about free will and destiny, about man's power of choosing and the contrary impulses that constrain him in the exercise of that power, but they are truths that are embodied in the Tale itself, and that will not allow themselves to be extracted by the mechanical procedure of *id est*. The Tale does not say one thing and mean another: it means what it says, and one of the things it says is that critics and cocks have much in common.

York Derek Pearsall

18. For an excellent study of the Tale from this point of view, see A. Paul Shallers, "The 'Nun's Priest's Tale': An Ironic Exemplum", *ELH* 42 (1975), 319-37.

Correction

Unfortunately at the top of p. 18 of *DQR* 1980/1 part of a sentence got lost. It should read after "experience,": "which calls for judgement, certainly, though it is Hamlet himself or Shakespeare speaking through Hamlet, ...". We apologize to Professor Knights for the mistake.

AS IF BY MAGIC

This is the very first time that I have ever spoken about one of my own books. I've talked about my work as a whole, but never about a single book like this and in a way it seems a very arrogant thing to do. As perhaps will come out of my talk, I have two sides to my character: one of which is very puritanical and that side feels very ashamed of talking about a book of my own; the other side is very hedonistic and that side is extremely pleased for once to be able to talk about one of my own books.

Regarding the title of the book and the book itself: the immediate subject of it is clear, it is that, although we may hope to do so, we cannot solve life's complex problems in a day. And certainly in the present day, we cannot solve those problems by reverting to various devices as though they were magical. We cannot, as the central male figure Hamo does, approach our problems by a kind of rationalistic, scientific, narrow magic. We cannot accept the suggestion that if we take science and reduce it to its most completely technical aspects and its most inhuman – without reference to its connections – we will somehow avoid any kind of moral danger that may attach to science. Nor can we accept that science will have magical results because we have confined it to its absolutely, purely academic quality. Nor may we, as Hamo also does, approach sex as though it was a magical thing which, if we denude it of all humane and emotional qualities and make it into something which is purely physical and without any actual human contact with people, will somehow act in a magical way to save us. I suppose this is the magic of my generation, of older people. But there is another kind of magic which has also grown up in opposition to that sort of rationalistic magic of my generation. The younger generations' magic, which is shown in the heroine, who approaches sex in the opposite way, as though it should be as vague as possible, that it should allow for as much possible emotional or physical connotations as can be allowed in it, and that somehow, if you do this, it will again produce magical results; or it may be found in the reversion to primitive magics, to Eastern gods, to religions which by their very vague quality, by the very nature that they say nothing which can be actually rationally examined, will somehow save us. The book on the surface is about the fact that we cannot be saved by magic. But it cannot save us because in life there are two things we have to make sense of. The one is to make sense of our own lives, to find some satisfaction for ourselves in our lives. And this cannot, I think, be done by magic. And the other is to make some communication with other human beings. This is a social quality, to have some relationship with other people, and this again cannot be solved by instant magic, whether it be rational magic or whether it be magical magic. But I shall go on to show how Hamo and Alexandra, each in their different way, become people running into magic, isolating themselves, cutting themselves off, not only from other human beings, but also in a way from themselves, that they somehow become lost; and then, how in some way, they are found again, which is the social and psychological centre of the book.

But there is another point that I want to make before I go any further: life does demand of us that we should find some purpose for ourselves and that that purpose should be something inside ourselves and also something within the outside world, with other human beings. But I believe there is another aspect of life which comes into this book and which is very important in relation to the book itself: that is that by the end of the book both Hamo and Alexandra realize that they've not only failed in finding a purpose in their own lives and in finding a connection with other human beings (and this they have tried to repair, Hamo tragically and without result, Alexandra with a limited result – but I shall come to that in a moment), but they do also realize that in being isolated, in being concerned with inside themselves, in being lost, and even also in trying to make some contact with the rest of society, with having social aims, with having personal aims in relation to other people they've missed something else. They have missed out on the actual, external physical world itself. At a very important moment in the book Hamo decides that he will go away to the hotel in the South of India and think up what he shall say about this magic rice, which he has brought to India and which in various ways has not performed the magic task that it is supposed to do. Before he does that he is told by Erroll, who is a kind of Sancho Panza to his Don Quixote, to go away and rest himself for a while and to take the field-glasses which he has with him and to watch the wild birds. Then he realizes "My God, all this time I haven't seen what is around me, I just haven't even been looking at the world that is round me". And when Alexandra goes to prevent the riot, her moment of courage when she goes to the fake Austrian swami to persuade him to get away so that the great riot doesn't take place, when she goes to the old city of Goa, with its wonderful Renaissance and Baroque churches, she thinks, "My God, I've never looked at this place; I've never looked at any buildings, I've never looked at the things that are around me. I've been worrying so much about myself and also about my duty to my neighbour that I haven't been looking at the visible world". And so at that moment they are suddenly overcome with the feeling that there is another thing in life, a third thing which is the world around us. And this is a plea for art itself, not as the magic that can transform our personal lives, except for the moment when it touches us, nor as a magic that can solve our relationship with society: but there is a quality of the world around us, the shapes and forms and colours which we neglect at our peril if we refuse to look at them at all, and also if we refuse to concern ourselves with learning them. When Hamo goes to look at the birds, they are a blur. He thinks "Those are probably cranes, that might be a stork, this might be an ibis, but I don't really know, I've never asked about the names of the birds". And when Alexandra sees the churches, she thinks "Baroque, I suppose, it's Baroque, I don't know, it's different to that one, that looks like Renaissance and that one looks like Byzantine, but it can't be in Goa".

The fact these words plea for is important: many people like to tell you that we can just go in and say "Ah, beauty, oh, lovely". But we must try to distinguish forms and shapes, and the meaning of words is important and so this is a plea, in a sense, for the book itself, which would have no importance in what it tells you about the relationship of human beings, one to another, or to themselves, unless it were for the words in which it is written, unless it were for the element of poetry which goes beyond what is being said, about society or about the individual. It is the words and the poetry which ultimately justify the existence of a book and to that extent there is some quality of magic in the book which is resident in words.

This sort of magic which we're calling art is not and cannot be a solution to our lives. People who have tried to live by art in this kind of way have found themselves lost really, I think, and certainly, it is no solution to our relationship with other human beings. But it is a satisfaction and many of the minor characters in the book, people who can be clearly seen to have failed in ways that neither Alexandra nor Hamo do, people with very false pursuits in life do have qualities and capacities for these moments of magical vision. Erroll, the young man who is the assistant of Hamo, in a way a rather cock-sure man, is constantly saying: "But you didn't see that. Why didn't you see it", because he can take photographs, because he has this sense. When they're in Ceylon he sees these pied kingfishers flying down into the canals to fetch fish and he has a vision of that. Erroll for all of this is a coarse-grained young man and afterwards is seen to be really more interested in money than in anything else: yet he has his moments of vision. And this is true of Alexandra's father, Perry the novelist. I think, he is a character treated perhaps rather unfairly by me, a kind of character I don't at all like, a sort of media-man, a kind of television man plus novelist. But he has his moments of vision. These people have moments, we could call it grace. These are moments of grace, I would not believe myself that man can live by grace alone, that is why the book is in some degree about works as well. But I want to point out that the book itself is the words in which it is composed and the shapes of which it is composed and this is a kind of magic. I don't believe it to be a magic which is only possessed by the maker. I think it's a thing which can be felt by the reader and should be felt by the reader and is something which the reader recreates when he reads the book.

But it is important to make this point, because otherwise it will look as though the novel is a book about society and psychology, but society and psychology are only in that book because of the words which make them up. And early on, I think, I try to suggest this by describing the laboratory, which in Hamo's eyes and the other scientists' is a place of scientific, rational work, in a way which gives it a totally different dimension, a purely visual and poetic dimension.

The difficulty about talking about one's own book is that it seems as though you are arguing for the thing being well done. I can't say whether it is well done. But this is what I'm trying to do in that passage, and I'm doing it on purpose, for instance:

> And on into another great glassed house, where box after box of antirrhinums offered now huge lips that threw proportion into limbo as do the artificially extended lips of some negresses in Central Africa; and then, as perhaps only among Venusians or

> the inhabitants of Andromeda, showed only the overhanging petal and no lips at all, mouthless velvet creatures. In an ever-changing range of colour from deepest red to deathliest white, through apoplexy, blood, blush, pallor and anemia, *pentstemon agate* showed her controlled rage. . . . But now, it grew warmer, and in the temperate air bougainvillaea tumbled its magenta streams as in any respectable Edwardian greenhouse, but the admired, showy, colourful bracts were vestigial, and the modest, usually unnoticed cruciform, cream-coloured flowers were monstrous and bold (p. 13).

This is seeing all of these plants, which in Hamo's eyes and the other scientists' are there purely for the scientific purposes, in quite another way, as a strange kind of expressionist painting if you like, a kind of monstrous picture. And I do this on purpose. So I start the book by saying: "Watch out, there is a kind of magic, but that magic is in this book and it is connected with seeing things in a special, poetical way, which is connected with the use of words and a vision". And early on in the novel too, we get this moment when the vicar, a Christian minister, whom grace has always evaded, a modern, rational vicar, who, when he comes to difficult things, produces humour and irony as a way of guarding himself against the deeper meaning of religion, sitting there, says to himself mechanically, because these young people are going to do a mime and this mime may contain mystery:

> Without mystery, our faith is nothing. Not by works alone. But *true* mystery, the *great* mysteries were never obscurantist, never foggy. The words of Saint John of the Cross burned through the soul with the clear Light of Love.

And he thinks:

> A light that I've never been quite able to face. He flushed at this thought, forcing it with a struggle back into its cage where only at long intervals was its desolate whimper heard to render his life waste. He closed his eyes and he summoned Keeper Humour and Keeper Self-mockery to his aid (pp. 10-11).

As if to say – "You know let's have a good laugh, then we needn't think about the fact that I've been a Christian minister all this time and I've never really known what mystery and magic mean." So this is a plea for the existence of some kind of real magic, which is connected, I think, with art. And it is noticeable that when a lot of little boys from the street come and crowd at the window, while the young people are dancing the mime of "Batteries", it says in the novel of one of the little poor boys from the nearby street, called Charlie Webster, who only comes in at that moment:

> Only Charlie Webster had realized that the mime meant something, that the loonies were poultry. And in his delight at this surprising unknown power of interpretation in himself, he winked through the window at the vicar, then ran off triumphantly, shouting, "Chicken! Chicken! " (p. 12).

He recognized what art meant, he had a sense of what something was which was more than just the actions that were being done. So this is an assertion from the start which is over and above the rest of the book, dealing with the question of how we can make some meaning in life for ourselves. It's a statement about the existence of the thing called art which is the book itself, which is the justification of the book and that justification lies ultimately not in the psychology of the characters, not in the social philosophy of the book, not in anything except the way it is put together and the words that are used. And this is the meaning of the magic of art which must be all there is in fiction, of any real value. Because fiction is not a social guide, nor is it a philosophical textbook, nor is it a psychological textbook, it is a creation of some kind of work of magic or of art, a collection of shapes and colours.

So I put that on one side and say that I want to think of that all the time as overriding anything else which we have to say about the book. But we live in society and I am, as many people of my generation, a social-democrat of the old-fashioned kind and for all the steady erosion that has taken place of liberal and social-democratic values in the last twenty years shall we say, I think a great number of people feel as I do, that they have to make some kind of sense, however limited, of a commitment to other human beings in terms of some sort of liberal, social-democratic code. And certainly they must see what can be salvaged about the meaning of their own life in a world in which, as I suggest, people have taken refuge in all sorts of magics because they cannot solve the meaning of their own existence there, let alone any kind of attempt to reach a connection with other human beings around them.

We are forced, as I say, to look again and see what we can salvage from this world, to satisfy the sense that nags most people, that we have a sense of responsibility, one for another. So in this book we take the fortunes of two gifted people, both Alexandra and Hamo imprisoned in themselves, unhappy people, they go round the world, one goes in one direction and one goes in the other and in the suitable conventional style of a picaresque novel they meet at a certain point. And we do so in a great degree in comic adventures. Because in the long run, if people are totally self-imprisoned, then they become comic. There is a certain quality about neuroticism, about neurosis, which is funny and absurd and it's best in a way to look at it from that point of view and one of the advantages of treating Hamo and Alexandra comically, as I do in the book, is, I think, that you are more likely to get some kind of sense of sympathy towards them in the long run, than you will if you try to make pleas for them. I've been struck by many people saying to me – and I think that perhaps the sexual adventures of Hamo are perhaps not everybody's cup of tea as the saying is, and one might have expected that many people would have taken against him, simply because of this – but I've been surprised at the number of people who've said to me "I think you are very unfair and unkind to Hamo". And I think I have succeeded in winning some sympathy for this character by treating him comically. But I have subjected him to what used to be called, you know, a kind of Laurel and Hardy-existence, a sort of Charlie Chaplin film-existence, because there's a certain amount of truth, I think, that when people come into a room and slip on a mat and fall down bang on their nose we all laugh and then afterwards we feel rather sorry for them because we feel ashamed of having laughed at them. So it's a way of getting a little sympathy for someone who might otherwise be rather repulsive to a number of people who might be reading the book. So that's to do with the comic side of that. This is a picaresque journey. It also has something like the form of a game of *Snakes and Ladders.* The stories of Hamo and Alexandra are a compound of the wandering of a picaresque novel such as you will get in the eighteenth century novels in Fielding or in Smollett or Sterne, or in *Don Quixote*, and also of snakes and ladders. Hamo lands in the uncle's picnic – go back twenty-seven places. Hamo lands in the Ceylon place – go back only five places and so on. Alexandra lands with the swami and shows herself courageous – go on twenty places. Let's look just for a moment first at the basic situation of Alexandra. I think it's important to do that. Alexandra is afraid. She engages in this sexual tripling because she is afraid not to do so, she is afraid to choose between the two men, because she feels – and it will become clear to you why this is so important later on – and she fears that if she chooses Rodrigo she will have chosen someone who will bully her, and if she chooses Ned she will choose someone who scrounges on her, who takes from her all the time. This is going to be, I shall hope to show you, the real social dilemma of the book: what are we to do about our fear of the strong? And what are we to do about our fear of the weak? How are we to deal with this? This seems to me one of the central social dilemmas of the modern world and I believe one of the reasons why in the sixties, when it was at its strongest and it still is very strong now, so many people resorted to various sorts of magic. But Alexandra is afraid. She is afraid to give up her tripling. She is afraid to go on with it, she is afraid to resolve it with Rodrigo, she is afraid to resolve it with Ned. She tries to create a world for herself for which she is only equipped by a sort of second hand magic of literature, made up of ideas taken from D. H. Lawrence and ideas taken from Tolkien's *Lord of the Rings.* This is a very second hand magic to manage life with. And she feels herself very much afraid of being refused love and yet she's afraid to give it. And she tries in fact to go mad. She tries to become mad as a refuge from the life that she fears so much. She moves towards hysteria, she play acts it always a little further so as to try and see if she can't get to a point that people can say you're not responsible, you don't have to do any more because you're mad. And she asks her grandmother, her great-grandmother, is there any madness in the family. She hopes that they will say yes, there is madness, then she can think "I'm no longer responsible, it's all right. I'm safe, I'm mad so it's all right. I don't have to worry". And yet she is nagged all the time by the knowledge that she's play acting, that the whole thing is a kind of play which she is doing and that it isn't really touching the reality of her life. Well, we'll come back to her in a moment.

Now we come to Hamo. Hamo has built up for himself what seems to be an absolutely impregnable fortress. Science for its own sake, technique, no reason given, just the technique. Sex for its own sake, no human connection, just sex. Nobody can blame you, it's just a thing which you do. You do sex, you do science. Nobody can say it's you. You are unblameable, you are not hurting anybody, you have no emotional connection. You are discovering this strain of rice because you have to work out certain scientific techniques, what is done with it is not your concern. You are unblameable. He has denied himself all possibility of impulsive life and it's to be noted that whenever he acts on impulse it becomes like Charlie Chaplin. In the plane when he gets up on impulse, he falls over. At the beginning, during that family party, when he suddenly feels that Alexandra is lost and unhappy, impulsively he goes to her and he offers her money. It's a disaster. The one thing he should not have done is to offer her money. And then in trying to recover from that he falls over and breaks Zoe's precious vase. Everything he does on impulse goes wrong. When he's been to the uncles' picnic and he's travelling back with one of the English uncles who's taken them there, they go to a Buddhist temple and the English uncle is very much attracted by the boy at the temple and goes away and he comes back having talked to him and says to Hamo:

> "Well, I shall have something to talk of at the club. Do you know what that chap was? I had my suspicions from the first that he wasn't a local Indonesian lad, though I tried him in each of the five local dialects. So I took a very long shot. My Batak's pretty rusty, but it acted like magic. He started jabbering away, God knows how he got here. One of our peasant lads looking for gold bricks again, I expect. They walk bloody hundreds of miles. Looks as if he could do with one of those chops, doesn't he? But then they're probably sacred."

And he goes on, saying that he pitched the story to him and obviously Hamo is thinking that he's made an assignation with this boy and he doesn't want to appear to be interested because he doesn't like it. But he feels he must say something and so he says:

> "What was his reply? " . . .
> "Well, it's difficult to give an exact translation for *imaguta-si.* But I suppose 'barmy' would be the right word. Yes, he said; 'You must be barmy' ".

And then Hamo sees that he can't help it, he laughs, on impulse, because he thinks it's so funny. All that this man reports of this great conquest is that the boy said he was barmy. And then Hamo commits a terrible thing because this man thinks that he is laughing at him for using old-fashioned slang, for he says in a very offended way:

> "We're not trendy here . . . But we're not fools either. You thought it very funny that I said 'barmy'. I'm quite aware that it's an out-of-date word. I use it because my father was very fond of it and that happens to be enough to make it a special pleasure for me" (pp. 184-5).

Now of course Hamo worships his father, so in a moment of impulse he's doing a terrible thing just because he laughed, because for once he has acted impulsively and he has lost the right to act impulsively having fenced himself round so that he need never feel. And if you've lost and denied yourself the power to feel then you've really denied yourself the right to any sort of impulse. And this happens all the way through with him. Everything that goes wrong is when he tries to do something impulsively.

So that by depreciating himself he can only give money, he can never give love. He makes these general rules, he's laid them all down in the past. Once or twice in the book he suddenly thinks of the time when he was a boy – it's all imaginary, he was a lonely boy with a father who was a soldier and a grandfather whom he worshipped, but he believes that at some time there was another boy, a working boy whom he played games with and they laughed and they were natural and they lived in a happy and natural way. And it's all a vision from which you can never get away, so he must forever make these sexual connections with working boys, but it can never have any kind of emotional reality. And the only time that he makes any real connection in his life is with a boy called Leslie (or a young man called Leslie), who is a working class boy and then that boy ceases to be working class. He's a very clever boy, he does very well, he's no longer a poor boy, which is what Hamo always romantically imagines, he becomes a fairly rich teacher and he's growing up. And then Hamo can't bear it. His romantic vision is gone. He has got to make some kind of relationship which is not a dream. And so he says I can't go on with this, because . . . And then he produces this formula, which is just like a scientific formula, he says he can only be in love with people of such a height and such an age and so broad across the shoulders and so big in the hips and so on. Which is a scientific formula which he has laid down, which will prevent him from ever really having to make any kind of human relationship at all.

So Alexandra and Hamo have, at the beginning of the book, cut themselves off from the rest of society, from the whole relationship – and this is important – from the whole relationship of society in distinguishing between who is a bully and who is a scrounger and what is a weak person and what is a strong: cut off from having to make this terrible decision which is what we all have to make, and which becomes increasingly complicated, about the nature of society: do we do harm to someone if we try to help them? Is help purely patronage, and do we ourselves assert a kind of bullying technique when we even announce that someone needs help? On the other hand, if we feel ourselves to be among the weak, if we ask for help, are we scrounging, are we refusing our own personality? And this is the whole complex of relationships which exists, I consider, in modern society, in so far as I've been able to see it in the communist world and certainly in the capitalist world today. These two people, like many other people have opted out with attempts at various magics. And the book is about how these magics do not work.

The problem is very much harder now than it was when I was younger, I think. One of the things that has happened is that people have developed a social conscience and also developed a kind of automatic technique for dealing with social conscience. I am not now making a plea for some kind of return to personal charity, not at all. But an enormously organized society which recognizes the existence of the helpless and the weak and the need for the strong and the powerful to help them make their way, inevitably has to have bureaucratic and remote rules for dealing with this. And so we are attempting to do something impersonally which is a matter of personal relationships. Recently a protest broke out in Cologne from many of the minority communities, particularly the Turkish community and also from some of the social-democratic groups, because two of the floats which were to be included in the carnival procession included one in which a young man is in bed with a young woman and it says: "I find it better in bed on social welfare". Another one showed a Turkish man and his wife with six Turkish children and it said: "I like having six children on welfare payment". Now you see, I think that this shocks a liberal person like me, but something must have gone wrong, when those people who are trying light-heartedly – and I don't believe them to be monstrous people who invented those particular floats – feel that in some kind of way their gifts and their right to have some recognition of their gifts is being drained away by the existence of people living on welfare. They have invented and given a new name to what I would have called when I was young and more especially when I was a young man, the needy. They will call them scroungers. People that I would tend to have called gifted people will now be seen by a great number of people as bullies. Now this is a thing which has grown and grown and grown I think, and is a terrible situation because on both sides, it means the end of all feeling. It is the underlying theme of the book and my suggestion is that this kind of conflict had by the sixties become so serious that people escaped, so they thought, by various sorts of magic.

Hamo, just before he goes to Ceylon, hears something which I think is very important. It's after the episode with the uncles, which upset him very much and I think for a very good reason; although he was deeply shocked, in a way, by this pederastic world, he also realized that there existed between the uncles and the nephews some kind of communication, whereas his high-minded determination to have sex without any connection meant that he was absolutely alone, so he was really almost worse than the people he felt uncomfortable with. And after that the world becomes very terrible for him for quite a while; wherever he went he heard "a high, distant overtone of perpetual, desperate woe. Could it be the natural noise of the world, as he began to fancy? " (p. 222) Now I think that we can get into the situation, which is a diseased one, of only hearing the high perpetual noise of woe. But I think you can get into a very much worse position, a very much worse noise and that is the noise made by Sir James, who represents the voice of the power, the voice of the bully. Sir James's answer to that high voice of woe, he gives at Hamo's funeral, when he turns everything that Hamo tried to do in the last months of his life upside down, to Alexandra's horror, giving a kind of social Darwinist address about Hamo:

> "Hamo Langmuir was one of the strong of this world. His life was given to discoveries, which would increase the number of

> those who are strong, by increasing the total amount of wealth at the disposal of society, by adding to the number of well-fed whose lot would naturally be cast on the side of a sane, organised, disciplined society. Science is knowledge and knowledge is order. But there are . . . the naturally unteachable, the naturally hopeless. Years of misguided sentimentalism, of capitulation to these elements, of paying of blackmail to the weak by the strong have brought us to a point where society is deeply threatened, where knowledge and science – the things for which Hamo Langmuir has lived – are in real peril" (pp. 409-10).

Now this is the voice of the opposite side and I believe them to be lost and diseased voices, but I would suggest that if we lose contact with that desperate sound of woe, then we are much more lost than if we hear it rather too loud, which is what Hamo came to do in the end. Hamo's fault is not the awareness of the voice of woe, which came to him at last when he changed his plans and decided that he would try to undo what had happened with his magic rice. That is not, I think, his fault. His fault is that he went on believing in magic even when he had come to realize that his magic rice had not profited those who lived on poor and rocky soil and on marshlands (which is I may say, an actual statement about the reality of certain rices which have done wonders for the urban populations of Asia). When he came to realize this he believed that somehow if he came forward and told these people who were desperate: "I'm sorry I made a mistake, I'm going to reverse it and I promise you we may be able to do something, I can't say we may do something, but we'll try and it may be rather late, you may have to wait a while". Now this was a belief in another magic, this voice coming to desperate people and giving them this rational message: wait a little bit longer and maybe it'll be all right. This was an impossibility, it's a kind of egotism and of course a hazard, which ironically fits with the fact that he gets killed by a mob which has nothing to do even with the people whom he thinks he is speaking to. So the answer he gives is an impossible and magical one to give just like that. But the discovery that he could not offer a magic as he had thought before, the discovery that there was this high and continuous voice of woe, was the beginning of some understanding of India. However, the use of comic forms (for example, in the Tokio brothel, – making fun of American folk literature; in the picnic of the uncles, a parody of Sade's *Hundred and Twenty Days of Sodom* and in the Ceylon household the parody of Feydeau's farces and of Nicolai Gogol's *The Inspector General*), the use of these kinds of farcical forms has disguised the degree to which he really has completely destroyed himself. But it really is too late when he comes to it. Those forms I chose, because most humorous literature, farce in particular, (a Feydeau farce, and nobody enjoys it more than me, or *The Inspector General,* which is a very funny play), is really about desperation. It's not about fulfilment, it's about loss and so I chose those farcical things and I chose Sade, because Sade's work is that of a person who believed that he was making a philosophical message, but all he was doing was to make a hollow noise and so these forms were chosen for their hollowness. And in each case Hamo ends even more alone than the awful people that he's involved with. He's more alone than the old, old American men in the Japanese bar. He's more alone than the uncles and the boys at the picnic and he's terribly alone when for once in his life he enjoys himself and this is the saddest part I think of his adventures, as I intended them to be. When he pretends to be various people at this Singhalese bourgeois household, when he pretends to be Dr. Malcolm (he's never done such a thing in his life before, he doesn't even know who Dr. Malcolm is) he feels his way and starts to enjoy himself. Then he invents another character called Roger Sudbury, and he really enjoy this. This is the first time he's let himself go and have some fun and although it's important to him because he really is doing it in order to have the kitchen boy, nevertheless he does invent these things and he begins to have fun. But what he has done is a very bad thing, because those people, even the subordinates and even the husband and his wife, but especially the old parents, these Singhalese people, though they are very conventional, though they are imitation-British and in some ways very comic, they are good and kind people, especially the old people. There is a moment when the old people turn on him and say something to him, which must come as a dreadful blow, much though he may have enjoyed the situation, which indicates what he has done, he who is a man of honour. When the old people come to see him at the hotel and tell him that the boy's run away and is completely lost, Hamo offers them money for him. But money is not really relevant for them and before they go, in the lounge of that hotel, the old man, Mr. Dissarwardene says:

> "Mr. Langmuir, I will tell you what Mr. Justice Carpenter used to say sometimes in the club after a day's work in the Court. 'Mr. Dissarwardene,' he would say, 'you failed today in your duty to your client. You did not master your brief properly. A professional man must always know the details of his job.'"

And then Mrs. Dissarwardene, who is a stately and honourable old lady, says with pride, filling out the rebuke:

> "Mr. Langford, we are here a *small* community. You have come among us here without respect" (p. 290).

Now this is a terrible blow for a man like Hamo. He's enjoyed himself for once in his life, but he's come and behaved without respect to a community of decent people. So you see all the way through, perhaps the humour hides the disaster of it all. When they say: he's a divine idiot, this is what Alexandra feels, when she feels she loves him in that moment in Goa, she suddenly says: "You're the divine idiot, you're Myshkin in Dostoyevski's book". This might be true, but we must remember that in *The Idiot* Myshkin fails. He fails everybody in the book, so divine idiocy may be a very pleasant thing to contemplate, but as a means of communication with human beings, it is finally a failure, and this is what Hamo has been. And she herself can't use his magic, as we see at the end of the book. She realizes that she can't use even what he has learned in life, she can't use his knowledge, she has to make her own knowledge. Well, now, what about her?

I'll just say a word about her and then I'm coming to the end. What of her journey? She is like her mother. She trusts too much. She doesn't, as Hamo does, cut herself away, but trusts too much. You remember that all the way through Zoe trusts too much in liberal cliches. She believes that if she talks to Concepcion, the cook, and tells her: you must take the pill and then she thinks, "Oh no, no, she's past child bearing, you must go and have a test taken for cancer of the cervix." Because she must bring her wonderful knowledge to this simple woman. She trusts that you can communicate whenever you want to and she trusts too much in the love of her husband. So Alexandra trusts too much in the boys, so that when they say to her: The real magic now is to do without the pill and she goes without the pill, then they turn in horror and say: "You didn't really believe us when we said it was magic, do you? " And then she has to make her decision. Now she makes a decision to have the baby and I want to make it clear that I think she made the right decision, a courageous decision. But having the baby doesn't solve Alexandra's problems. It takes her a step on, she's better off than Hamo for this reason, that when she is at Morocco with the baby and where they're compared all the time to the sea moving backwards and forwards and her life is a kind of monotony, this gives her rest. While poor Hamo never has any rest. He's like Charlie Chaplin, he's on the move all the time and round and round, so that he has no time to sit back and get the strength to make a decision. Alexandra is in a way very lucky, she makes a courageous decision, she has that baby, but then as Elinor, the American girl, says to her: "My God, you know, you think that life is all just simply baby's teats and changing their nappies, that isn't what life is about! " And motherhood is a temporary rest for her and it gives her the strength and the courage to carry on later. But she is due for a double shock, because she sat there with her baby, listening to the hippy-community as they came to talk to her, but not really caring about what the nature of this hippy community is at all. In particular not caring a bit about what the Moroccan population is like, what their lives are, so that she is quite amazed when she and the others are arrested, and she discovers that the hippy people believe in the magic of primitive communities but do not care twopence about the community which they have come among. Exactly like Hamo when he goes among the Singhalese people and they say, "you come without respect", the hippy community go to Morocco without respect and when their children are cold they kill the goats which are the only things that the Moroccans have to live on. Alexandra because of her motherhood, because of her absorption with the baby, has not known this. And so she is arrested and she realizes that she has been part of a very abominable deed. And then she goes to India and there she finds herself involved, against her will, because of her love of Ned, with the Swami and only wakes up very late to the fact that if the Swami is going to test out his powers, which he feels he must do since he's got to the state of half-belief where he feels that if he doesn't satisfy his followers that he has the power to raise St. Francis Xavier from the coffin he would be lost, then there will be very large riots. Then, only then, does she have the courage to act. She is ready, I think, only to be brave, but she isn't ready to be resourceful. I use, as I've often used in other books, as in my novel *Hemlock and After,* a Dostoyevskian device here – you suddenly go right away from the situation when you get this climax coming and all the people are there together and you know, all these tensions have grown up. I move away and speak from outside. Dostoyevsky does it very often, you'll find, especially in *The Possessed.* It suddenly changes tone – we have the episode of the rape of Elinor which ends "gathering her long towelling bathrobe about her trembling body, [she] fled, faster even than the avenging citizens running from the blood they had so suddenly shed". Then it changes:

> The situation for the local authorities in the following weeks was enough to daunt even the best-trained bureaucrats. It was all that the British in the days of Raj had meant by "out of hand".
>
> To begin with, the stonebreakers and indeed all the lower castes were roused to a sullenness . . . (p. 350).

We come once or twice to situations like that, so we see the situation from outside. When Hamo has been stoned to death and thrown into the river by the mob and Alexandra just managed to prevent the Swami from sparking off an enormous riot we get an ironic note:

> The authorities, on the whole, had good reason to be satisfied with the day's events. Some disturbances had taken place at the great temple of Vishnu at Shri Mangesh. Two worshippers had been injured by stones . . . The agrarian rioters, against whom the main forces of authority had been levelled, had never come within miles of the confines of the city; and only one death and two severely injured were reported from their confrontation with the police. A plant geneticist, who had shown himself unfriendly to India and uncooperative to Goa in particular, had mysteriously drowned in the Mandovi, killed, it was said, by followers of Vishnu. A hotel porter, a Bengalee immigrant, who'd disobeyed the curfew, had been burned to death in a bus. The Austrian Swami, long a figure of the greatest controversy, had disappeared from the scene. The larger part of his followers, including many of these offensive hippies, had been expelled –

> one, the red-bearded young leader of some dangerous mass-ritual, had suffered injury on arrest, but he was leaving on an aeroplane with his leg in plaster. The Jesuit Father in charge of the organisation of the processions in old Goa had written to the Chief of Police to thank him for his efficiency. There were a number of letters to the paper next week comparing the sense of order there with the lawlessness to be seen in so many far richer Indian cities. An account strongly on the credit side (pp. 386-7).

Well, that of course is the end of Hamo and the end of all his hopes. And you suddenly see from the outside the situation in which Hamo has shown his lostness and Alexandra has shown her courage and also she has shown, a strange thing, that nothing is completely useless. She'd thought that English Literature, learning Eng. Lit. as many people no doubt here are doing and I teach, that English Literature was of no service to her (indeed, a knowledge of *Women in Love* had hardly helped her in her life), but when she comes to rescue the Swami she suddenly remembers a scene from *Little Dorrit,* where Mr. Casby is made a figure of fun by cutting his hair. So she dresses the Swami up as an old woman and then at a certain moment she pulls his hat off and he looks a comic figure and the people who might have been violent burst into laughter. So English Literature was some use. And she comes back and she tries to fight Sir James and she's left with a sense of the limits of what she can do; a knowledge that she is, with all this money, in danger of becoming some kind of a bully, a nice kind of bully like her mother, not a nasty kind of bully like Sir James, but something of a bully maybe. She can't do what Hamo wanted to do, she's got to do her own thing. And her own thing is connected with this nice vision she has of the world outside, with not having hideous, ugly buildings destroying the line of a city, and of making houses for people, where they want them, which is the social part. But still she is left without any solution to her own function. She says that she doesn't really want to go on being a very successful unmarried mother, but there's nothing much else left on her hands at that moment. She's got two people that she might marry, one of them is obviously in danger of becoming a bully, the successful Rodrigo, charming though he is. And the other one, Ned, is obviously likely to scrounge on her for the rest of her life. On the other hand, when she says that he's gone off to the temple in Pondicherry to talk to the Great Mother, her mother, Zoe, in her usual cliché, says: "Oh, how terrible", Alexandra replies: "Not at all, we don't know. The Great Mother may have some message for him! " She has her mind open but she has no answer. She knows that all that is left to her is a limited capacity and that limited capacity must be the result of constant hard work, constant thinking and pleasure. If she does not get pleasure in the world around her then she has also failed. And one thing that she doesn't do, and this is a very important point to me. I don't know how many of you have read E. M. Forster's novels, but I come here to *Howards End,* where at the end of that novel one of the sisters, seeing the son making hay, looks out to the younger generation and says: "It's all right, it's going to be such a harvest as never was". What Forster is doing there and what I strongly object to is the idea that we don't try and do the thing ourselves, limited as that may be, but we will put it all onto a future generation. At the end of Forster's *Passage to India,* he says: ". . . not now and not in this place . . ." but he implies that it'll come, it'll come. I believe that this kind of fervent progressive hope is an evasion and when Alexandra's parents, all the old ladies at the end of the book look down at the baby and say: "Well, you know, it's all right, there's a baby there, the future generations will do it! ", she turns on them, rightly in my opinion and says in effect: "No, I won't have this E. M. Forster thing, putting it all onto the future. It's a limited amount we can do, but we shall do it now". And so it ends on a rather pragmatic note and that roughly is what the book is about.

Angus Wilson

This article is an edited transcript of a talk given by Angus Wilson on his own novel, *As If By Magic,* in Amsterdam on the 23 February 1976. The editors of *DQR* would like to thank not only Angus Wilson for allowing us to tape his lecture, but also Kees Helsloot and the English Department of *D'Witte Leli* for their help in recording and transcribing it. All page references are to the Penguin edition (1976) of *As If By Magic.*

EVELYN WAUGH'S SWORD OF VOLGOGRAD

Evelyn Waugh's novel of the Second World War, *Sword of Honour*, is a recension of three novels: *Men at Arms* (1952), *Officers and Gentlemen* (1955), and *Unconditional Surrender* (called *The End of the Battle* in the U.S.A., 1961).[1] In May 1960 Waugh wrote to Anne Fleming:

> I am slowly composing a third volume of the War novels – not bad, so far. All about the "Sword of Stalingrad." Do you remember that? Does anyone? It is the theme of the first part of the book and it will fall pretty flat if it is quite forgotten. Ask representative younger people such as O'Neill [Mrs. Fleming's son] if they have heard of it. Well I suppose the young don't read my books anyhow.[2]

Had the question been put to me, the answer would have given disappointment. I do read his books, and I was born in England in the second year of the war, which means that I had every opportunity to share the reminiscences with which all kinds of Britons celebrated their unlikely survival and the Allied victory. World War II is still Britain's favourite historical event, as television, from *Dad's Army* to *A Family at War*, will prove. I know about the *Altmark* incident, A.R.P., Woolton pies, the repeated sinkings of

1. A recension is a careful and critical revision of a text and Waugh, in using the term in the "Preface" to *Sword of Honour*, means a version of his three novels with the revisions, mostly cuts, which he made to shape the three books into one. These cuts are sometimes regretted by his critics, but to ignore their existence causes problems. In a good essay on the theme of chivalry in *Sword of Honour*, for example, B.W. Wilson seems to assume that *Sword of Honour* is simply the three novels laid end to end, and makes major use of several passages which have disappeared from the recension ("*Sword of Honour*: The Last Crusade," *English*, XXIII [1974], 87-93). I take the recension to be Waugh's final intention for the book which must be honoured and have made no use of passages excised.

2. *Evelyn Waugh and His World*, ed. David Pryce-Jones (Boston: Little, Brown, 1973), pp. 240-41.

the *Ark Royal*, Lord Haw-Haw, and Mulberry harbours – but until I read Waugh I had never heard of the Sword of Stalingrad; it could have been for me a fictional production.

Waugh's fear that a response such as mine would entail the failure of the opening of *Unconditional Surrender* is, however and of course, unfounded. He was careful to incorporate enough facts concerning the sword to place any reader in command of all the details he would need to appreciate the symbolic and ironic functions of that weapon. Yet a knowledge of the facts derived from sources other than Waugh does add something to one's appreciation, particularly since it throws illumination on Waugh's working methods and on his intentions. The sword's place in the scheme of the novel is truly important, and Waugh's concern about it was quite justified.

Waugh wrote a foreword to *Officers and Gentlemen* in which he stated that the work was to be considered finished, but as Christopher Sykes has pointed out, such a termination would not have been an artistic ending: "Too many loose ends would have remained; the full intention would have been but vaguely discernible."[3] *Unconditional Surrender* is in many ways predicted by *Men at Arms*, and the most striking of these predictions is the title of what became the first chapter of the recension and the title of the whole work – "Sword of Honour."[4] The sword so called is that of Sir Roger of Waybroke, the crusader whose tomb in the church of Santa Dulcina delle Rocce is visited by Guy Crouchback as he leaves his family's villa, the Castello Crauccibac, to return to England and the war. "Now on his last day, he made straight for

3. Christopher Sykes, *Evelyn Waugh: A Biography* (London: Collins, 1975), p. 375.

4. The manuscript of *Men at Arms*, now at the Humanities Research Center of the University of Texas at Austin, shows that Waugh planned to call the book simply *Honour*, so the theme was present in his mind from early on. *Unconditional Surrender* was earlier to have been called *Conventional Weapons*, a category which presumably includes swords. The best-known "Sword of Honour" in British life is that awarded each term to the top cadet passing out from the Royal Military Academy, Sandhurst. I am grateful to the Estate of Evelyn Waugh (represented by A.D. Peters and Co., Ltd.) and to the Humanities Research Center of the University of Texas at Austin for permission to consult Waugh's manuscripts and books from his library and to quote extracts and employ information thus obtained in this paper.

the tomb and ran his finger, as the fishermen did, along the knight's sword. 'Sir Roger, pray for me', he said, 'and for our endangered kingdom'."[5] The sword motif, introduced thus quietly, returns clamorously and discordantly, in distorted restatement, at the beginning of *Unconditional Surrender* where Sir Roger's "sword of honour" finds a competitor, the Sword of Stalingrad.

The Hitler-Stalin pact, in which Guy Crouchback has rejoiced since it brought the enemy, "the Modern Age in arms", into clear view, has been discarded for an alliance of the Western Powers and Russians against Hitler. To Guy this alliance poisons the cause for which he had hoped to fight, since what should have been an enemy is now an ally, and Waugh uses the Sword of Stalingrad to indicate the loss of honour and the pragmatical compromises which now pertain. Chapter eight of the recension, which had been the prologue of *Unconditional Surrender*, is called "State Sword". The Sword of Stalingrad is referred to in this manner partly to suggest such a phrase as "reasons of state", implying cynical power politics, partly to allude sardonically to the Swords of State of the English monarch's regalia, and partly to connect it with the cavalry sword which had been one of Corporal Ludovic's accoutrements when he soldiered with the Blues. To unweave this web of allusions, it is necessary to set out some facts.

Russian popularity in Britain became very great at the time of the Battle of Stalingrad at the end of 1942 and grew to amazing proportions in the following year.

> Frustrated in its desire for an invasion of France, the public became even more frenzied in its admiration of all things Russian. The BBC, which in June 1941 had refused to broadcast *The Internationale*, was by December mounting a special concert in honour of Stalin's birthday . . . and later there were frequent programmes about Russian history and a highly successful serialisation of *War and Peace*. But the public mania was insatiable . . . The government, unable to restrain the national hysteria, wisely took advantage of it. In September 1941 production was boosted by Tanks for Russia week . . . In

5. Evelyn Waugh, *Sword of Honour* (Boston: Little, Brown, 1966), p. 16. Page references in the text are to this edition.

> Croydon Russian droshkys toured the streets collecting donations . . . in London one borough, in a frenzy of pro-Russian sentiment, painted its dustbins bright red.[6]

Some acts of acknowledgement to the Russians were more ceremonial. The twenty-fifth anniversary of the Red Army, for example, provided one notable opportunity. There was, said Molly Panter-Downes in a London letter to *The New Yorker*, "a vast program including an Albert Hall pageant, called 'Salute to the Red Army' and composed by Louis MacNeice, with lots of symphony orchestras and Guards' bands to provide the sound effects".

This pro-Russian euphoria gave ironists much matter. "The Soviet flag flew gaily in the calm Sabbath air over a number of cities, whose honest bourgeoisie were as pleased to tip their hats to it as they would have been surprised to see it there three years ago."[7] King George VI, too, was moved by the Soviet resistance and indeed helped to build up the response. On February 22nd, 1943, *The Times* published the text of a telegram sent by the King to Kalinin, Chairman of the Praesidium of the Supreme Soviet of the U.S.S.R.:

> It was the unyielding resistance of Stalingrad that turned the tide and heralded the crushing blows which have struck dismay into the foes of civilization and freedom. To mark the profound admiration felt by myself and the peoples of the British Empire, I have given commands for the preparation of a Sword of Honour, which it would give me pleasure to present to the city of Stalingrad.[8]

The phrase "Sword of Honour" is therefore as much the King's creation as the sword itself, and it is instructive to observe Waugh's handling of this fact.

In the novel, the phrase "Sword of Honour" is never directly applied to any weapon. By its title, however, the first chapter applies the phrase to Sir Roger's sword, and this application is scrupulously denied by Waugh to the Sword of Stalingrad. The

6. Norman Longmate, *How We Lived Then: A History of Everyday Life during the Second World War* (London: Hutchinson, 1971), p. 486.

7. Molly Panter-Downes, *London War Notes, 1939-1945,* ed. William Shawn (New York: Farrar, Straus and Giroux, 1971), p. 271.

8. *The Times* (London), 22 Feb. 1943, p. 4.

headlines over the announcement in *The Times* included "The King's Gift to Stalingrad" and "A Sword of Honour", and it was some time before the paper began to substitute the more self-explanatory "Stalingrad Sword" for the original description. In anything faintly resembling an official document – such as Churchill's account of the presentation of the sword to Stalin – it is always the "Sword of Honour". To Guy Crouchback, however, and certainly to his creator, honour was precisely what had been sacrificed for the alliance with Russia. In Egypt, after the fall of Crete, Guy thinks back to his last day in Italy and of his happiness at the Hitler-Spain pact:

> Now that hallucination was dissolved . . . and he was back after less than two years' pilgrimage in a Holy Land of illusion in the old ambiguous world, where priests were spies and gallant friends proved traitors and his country was led blundering into dishonour (pp. 531-2).

Waugh's refusal to grant the Stalingrad Sword its official title, and his appropriation of that title for his own purpose are not his only acts of resistance to the official line. Another very Wavian stroke is the invention of a rumour which makes Trimmer, the hairdresser now become an utterly bogus "war hero", responsible for the sword. Ian Kilbannock, an official propagandist, confides the story to his wife:

> "By the way, do you realize it was Trimmer who gave the monarch the idea for this Sword of Stalingrad? Indirectly, of course. In the big scene of Trimmer's landing I gave him a 'commando dagger' to brandish. I don't suppose you've ever seen the things . . . A few hundred were issued. To my certain knowledge none was ever used in action. A Glasgow policeman got a nasty poke with one. They were mostly given away to tarts. But they were beautifully made little things. Well, you know how sharp the royal eye is for any detail of equipment. He was given a preview of the Trimmer film and spotted the dagger at once. Had one sent round to him. Then the royal mind brooded a bit and the final result was that thing in the Abbey. An odd item of contemporary history" (p. 577).

Waugh must have greatly enjoyed providing this sordid and spurious pedigree for the sword; it is the first of the two bastards Trimmer fathers in the book.

Westminster Abbey, where the sword was exhibited from October 29th to 31st, 1943, and where it attracted great crowds of visitors, provides Waugh with further opportunities to descant upon the sword as the symbol of dishonour and degradation. He moves into the matter carefully by recounting the difficulties Guy has in finding employment for himself as an officer. He ends up as a rather loosely attached and defined liaison officer with H.O.O.H.Q. and the author comments: "But it was not for this that he had dedicated himself on the sword of Roger of Waybroke that hopeful morning four years back". Then comes a set-piece description, not of the Abbey itself, but of one of its monuments:

> In all the hosts of effigies that throng the aisles of Westminster Abbey one man only, and he a sailor, strikes a martial attitude. The men of the middle ages have sheathed their swords and composed their hands in prayer; the men of the age of reason have donned the toga. A Captain Montagu alone, in Flaxman's posthumous statue, firmly grips his hilt, and, because they had so many greater treasures to protect, the chapter left him to stand there throughout the war unencumbered by sand bags, gazing across the lower nave as he had gazed at the ships of revolutionary France in the waters of Ushant on the day of victory and death.
>
> His name is not well remembered and his portrait, larger than life and portly for his years, has seldom attracted the notice of sightseers. It was not his sword but another which on Friday, 29 October 1943, drew the column of fours which slowly . . . (pp. 549-50).

Captain Montagu, therefore, has found renewed immortality in Waugh's novel because he grasps his sword, which is a sword of honour since it was borne into battle against a revolutionary and atheistical foe.

The Senior Service had a history of emphatic resistance to the types of political and social philosophies being "sanctified" in the Abbey on this day in October 1943, and it is interesting to note that on 2 August 1943 Waugh's friend the historian and later archbishop David Mathew presented to Waugh a copy of his book *British Seamen*, which includes the following passage:

> The old English commanders with their oaken competence and that self-reliance which was at once so stern and petrified could

> not abide the men of the Revolution, nor their atheistical and bloody principles. There was something monstrous in those officers who had been disloyal to their lawful sovereign ... Jacobin doctrines did not consort with the wrought snuff boxes and the demi-johns within the cupboard and the jewelled swords of honour of the Hanoverian Admiralty.[9]

Captain Montagu is estimable, too, in that he is *not* an officer of the Royal Air Force, a service which in Waugh's view had no history and an inflated contemporary reputation. All the R.A.F. men in the novel are bogus, such as Ian Kilbannock, for example; and B.W. Wilson aptly quotes George Orwell who saw "the need to raise a large air force" as having created "a serious breach ... in the class system".[10] The R.A.F. is politically and socially suspect, and Waugh finds an effective contrast in the Navy of the late eighteenth century. Though the total effect of the captain's effigy may be slightly fatuous, his presence in the Abbey is deserved and appropriate; that of the Sword of Stalingrad is a disgrace.

But Waugh does not say so openly. Instead he presents an ostensibly objective description of the scene which easily contrives to make his feelings felt. The queue of visitors to the Abbey, for example, includes some who smoke, or, as Waugh puts it: "[suck] cigarettes made of the sweepings of canteen floors". The quasi-religious elements – "a table counterfeiting an altar" – culminate in a virtually direct statement of the idolatry and sacrilege of the scene. The sword has "reached its apotheosis, exposed for adoration hard by the shrine of St. Edward the Confessor and the sacred place of the kings of England" (p. 552). It is a rival of the five Swords of State of the regalia, and particularly of the Jewelled Sword of Offering which, during the coronation ceremony, is laid on the altar and then girded on a King (or presented to a Queen regnant) with the words:

> Receive this kingly sword, brought now from the altar of God .... with this sword do justice, stop the growth of iniquity, protect the Holy Church of God, help and defend widows and orphans, restore the things that are gone to decay, maintain the

9. David Mathew, *British Seamen* (London: Collins, 1943), pp. 37-38.
10. B.W. Wilson, p. 91. Orwell's remarks were published in *Partisan Review*, July-August, 1942.

> things that are restored, punish and reform what is amiss, and confirm what is in good order.[11]

This particular "state sword", however, will be presented to a characteristically modern "sovereign" and clearly represents for Waugh English complicity in "the growth of iniquity".

Craftsmanship was a quality particularly dear to Waugh, but the fact that the making of the Sword of Stalingrad was the occasion for a demonstration that traditional crafts, too, were surviving the war was of no comfort to him. He cannot impugn the workmanship (though he notes and makes use of one error), but by using details provided for him by the publicity machine he is able to suggest a self-infatuation and silliness which are more sinister than the naive hopefulness which might seem today to be the characteristic note of the whole episode. One might, for example, contrast two accounts of the forger of the sword. Waugh says: "An octogenarian, who had made ceremonial swords for five sovereigns, rose from his bed to forge it . . . ." Molly Panter-Downes says: "[It] will almost certainly be the work of the famous eighty-four-year-old swordsmith Tom Beasley, who once made, among other notable blades, a flaming 'Garden of Eden' sword for Emperor Haile Selassie".[12] Waugh contrives to suggest senile enthusiasm, Panter-Downes veteran competence. "In this year of the Sten gun", says Waugh, "it was a notable weapon", and the phrase "year of the Sten gun" hints at grim political realities about which the British are deceiving themselves with twaddle about swords. Waugh's summary of his view of the motives of the "worshippers" follows at once. "The people were

11. *The Historical Record of the Coronation of their Most Excellent Majesties King Edward VII and Queen Alexandra Solemnized in the Abbey Church of Westminster on Saturday the Ninth Day of August in the Year of Our Lord 1902*, Compiled by H. Farnham Burke (London: Harrison and Sons, 1904), pp. xvii-xviii. Waugh owned a copy of this book, which is now at the Humanities Research Center, University of Texas at Austin.

12. Panter-Downes, p. 271. Had Waugh known of it, he would have enjoyed this connection with Haile Selassie, who was to him a bogus and comic figure, another product of publicity in the service of barbarism. His coronation was one of the two which Waugh attended. See his *Remote People* (London: Duckworth, 1931) and *Waugh in Abyssinia* (London: Longmans, Green, 1936). For an account of the second coronation, see *Tourist in Africa* (Boston: Little, Brown, 1960), pp. 88-91.

suffused with gratitude to their remote allies and they venerated the sword as the symbol of their own generous and spontaneous emotion". Self-regarding, self-deceiving.

The next item of the indictment involves poetry. On October 11th, 1943, *The Times* published a poem of twenty lines, "At Goldsmith's Hall", and Waugh, remarking that "The Times 'dropped into poetry' ", quotes eight lines from it (stanzas 3 and 5). By omitting the title, and by inserting his excerpts after the scene in the Abbey, Waugh gives the impression that the poet, F. Willis Abbot, is describing that scene rather than the purely secular occasion in Goldsmith's Hall. The stanzas quoted then reinforce Waugh's view that the sword is an element in a new religion of state, a competitor for the true religion:

> . . . I saw the Sword of Stalingrad,
> Then bow'd down my head from the Light of it,
> Spirit to my spirit, the Might of it
> Silently whispered – O Mortal, Behold . . .
> I am the Life of Stalingrad,
> You and its people shall unite in me,
> Men yet unborn, in the great Light in me
> Triumphs shall sing when my Story is told.[13]

But the poem is not quoted merely to exemplify the extent of pro-Russian silliness, for it allows Waugh to bring literature within the atmosphere of corruption represented by the sword.

The visitors to Westminster Abbey to see the sword are all tainted in some way. (Guy Crouchback, it might be noted, escapes taint here. He drives past the line of "devotees" but is "not

13. Waugh omits the first two stanzas, which are descriptive, and the fifth:

> I am the Soul of Stalingrad,
> The Hope and the Courage, and the Fears of it,
> The Blood and the Sweat, and the Tears of it
> Young tho' my form may be, ageless and old.

One might speculate that this was omitted because it focuses on the actuality of Stalingrad, linking the battle via the Churchillian echoes with the Battle of Britain, a parallel which was present to many minds at the time and which gave rise to emotions less self-serving, perhaps, than Waugh wishes to emphasize. Waugh's distaste for Churchillian rhetoric and his ironic use of echoes of it are presented by B.W. Wilson (see footnote).

tempted to join them in their piety. 29 October 1943 had another and more sombre significance for him. It was his fortieth birthday . . . ." Waugh himself was forty on October 28th, 1943.) One sinister "devotee" is the mysterious and mad Major Ludovic, formerly a member of the same Commando as Guy. They escaped together from Crete, where the brigade major, Hound, who like Ludovic has deserted his unit, has disappeared. In the words of Waugh's "Synopsis of Preceding Volumes" which prefaced *Unconditional Surrender*: "It is to be supposed that Ludovic perpetrated or contrived at [sic] his murder . . . . On the morning of the surrender Guy meets Ludovic on the beach. They join a small party escaping by boat. They suffer acutely from privation and exposure. Ludovic alone remains capable. The delirious sapper officer who was originally in command disappears overboard during the night. It is to be supposed that Ludovic precipitated him". Ludovic's avocation is literature, and he "keeps a volume of *Pensées*," maliciously modelled on Cyril Connolly's *The Unquiet Grave.*[14] He visits the sword in the Abbey hoping to gain some inspiration for a sonnet he intends to compose for a literary competition in the magazine *Time and Tide.*[15] Ludovic's metamorphoses from corporal of horse to field rank and from desk soldier to war hero (he gets the Military Medal for "saving" Guy) are soon to be accompanied by his metamorphosis from author of *pensées* and sonnets to big-time best-seller when his novel *The Death Wish* is published. There is an equation of bad taste with cultural decay, and this triumph of dullness is perhaps embodied

14. The manuscript reveals that, before he decided on "Ludovic", Waugh intended to call the character "Connolly". Since Cyril Connolly appears as "Everard Spruce" in the novel (earlier he was to have been called "Kenneth Willoughby" then "John [Jack] Spruce"), this use of his name once again for another repulsive character was cruel and unusual punishment even by Wavian standards. It is perhaps worth noting that in 1923 Waugh had done an illustration for an article in the *Isis* which told of a visit to Oxford by three creatures – an ant, a bumblebee, and a snail. The snail was called "Ludovic". Major Ludovic's molluscan features include his "oyster eyes" (p. 586).

15. Pedantry rejoices to point out that Ludovic is in fact too late. The sonnet competition was announced in *Time and Tide* on 16 October 1943 (p. 843) and the closing date was 26 October. The winning entry, by "Denvil", from which Waugh quotes some lines (p. 588) appeared in the magazine on 6 November.

in the fact that eventually Ludovic becomes the owner of the Castello Crauccibac. By bringing him into Westminster Abbey to look for "inspiration" in the sword, Waugh makes him another bogus worshipper at this false shrine, and corruption is shown to be spreading.

But Ludovic's presence in the circle around the sword lays bare a further area of corruption, one perhaps more important than the colonization of letters. As he passes St. Margaret's Westminster, Ludovic remembers a fashionable wedding at which he was one of the guards of honour. At the reception afterwards, Ludovic was picked up by Sir Ralph Brompton, a crypto-homosexual and crypto-communist member of the diplomatic service. As a corporal of the Blues, the Royal Horse Guards (the regiment to which Waugh transferred from the Royal Marines), Ludovic is in this following regimental tradition, albeit one less glorious than that of the battlefield. Male prostitution is a custom of long-standing among the Other Ranks of the Household Brigade, but Ludovic is unusually fortunate in his protector. He becomes Sir Ralph's "valet" and "secretary", accompanying him abroad and receiving an education at his hands. "The marriage, at which they met, did not last long. There was an unusually early divorce. Ludovic, as he now was, constituted the sole progeny of that union" (p. 565).

Ludovic's mind runs on swords as he passes St. Margaret's, for the guard of honour had held up an arch of swords under which the newly wedded couple had passed. Later, at a party given by the editor of *Survival,* Everard Spruce, Ludovic recognizes the bride:

> "I was at your wedding," said Ludovic.
> "Surely not? No one was."
> "Your first wedding."
> "Oh yes, of course, everyone was *there*."
> "I held my sword over your head when you left the church."
> "That was a long time ago," said Lady Perdita. "Think of it: *swords*." (p. 574).

Waugh's views on divorce were uncompromising, and it is clear that Lady Perdita is perhaps as "lost" as her Shakespearian namesake, but not as innocent. The swords at her wedding are enormously remote in their chivalrous symbolism, but the real meaning of marriage is no less remote, and marriage too comes into the atmosphere of decay.

From the Abbey, Ludovic makes his way to an assignation with Sir Ralph and at one point in their talk he refers to his visit:

> "I went to the Abbey before I came here – to see the sword."
> "Yes, I suppose like everyone else you are coming to appreciate the Soviet achievement."

Ludovic makes clear his real purpose and remarks that "it set me thinking – about swords". Sir Ralph says: "You were meant to think about tanks and bombers and the People's Army driving out the Nazis":

> "I thought of my sword," said Ludovic stubbornly.
> "Technically, I suppose, it was a sabre. *We* called them 'swords' – 'state swords.' Never saw it again after I left the regiment" (p. 568).

This conversation (I have not quoted it all) is created by Waugh principally to allow him to plant the term "state swords". The resonance with "sword of state" and the coronation ceremony now acquires the political strain – of subversion and totalitarianism – which Sir Ralph contributes. The great theme of betrayal, found throughout *Sword of Honour*, here becomes specific and political, and it is clear that the revelations of the 1960's concerning Burgess, Maclean, and Philby have greatly influenced Waugh. (The novel is, of course, a product of the postwar and Cold War years.) Sir Ralph is described when first introduced as "a figure of light comedy rather than of total war", but even so Waugh intends his subversive activities to be taken seriously. Later, he says of him: "Wherever those lower than the Cabinet and Chiefs of Staff adumbrated the dismemberment of Christendom, there Sir Ralph might be found", and Sir Ralph is seen assisting those who wish to use the European partisan and resistance movements to facilitate the advance of Communism. When he first appears in the novel, visiting a boy-friend nicknamed "Susie" at H.O.O.H.Q., the emblematic subject of conversation is, of course, the sword:

> "Been to see the Stalingrad sword? " Susie asked. "Nice bit of work. But I reckon a few machine guns would have been more to the point."
> . . . "It affords the People an opportunity for self-expression," said Sir Ralph (p. 559).

Sir Ralph and his adherents thus take their places around the sword. One more figure completes the circle, "the Loot".

Lieutenant Padfield is an ubiquitous American, "a portent of the Grand Alliance".[16] The Loot is affable and highly gregarious, and at first the narrator's measurable distaste for him seems no more than routine anti-Americanism. But gradually we learn of a pattern of "betrayals" perpetrated by him which makes him an unusually sinister figure. He is an intimate of Sir Ralph's, and Kerstie Kilbannock says: "I don't think the Loot likes women". It is the Loot whose evidence enables Mr. Troy, a later husband of Guy's former wife, Virginia, to divorce her without alimony. The Loot finds the bogus *Survival* "significant". He is in Italy when Guy arrives there and is friendly with Cattermole, a pro-Tito fanatic at Bari, headquarters of the British Mission to the Anti-Fascist Forces of National Liberation (Adriatic). The Loot is very probably the "young American I know" who tips off Cattermole that a Serb on a mission to the Communist partisans is carrying a gold watch for Mihajlovic, the chetnik leader, inscribed with the title of Minister of War in King Peter's government in exile. (The Serb is killed by the partisans.) After the war, the Loot becomes Ludovic's "factotum" and negotiates his acquisition of the Castello Crauccibac from Guy.

When Padfield first enters the novel, he too alludes to the sword:

> "I think it is a very lovely gesture of your king's, but there was a feature no one could explain to me – the escutcheon on the scabbard will be upside down when it is worn on a baldric."
>
> "I don't suppose Stalin will wear it on a baldric."
>
> "Maybe not. But I was certainly surprised at your College of Arms passing it."

16. The Loot seems to be based on Stuart Preston who "came to England in the van of the American troops . . . he was much fêted in London social and literary circles owing to his charm and intelligence". He "was known to his English friends as the Sergeant, because he was a sergeant in the U.S. army" (James Lees-Milne, *Ancestral Voices* [London: Chatto and Windus, 1975], pp. 137n, 157n). Harold Acton quotes a reference of Waugh's to Heywood Hill's bookshop as a place "at least one American Sergeant will remember" and identifies the sergeant as Stuart Preston, "much lionized in London towards the end of the war" (*Nancy Mitford: A Memoir* [London: Hamish Hamilton, 1975], pp. 82-83.)

> . . . "Pretty fair cheek that young American finding fault with the sword," said Jumbo as they left the restaurant. "What's more he didn't discover the mistake. There was a letter about it in *The Times* weeks ago." (pp. 555-6).

"Weeks ago" was nearly four months earlier when, on June 29th, 1943 *The Times* published an extract from a letter from Mr J.A. Collins of Ashdon Hall, Essex:

> Your illustration of this beautiful weapon discloses a somewhat singular feature. The royal coat-of-arms on the scabbard is depicted with the top of the shield towards the point instead of towards the hilt. Slung from the belt or baldrick of the knight the emblazonment would appear to be upside down. It would be interesting to have this explained, for the emblems, including the Royal Arms, on the scabbard of the Sword of State of the Regalia are otherwise imposed.

Waugh, one may easily surmise, was delighted to discover this error in design which emphasizes the falseness of the Sword of Stalingrad, but he makes the introduction of the fact into the narrative revelatory also of the Loot's assiduous, unscrupulous, but very successful penetration of English society. His nationality, underlined by the nickname which hints of plunder, added to the hints concerning his sexual, political, and literary proclivities, and combined with his strangely ominous ubiquity, makes him perhaps the most threatening of the swordsmen.

Martin Green suggests that by splitting up and distributing characteristics which were united in the character of a Guy Burgess, for example, Waugh has perhaps weakened his novel by diffuseness.[17] This may be so, but the need to create a number of figures with harmonious and overlapping characteristics was surely essential. Waugh's attempt to create a central emblem to hold his figures in pattern is the sword. And while it is possible to argue that this device is flawed by factitiousness, it is typical of Waugh's methods that the sword itself should be a fact and one which needed only a few touches of literary improvement to make it fit the novel. The love of fact is one aspect of Waugh's deep-seated

17. Martin Green, *Children of the Sun* (New York: Basic Books, 1976), p. 371.

literalism; as with many artists of a satirical bent, the surface fact is valued as a reliable clue to hidden truths.

None of the swordsmen is an inconsequential figure in the later stages of *Sword of Honour*; each of them has an effect on Guy Crouchback's destiny. Yet, placed as they are around the sword, these figures have an important secondary function as the collective embodiment of an upstart culture. Another theme of *Sword of Honour*, one it shares with Ford Madox Ford's *Parade's End*, is "who shall inherit England? " Waugh predicts that the swordsmen, these crusaders of darkness, will do so, and it is interesting to observe that in making his prediction he creates – quite inadvertently, I presume - a series of parallels with another and much earlier prediction of the triumph of ignorance, Alexander Pope's *The Dunciad*.

Pope's poem, for example, depicts a society in which all the strata, from the Hanoverian court to the depths of Grub Street, conspire together to promote dullness. Waugh links King George VI to Trimmer, the near-plebeian phoney, in the begetting of the sword, and all levels from aristocracy to the masses are shown to be promoting the values the sword represents. Pope's mob becomes the stream of repulsive "worshippers" queueing for a glimpse of the sword, and the ceremonies around which Pope constructs his poem – the Coronation procession, the Lord Mayor's pageant, and the proclamation of a prophet-Messiah – are subsumed into a pseudo-religious ceremony in Westminster Abbey itself. Pope makes much of the geographical "progress" of dullness from the East of London – the City of London, the home of Whig commercialism, of the cash nexus and unorthodox religion – to the West End, where the Court should, but does not, maintain the values of civilization. Waugh's sword moves from the hall of the Goldsmith's Company to the western minster and brings with it a mob of which "many were entering for the first time in their lives" and who "knew no formal act of veneration". (In another context, American responsibility includes encouragement of this migration from the East End to the West. "For [the comfort of U.S. servicemen] there swarmed out of the slums and across the bridges multitudes of drab, ill-favoured adolescent girls and their aunts and mothers, never before seen in the squares of Mayfair and Belgravia.") Sexual and political deviations appear in the indictments made by both authors. Most of all, Waugh's linking of the sword via Ludovic to the world of modern literature is an Augustan equation of cultural decline and bad taste with the failure of civilization.

After the scene in Westminster Abbey and the conversations to which that gives rise, the Sword of Stalingrad disappears from the novel, though Waugh's allusions help sustain its symbolic resonance, as when he remarks that some of the Allied troops in Italy wore "ironically enough, the woven badge of the crusader's sword" (p. 716). But in fading from the novel, the sword did not cease to exist but continued in the world of fact, where, of course, by one of the strange paradoxes of life's relation to art, it has a more tenebrous existence than it has in fiction. Such, at least, is the case in the Western world. In Russia, the situation is reversed, for there the Sword of Stalingrad is widely known while Evelyn Waugh is but the most shadowy of presences.

At the Teheran Conference in late November 1943, Winston Churchill presented the Sword of Honour to Stalin:

> When, after a few sentences of explanation, I handed the splendid weapon to Marshal Stalin, he raised it in a most impressive gesture to his lips and kissed the scabbard. He then passed it to Voroshilov, who dropped it. It was carried from the room in great solemnity, escorted by a Russian guard of honour.[18]

In Waugh's novel there is only one reference to Teheran. Guy Crouchback re-reads the letter from his recently dead father which contains the sentence which Waugh intends should apply to all the experience his novel depicts: "Quantitative judgements don't apply". The narrative then states: "There was a congress at Teheran at the time entirely occupied with quantitative judgements" (p. 672). Waugh must have known that the sword was presented at Teheran, for he next mentions, with irony, the visit of Churchill and Roosevelt to the sphinx that occurred when the "two puissant old gentlemen" were returning from Teheran – an account which draws on Churchill's own recollection. To mention the sword in connection with Teheran, however, might have overshadowed "quantitative judgements" or even have strained credulity.

18. Winston S. Churchill, *The Second World War: Volume V, Closing the Ring* (London: Cassell, 1952), p. 321.

The sword travelled back from Teheran with the Russian delegation and in 1948 went on display in what is now the State Defence Museum in Volgograd, formerly Stalingrad. There, according to *Nagel's U.S.S.R.*, it reposes among many other tokens of esteem, such as a flag "clandestinely embroidered by Norwegian women", "a miner's lamp given by Polish workers" and "a shield presented by the Negus Haile Selassie".[19]

I thought it would be interesting to try to obtain a picture of the Sword of Stalingrad *in situ* and considered writing to the Russian authorities. I wondered, however, whether I should mention anything of Waugh's employment of the sword and decided first to check on the Soviet opinion of him. A colleague in the Russian Department at Dartmouth College, George M. Young Jr., investigated on my behalf, and I gratefully quote from his memorandum:

> I've had a chance to check the Soviet source on Waugh. As might be expected, he isn't a favorite with them – not a Jack London, a Dreiser, or a Howard Fast. The first thing that interested me was their spelling of his name. The Cyrillic alphabet is more nearly phonetic than ours, so what they usually do in transcribing English names is to figure out how they're pronounced and spell them accordingly. I expected Waugh to come out Ua in Cyrillic (as in Ualt Uitman), but it turned out to be Vo. Now, playing Sherlock Holmes, I would venture two possible explanations. Either they didn't have anyone who knew enough about Waugh to know how his name is pronounced in English, or someone knew but wanted to give the impression that he didn't, thus sparing himself from charges of being overly interested in the work of reactionaries and decadents. Usually they are quite careful about how they spell foreign names, and, working within a centralized system, they are absolutely consistent. Once it is spelled Vo it must remain Vo forever. So I was a bit surprised that

19. *Nagel's Encyclopedia Guide: U.S.S.R.*, 4th ed. revised (Geneva, 1973), p. 687. Waugh might have been delighted to learn that Haile Selassie had presented a shield to complement George VI's sword. See note 8 above. A full description of the Stalingrad Sword is given in *The Times,* 25 July 1943, p. 4. Good pictures appear in *The Illustrated London News*, 3 July 1943, p. 21 and 9 Oct. 1943, p. 412.

the normally meticulous editors of the Literary Encyclopedia settled on Vo as the official spelling.

Now here's what they say about your man. First, under the Vo heading, they indicate that there are two, Alec and Evelyn. Alec is polished off first, then Evelyn:

"Waugh, Evelyn, born X/28/03, brother of Alec, began literary activity in 1928. In the 1930's he advanced and supported Italian fascism. In the novel *Brideshead Revisited*, 1945, his mystical views are reflected. During the Second World War he published the novel, *Put Out More Flags*, (1942) about the adventures of a high-society blackmailer. *The Loved One* (1948) bears [carries, displays, wears – the word in Russian means all of these] a pathological character. In the novels *Men at Arms*, 1952, and *Officers and Gentlemen*, 1955, devoted to the events of the Second World War, E. Waugh's reactionary position is laid bare. In the novel, *The Ordeal of Gilbert Pinfold*, 1957, he continues the antidemocratic tendency of modernism."

Kratkaja literaturnaja enciklopedija (Short Literary Encyclopedia), Volume I, Moscow, 1962, p. 999.

George Young's information convinced me that I was unlikely to ingratiate myself at all by mentioning Evelyn Waugh to the Russians, so I settled merely for asking how the sword had made its way to Russia, when it had gone on display, and if there was available a picture of it. I received a polite reply giving me the information but making no reference to a photograph or postcard. The letter did, however, give me one intriguing fact. What, I wondered, did the Russians call the sword? – "pochetnyi mech", is the answer, "sword of honour". And so, if the time ever comes when the book is translated into Russian, the title at least will be easy.[20]

Dartmouth College — David Wykes

20. The *Times* "diary" of September 24th, 1976, announced a translation, under the heading "Hard Line".

THE DUTCH QUARTERLY REVIEW OF ANGLO-AMERICAN LETTERS

Index to Volumes 1-10 (1971-1980)

Compiled with the Aid of Tejo Borm

1. ARTICLES AND REVIEW ARTICLES

II. SURVEYS

1. *A Critical Bibliography of American Literature*

2. *A Critical Bibliography of English Literature*

Bronzwaer, W.F. Diekstra and G. Janssens	A Critical Bibliography of English Literature: The Middle Ages to the Eighteenth Century	1 (1971/1)	27- 40
Diekstra, F.N.M.	A Critical Bibliography of Old and Middle English Literature	2 (1972/1)	21- 30
Dorsten, J. van	A Critical Bibliography of English Literature: The Sixteenth and Seventeenth Centuries	5 (1975/1)	54- 60
—	A Critical Bibliography of English Literature: The Sixteenth and Seventeenth Centuries	7 (1977/3)	214- 26
Janssens, G.A.M.	A Critical Bibliography of English Literature: The Seventeenth and Eighteenth Centuries	2 (1972/3)	97-103
Janssens, G. and W. Bronzwaer	A Critical Bibliography of English Literature: The Eighteenth to the Twentieth Century	1 (1971/2)	82- 97
Loop, A. van der and W. Bronzwaer	A Critical Bibliography of English Literature: The Nineteenth and Twentieth Centuries	3 (1973/3)	123- 34
Loop, A. van der	A Critical Bibliography of English Literature: The Eighteenth and Nineteenth Centuries	5 (1975/3)	206- 17
—	A Critical Bibliography of English Literature: The Nineteenth Century	8 (1978/2)	137- 49
Schulte, F.G.F.	A Critical Bibliography of English Literature: The Twentieth Century	7 (1977/1)	50- 65
—	A Critical Bibliography of English Literature: The Twentieth Century	9 (1979/2)	129- 48

3. *Shakespeare Criticism*

Bronzwaer, W.	A. Survey of Recent Shakespeare Criticism	3 (1973/1)	32- 8
—	A Survey of Recent Shakespeare Criticism	4 (1974/1)	28- 37

4. *Poetry*

5. *Drama*

6. *Linguistics and Stylistics*

III. INTERVIEWS

IV. BOOKS REVIEWED

Bolton, W.F. and D. Chrystal, eds.	*The English Language: Essays by Linguists and Men of Letters* (1858-1964) (1969)	1 (1971/3-4)	186- 7
Booth, W.C.	*A Rhetoric of Irony* (1974)	5 (1975/1)	76- 9
Bowman, E.	*The Minor and Fragmentary Sentences of a Corpus of Spoken English* (1966)	1 (1971/1)	5- 6
Bradbury, M.	*The Social Context of Modern English Literature*	2 (1972/2)	89- 93
Brady, F., J. Palmer, and M. Price eds.	*Literary Theory and Structure: Essays in Honor of William K. Wimsatt* (1973)	5 (1975/2)	154- 61
Brett, R.L., gen. ed.	*Writers and Their Background* (series)		
–	*S. T. Coleridge* (1971)	5 (1975/2)	145- 53
Brewer, D., ed.	*Geoffrey Chaucer* (1974)	5 (1975/2)	138- 45
Brower, R., H. Vendler, and J. Hollander, eds	*I.A. Richards: Essays in his Honor* (1973)	5 (1975/3)	218- 24
Bruns, G.L.	*Modern Poetry and the Idea of Language* (1974)	6 (1976/1)	79- 81
Budgen, F.	*James Joyce and the Making of "Ulysses"* (1972)	3 (1973/4)	185- 7
Burgess, A.	*Joysprick: An Introduction to the Language of James Joyce* (1973)	5 (1975/3)	225- 8
Burkhart, C., ed.	*The Art of Ivy Compton-Burnett* (1972)	3 (1973/4)	183- 4
Butscher, E.	*Sylvia Plath, Method and Madness* (1976)	8 (1978/1)	58- 62
Calderwood, J.L. and H.E. Toliver, eds.	*Perspectives on Fiction; Perspectives on Poetry; Perspectives on Drama* (1968)	1 (1971/1)	62- 4
Campion, T.	*The Works* (1969)	1 (1971/2)	120- 2
Carey, J.	*The Violent Effigy: A Study of Dickens' Imagination* (1973)	4 (1974/3)	1390 40
Carey, J. and A. Fowler, eds.	*The Poems of John Miltion* (1968)	1 (1971/3-4)	179- 81
Chapman, R.	*Linguistics and Literature* (1973)	4 (1974/4)	187- 9

	cal Imagination in American Fiction (1975)	5 (1975/4)	305- 12
Henke, A.	*Joyce's Moraculous Sindbook. A Study of "Ulysses"*	10 (1980/1)	75
Henn, T.R.	*The Harvest of Tragedy* (1966)	1 (1971/1)	60- 2
Hernadi, P.	*Beyond Genre: New Directions in Literary Classification* (1972)	5 (1975/1)	79- 81
Herndon, J.H.	*A Survey of Modern Grammars* (1970)	2 (1972/3)	141- 3
Hewitt, B.	*History of the Theatre: From 1800 to the Present* (1970)	1 (1971/2)	127- 8
Hewitt, D.	*The Approach to Fiction* (1972)	4 (1974/1)	46- 8
Hindus, M., ed.	*Walt Whitman: The Critical Heritage* (series) (1971)	4 (1974/3)	133- 9
Hodgart, M.	*James Joyce: A Student's Guide* (1978)	10 (1980/1)	73- 4
Holbrook, D.	*Sylvia Plath: Poetry and Existence* (1976)	8 (1978/1)	58- 62
Hollis, J.R.	*Harold Pinter: The Poetics of Silence* (1970)	2 (1972/1)	31- 2
Hornby, A.S.	*Guide to Patterns and Usage in English* (1975)	6 (1976/2)	157- 61
Huddleston, R,D.	*The Sentence in Written English: A Syntactic Study Based on an Analysis of Scientific Texts* (1971)	4 (1974/1)	41- 5
Hughes, A. and A. Trudgill	*English Accents and Dialects. An Introduction to Social and Regional Varieties of British English* (1979)	10 (1980/2)	156- 61
Jakobson, R. and L.G. Jones	*Shakespeare's Verbal Art in "Th' Expence of Spirit"* (1970)	1 (1971/1)	59- 60
James, E.A.	*Daniel Defoe's Many Voices: A Rhetorical Study of Prose Style and Literary Method* (1972)	5 (1975/3)	239- 43
Janssens, G.A.M.	*The American Literary Review: A Critical History 1920-1950* (1968)	2 (1972/1)	38- 9
Jump, J.D., ed	*The Critical Idiom,* 27 Vols. (1969)	1 (1971/3-4)	190- 1
Kean, P.M.	*Chaucer and the Making of English Poetry: Vol. 1* (1972)	3 (1973/4)	191- 2

Mack, M.	*The Garden and the City: Retirement and Politics in the Later Poetry of Pope 1731-1743*	2 (1972/1)	40- 2
Man, PDe			
Man, P.De	*Blindness and Insight: Essays in the Rhetoric of Contemporary Criticism* (1971)	2 (1972/4)	189- 91
Mariani, P.L.	*A Commentary on the Complete Poems of Gerard Manley Hopkins* (1970)	1 (1971/2)	116- 7
Martin, G., ed.	*Eliot in Perspective: A Symposium* (1970)	2 (1972/1	33- 5
Martin, R.B.	*The Triumph of Wit, A Study of Victorian Comic Theory* (1974)	7 (1977/2)	154- 6
Matthews, P.H.	*Morphology: An Introduction to the Theory of Word-Structure* (1974)	8 (1978/3)	225- 33
McCormick, J.	*American Literature 1919-1932* (1971)	3 (1973/1)	39- 44
McHugh, R., ed.	*Ah, Sweet Dancer: W.B. Yeats and Margot Ruddock, A Correspondence* (1970)	1 (1971/1)	42- 3
—	*The Sigla of "Finnegans Wake"* (1976)	10 (1980)	76- 7
McKinnon, W.T.	*Apollo's Blended Dream: A Sudy of the Poetry of Louis MacNeice (1972)*	2 (1972/4)	178- 81
Meys, W.J.	*Compound Adjectives in English and the Ideal Speaker-Listener* (1975)	7 (1977/3)	227- 31
Minter, D.L.	*The Interpreted Design as a Structural Principle in American Prose* (1969)	3 (1973/3)	142- 4
Moore, D.B.	*The Poetry of Louis MacNeice* (1972)	2 (1972/4)	178- 81
Muecke, D.C.	*The Compass of Irony* (1969)	1 (1971/2)	126- 7
Mukařowský, J.	*The Word and Verbal Art: Selected Essays* (1977)		
—	*Structure, Sign and Function: Selected Essays* (1978)	9 (1979/2)	153- 6
Murdoch, I.	*The Fire and the Sun: Why Plato Banished the Artists* (1977)	8 (1978/2)	155- 2

Nash, W.	*Our Experience of Language* (1971)	3 (1973/2)	94- 6
Nathanson, L.	*The Strategy of Truth: A Study of Sir Thomas Browne* (1967)	1 (1971/2)	120- 2
Newman, E.	*Strictly Speaking: Will America Be the Death of English?* (1974)	8 (1978/3)	223- 5
O'Connor, J.D.	*Phonetics* (1973)	5 (1975/4)	317- 19
Olderman, R.M.	*Beyond the Waste Land: The American Novel in the Nineteen-Sixties* (1972)	3 (1973/4)	177- 9
Osborne, H.	*Aesthetics and Art Theory: An Historical Introduction* (1968)	1 (1971/2)	123- 4
Osselton, N.E.	*The Dumb Linguists: A Study of the Earliest English and Dutch Dictionaries* (1973)	7 (1977/1)	73- 6
Page, N.	*Speech in the English Novel* (1973)	4 (1974/3)	140- 1
Palmer, D.J., ed.	*Tennyson* (1973)	5 (1975/2)	145- 53
Peake, C.H.	*James Joyce: The Citizen and the Artist* (1977)	10 (1980/1)	74- 5
Pearsall, R.B.	*The Life and Writings of Ernest Hemingway* (1973)	4 (1974/2)	94- 6
Pouillard, M.	*T. F. Powys (1875-1953): La Solitude, Le Doute, L'Art* (1978)	10 (1980/3)	230- 4
Preminger, A. F.J. Warnke, and O.B. Hardison, Jr., eds.	*Princeton Encyclopedia of Poetry and Poetics* (1975)	7 (1977/2)	140- 3
Prins, A.A.	*A History of English Phonemes from Indo-European to Present-Day English* (1972)	3 (1973/2)	92- 4
Puttenham, G.	*The Arte of English Poesie* (1970)	1 (1971/2)	119- 22
Quennell, P.	*Romantic England: Writing and Painting 1717-1851* (1970)	1 (1971/3-4)	173- 5
Quirk, R.	*The English Language and Images of Matter* (1972)	4 (1974/4)	185- 7
Ray, P.C.	*The Surrealist Movement in England* (1971)	2 (1972/1)	36- 7
Rabkin, E.S.	*The Fantastic in Literature* (1976)	8 (1978/4)	316- 8
Richards, J.C., ed.	*Error Analysis: Perspectives on Second Language Acquisition* (1974)	5 (1975/4)	319- 24
Ricks, C.	*Keats and Embarrassment* (1974)	5 (1975/3)	235- 9

Rigter, G.H.	*First Explorations in English Syntax, Part 1* (1978)	10 (1980/2)	147- 52
Robinson, I.	*Chaucer's Prosody: A Study of the Middle English Verse Tradition* (1971)	2 (1972/3)	127- 9
Rockwell, J.	*Fact in Fiction: The Uses of Literature in the Systematic Study of Society* (1974)	5 (1975/4)	313- 6
Rogers, P.	*Grub Street: Studies in a Subculture* (1972)	3 (1973/2)	86- 91
Rooke, B.E., ed.	*S. T. Coleridge: "The Friend"* (1969)	1 (1971/1)	45- 8 157- 60
Scheffer, J.	*The Progressive in English* (1975)	7 (1977/2)	
Schiller, J.P.	*I. A. Richard's Theory of Literature* (1969)	1 (1971/2)	124- 6
Schmerling, S.F.	*Aspects of English Sentence Stress* (1976)	8 (1978/3)	233- 40
Silverberg, R., ed.	*The Mirror of Infinity: A Critic's Anthology of Science Fiction* (1970)	1 (1971/3-4)	167- 9
Simon, J.K., ed.	*Modern French Criticism: From Proust and Valéry to Structuralism* (1972)	2 (1972/4)	189- 91
Sinclair, J.M. and R.M. Coulthard	*Towards an Analysis of Discourse. The English Used by Teachers and Pupils* (1975)	6 (1976/2)	154- 7
Slater, M., ed.	*Dickens 1970* (1970)	1 (1971/3-4)	170- 2
Smalley, D., ed.	*Trollope: The Critical Heritage* (1969)	1 (1971/2)	117- 9
Smith, E.	*Some Versions of the Fall* (1973)	4 (1974/4)	177- 80
Smith, G., ed.	*Letters of Aldous Huxley* (1969)	2 (1972/4)	177- 8
Sparshott, F.	*The Concept of Criticism* (1967)	1 (1971/1)	58- 9
Spearing, A.C.	*The Gawain-Poet: A Critical Study* (1970)	2 (1972/2)	86- 8
Spender, S.	*Eliot* (1975)	7 (1977/2)	146- 50
—	*The Thirties and After: Poetry, Politics, People (1933-1975)* (1978)	10 (1980/3)	236- 9
Spenser, E.	*A View of the Present State of Ireland* (1979)	1 (1971/2)	120- 2
Sprigge, E.	*The Life of Ivy Compton-Burnett* (1972)	3 (1973/4)	183- 4

V LIST OF CONTRIBUTORS

VI INDEX OF WRITERS DISCUSSED